ISBN 0-8373-5098-0

98 ADMISSION TEST SERIES

 RUDMAN'S QUESTIONS AND ANSWERS ON THE...

HOAE

HEALTH OCCUPATIONS APTITUDE EXAMINATION

Intensive preparation for the examination including...

- **Academic Aptitude**
  - **Verbal Ability**
  - **Arithmetical Reasoning**
  - **Figure Analogies**
- **Spelling**
- **Reading Comprehension**

NLC
NATIONAL LEARNING CORPORATION

(516) 921-8888
(800) 645-6337
FAX: (516) 921-8743
www.passbooks.com
sales @ passbooks.com
info @ passbooks.com

PRINTED IN THE UNITED STATES OF AMERICA

PASSBOOK®
NOTICE

This book is *SOLELY* intended for, is sold *ONLY* to, and its use is *RESTRICTED* to *individual*, bona fide applicants or candidates who qualify by virtue of having seriously filed applications for appropriate license, certificate, professional and/or promotional advancement, higher school matriculation, scholarship, or other legitimate requirements of educational and/or governmental authorities.

This book is *NOT* intended for use, class instruction, tutoring, training, duplication, copying, reprinting, excerption, or adaptation, etc., by:

    (1) Other Publishers

    (2) Proprietors and/or Instructors of "Coaching" and/or Preparatory Courses

    (3) Personnel and/or Training Divisions of commercial, industrial, and governmental organizations

    (4) Schools, colleges, or universities and/or their departments and staffs, including teachers and other personnel

    (5) Testing Agencies or Bureaus

    (6) Study groups which seek by the purchase of a single volume to copy and/or duplicate and/or adapt this material for use by the group as a whole without having purchased individual volumes for each of the members of the group

    (7) Et al.

Such persons would be in violation of appropriate Federal and State statutes.

PROVISION OF LICENSING AGREEMENTS. — Recognized educational commercial, industrial, and governmental institutions and organizations, and others legitimately engaged in educational pursuits, including training, testing, and measurement activities, may address a request for a licensing agreement to the copyright owners, who will determine whether, and under what conditions, including fees and charges, the materials in this book may be used by them. In other words, a licensing facility *exists* for the legitimate use of the material in this book on other than an individual basis. However, it is asseverated and affirmed here that the materials in this book *CANNOT* be used without the receipt of the express permission of such a licensing agreement from the Publishers.

NATIONAL LEARNING CORPORATION
212 Michael Drive
Syosset, New York 11791

Inquiries re licensing agreements should be addressed to:
    The President
    National Learning Corporation
    212 Michael Drive
    Syosset, New York 11791

PASSBOOK SERIES®

THE *PASSBOOK SERIES®* has been created to prepare applicants and candidates for the ultimate academic battlefield – the examination room.

At some time in our lives, each and every one of us may be required to take an examination – for validation, matriculation, admission, qualification, registration, certification, or licensure.

Based on the assumption that every applicant or candidate has met the basic formal educational standards, has taken the required number of courses, and read the necessary texts, the *PASSBOOK SERIES®* furnishes the one special preparation which may assure passing with confidence, instead of failing with insecurity. Examination questions – together with answers – are furnished as the basic vehicle for study so that the mysteries of the examination and its compounding difficulties may be eliminated or diminished by a sure method.

This book is meant to help you pass your examination provided that you qualify and are serious in your objective.

The entire field is reviewed through the huge store of content information which is succinctly presented through a provocative and challenging approach – the question-and-answer method.

A climate of success is established by furnishing the correct answers at the end of each test.

You soon learn to recognize types of questions, forms of questions, and patterns of questioning. You may even begin to anticipate expected outcomes.

You perceive that many questions are repeated or adapted so that you can gain acute insights, which may enable you to score many sure points.

You learn how to confront new questions, or types of questions, and to attack them confidently and work out the correct answers.

You note objectives and emphases, and recognize pitfalls and dangers, so that you may make positive educational adjustments.

Moreover, you are kept fully informed in relation to new concepts, methods, practices, and directions in the field.

You discover that you are actually taking the examination all the time: you are preparing for the examination by "taking" an examination, not by reading extraneous and/or supererogatory textbooks.

In short, this PASSBOOK®, used directedly, should be an important factor in helping you to pass your test.

SPECIMEN QUESTIONS FOR THE
PSB - Health Occupations Aptitude Examination - REVISED

ACADEMIC APTITUDE - Part I

DIRECTIONS: Part I measures how well you think and learn. The three sample exercises, demonstrating the three types of questions you will be expected to answer in this part of the Examination, are given below so that you may see how to do Part I of the Examination.

Sample 1. (A) Bad   (B) Evil   (C) Wicked   (D) Good   (E) Naughty

1. (A) (B) (C) (D) (E)

In the above "set" of words, which word is most different in meaning from that of the other words? GOOD is the correct answer. What is the letter in front of the word GOOD? The letter is D. The circle with the letter D in the center should be blackened in the answer row for sample question 1.

1. (A) (B) (C) ● (E)

REMEMBER that in the "sets" of words that follow in this part of the Examination, you are always to select the word that is most DIFFERENT in meaning.

Sample 2. You have $10 and give $3 to your mother. How much money do you have remaining?
(A) $1   (B) $2   (C) $4   (D) $5   (E) $7

2. (A) (B) (C) (D) (E)

Ten dollars minus three dollars is seven, so the circle with the letter E in the middle should be blackened in the answer row for sample question 2.

2. (A) (B) (C) (D) ●

Sample 3. ○ is to ○ as □ is to
(A) △ (B) □ (C) ▭ (D) ○ (E) ▯

3. (A) (B) (C) (D) (E)

The letter B, □ , is the correct answer

A large circle ○ is to a smaller circle ○

as a large square □ is to a smaller square □

You should blacken the circle with the letter B in the middle in the answer row for sample question 3.

3. (A) ● (C) (D) (E)

This is the way you mark all of your answers for the questions that follow.

---

1. (A) Vital   (B) Wither   (C) Fade   (D) Vanish   (E) Insipid

2. Five health professionals earned the following scores on an anatomy test: 65, 82, 77, 89, 72. What was the average score?
(A) 81   (B) 78   (C) 77   (D) 72   (E) 69

3. ○ is to △ (in circle) as □ is to - A (□ in circle) B (○ in square) C (□ in circle overlapping) D (○ in square overlapping) E (△ in square)

4. (A) Wane   (B) Dwindle   (C) Amplify   (D) Ebb   (E) Fade

5. A 72 inch roll of bandage at $1.08 per yard would cost?
(A) $1.08   (B) $1.96   (C) $2.16   (D) $2.96   (E) $3.24

6. △ □ < is to as is to - A ∠ B ⌐ C ∪ D ∟ E ⊥

7. (A) Hasty   (B) Serene   (C) Placid   (D) Still   (E) Calm

8. The first minute of a telephone call costs .24 and each additional minute .13. What is the cost of a 5 minute call?
(A) $1.20   (B) $1.12   (C) .96   (D) .76   (E) .63

9. ⌒ is to ◠ as ⬠ is to - A ⬠ B ◣ C ⬠ D □ E △

1 (A) (B) (C) (D) (E)
2 (A) (B) (C) (D) (E)
3 (A) (B) (C) (D) (E)
4 (A) (B) (C) (D) (E)
5 (A) (B) (C) (D) (E)
6 (A) (B) (C) (D) (E)
7 (A) (B) (C) (D) (E)
8 (A) (B) (C) (D) (E)
9 (A) (B) (C) (D) (E)

Go on to next page

SPELLING - Part II

DIRECTIONS:

Part II measures how well you can spell and what you know about the various rules of grammar as they are reflected in the spelling of certain words. Each line below contains a word with three different spellings. Only one spelling is correct. Select the correctly spelled word from each line.

Sample 1. (A) acheive   (B) achieve   (C) achive

What is the letter in front of the word spelled correctly? The answer is the letter B. ACHIEVE. In the answer row to the right, the circle with the letter B in the center has been blackened. You will mark your answers in a similar fashion in the section headed, Spelling - Part II.

1. Ⓐ Ⓑ Ⓒ

1. Ⓐ ● Ⓒ

1. (A) emergancy   (B) emergancie   (C) emergency
2. (A) infectious   (B) enfecteous   (C) enfectious
3. (A) deoderizing   (B) deodorizing   (C) deodarizing
4. (A) densitty   (B) densitie   (C) density
5. (A) detergents   (B) detergants   (C) detergantes
6. (A) caffene   (B) caffine   (C) caffeine
7. (A) ageing   (B) aging   (C) agging
8. (A) erroneous   (B) eroneous   (C) eronious
9. (A) vitamine   (B) vitimine   (C) vitamin
10. (A) paralisis   (B) paralysis   (C) paralzsis

1 Ⓐ Ⓑ Ⓒ
2 Ⓐ Ⓑ Ⓒ
3 Ⓐ Ⓑ Ⓒ
4 Ⓐ Ⓑ Ⓒ
5 Ⓐ Ⓑ Ⓒ
6 Ⓐ Ⓑ Ⓒ
7 Ⓐ Ⓑ Ⓒ
8 Ⓐ Ⓑ Ⓒ
9 Ⓐ Ⓑ Ⓒ
10 Ⓐ Ⓑ Ⓒ

READING COMPREHENSION - Part III

DIRECTIONS:

Part III is a test of your ability to understand what you read. It is a measure of some of the skills and abilities you have been developing ever since you entered school. You will be asked to answer questions based on the material contained in written passages.

Begin by reading each passage carefully. Each of the questions if followed by four suggested answers. You are to decide which one of these answers you should choose based upon the material in the passage. You must mark all of your answers by blackening the circle having the same letter as the answer you have chosen.

Answer the questions about one passage before going on to the next. You may look back at the passage while you answer the questions. Work carefully but rapidly.

Sample: You will have 30 minutes to work on this test. There are 4 passages and 50 sets of questions.

    1. In the sample passage above it states that the number of sets of questions is
       (A) 50   (B) 30   (C) 25   (D) 20

1. Ⓐ Ⓑ Ⓒ Ⓓ

The answer is 50 with a letter A in front of it. So the circle with A in the center should be blackened in the answer row for sample question 1.

1. ● Ⓑ Ⓒ Ⓓ

Be sure to mark your answers in the section headed, Reading Comprehension - Part III.

A few years ago, although no one knew it, the gases in spray cans were harming the ozone layer. The ozone layer is a part of the atmosphere, a thick blanket of air that covers the world. The atmosphere is made up of many gases, especially nitrogen and oxygen. Close to the earth, the atmosphere is thick and heavy, but as it gets farther away from the earth, the atmosphere gets thin. There, the energy from the sun changes the way gases behave. For example, oxygen atoms usually travel in the air connected together in pairs, but high in the atmosphere, the sun's energy causes three oxygen atoms to connect together instead of two. These groups of three oxygen atoms are called ozone. The place high in the air where regular oxygen changes to ozone is called the ozone layer. The ozone layer is very important to life on earth. It soaks up dangerous rays from the sun that harm plants and animals. Even more important, the ozone layer helps keep the earth cool. Without it, the earth might become so hot that the icecaps would melt and flood much of the earth. Fortunately, safe gases are now used in spray cans, but some of the ozone layer has been destroyed.

Go on to next

1. High in the sky the atmosphere is
   (A) thick   (B) heavy   (C) unchanged   (D) thin

2. High in the atmosphere regular oxygen changes to
   (A) solar rays   (B) oxygen rays   (C) ozone   (D) nitrogen

3. Without the ozone layer the earth would become
   (A) cold   (B) hot   (C) dark   (D) frozen

4. The ozone layer serves to screen dangerous rays from
   (A) oxygen atoms   (B) spray cans   (C) the sun   (D) the gases

5. The chief concern of the paragraph deals with the importance of the
   (A) sun rays   (B) spray cans   (C) icecaps   (D) ozone layer

1 Ⓐ Ⓑ Ⓒ Ⓓ
2 Ⓐ Ⓑ Ⓒ Ⓓ
3 Ⓐ Ⓑ Ⓒ Ⓓ
4 Ⓐ Ⓑ Ⓒ Ⓓ
5 Ⓐ Ⓑ Ⓒ Ⓓ

INFORMATION IN THE NATURAL SCIENCES - Part IV

DIRECTIONS: Part IV is concerned with measuring your accumulated knowledge or information in the area of the natural sciences. Below is a sample exercise to show you how to do this part of the Examination.

Sample 1. Discoveries in the operation of the force of gravity were made by
    (A) Lamarek   (B) Fields   (C) Wells   (D) Newton   (E) Bonet

1. Ⓐ Ⓑ Ⓒ Ⓓ Ⓔ

The answer is Newton. In the answer row of circles to the right, the circle with a D in the center has been blackened.

1. Ⓐ Ⓑ Ⓒ ● Ⓔ

o the following items in the same manner, marking your answers in the section headed, Information in the Natural Sciences - Part IV

1. The lower jaw in vertebrates is known as the
   (A) mandible   (B) hyoid   (C) pelvis   (D) coccyx   (E) ulna

2. In old age bones may become
   (A) porous   (B) flexible   (C) ductile   (D) pliable   (E) supple

3. About one quart, 0.908 dry quart, is equivalent to one
   (A) gram   (B) kilogram   (C) milligram   (D) calorie   (E) liter

4. Normal body temperature, expressed in degrees centigrade is
   (A) 212   (B) 120   (C) 98.6   (D) 37   (E) 22.8

5. The pH of a neutral solution is
   (A) 0   (B) 1   (C) 5   (D) 7   (E) 10

6. An individual who played a large role in smallpox vaccination was
   (A) Lister   (B) Jenner   (C) Salk   (D) Pasteur   (E) Dubos

7. The nutrient that yields the most energy per ounce is
   (A) fat   (B) protein   (C) starch   (D) sugar   (E) water

8. Of the following, the scientist who was a Nobel Prize winner was
   (A) Darwin   (B) DeVries   (C) Mendel   (D) Muller   (E) Galen

9. Approximate percent of nitrogen in the earth's atmosphere is
   (A) 78   (B) 68   (C) 58   (D) 48   (E) 38

10. An example of a good insulator of electricity would be
    (A) copper   (B) iron   (C) wood   (D) bronze   (E) tin

11. A type of mechanical wave motion in an elastic medium is
    (A) light   (B) radar   (C) heat   (D) X-rays   (E) sound

12. Type of radiation which tans the human skin (sunlight) is called
    (A) X-ray   (B) infra-red   (C) microwave   (D) isotopes   (E) ultraviolet

1 Ⓐ Ⓑ Ⓒ Ⓓ Ⓔ
2 Ⓐ Ⓑ Ⓒ Ⓓ Ⓔ
3 Ⓐ Ⓑ Ⓒ Ⓓ Ⓔ
4 Ⓐ Ⓑ Ⓒ Ⓓ Ⓔ
5 Ⓐ Ⓑ Ⓒ Ⓓ Ⓔ
6 Ⓐ Ⓑ Ⓒ Ⓓ Ⓔ
7 Ⓐ Ⓑ Ⓒ Ⓓ Ⓔ
8 Ⓐ Ⓑ Ⓒ Ⓓ Ⓔ
9 Ⓐ Ⓑ Ⓒ Ⓓ Ⓔ
10 Ⓐ Ⓑ Ⓒ Ⓓ Ⓔ
11 Ⓐ Ⓑ Ⓒ Ⓓ Ⓔ

Go on to next page.

VOCATIONAL ADJUSTMENT INDEX - Part V

DIRECTIONS:

In Part V there are statements that concern how you feel about yourself and certain situations in relation to a potential work environ This is not a test, but rather an inventory of your feelings, attitudes, and opinions which is designed to assist in placing you in a situation where you will find satisfaction and be happy. There are probably no "right" answers nor "wrong" answers - some pe feel one way; other people feel another way. Agreement or disagreement with the statements that follow will simply show you usually think, how you usually feel, or what you usually do about things.

If you agree with the statement, blacken the circle with the letter A in the center (A) in the correct row. If you disagree, blacke circle with the letter D in the center (D)

WORK RAPIDLY - On the answer section headed Vocational Adjustment Index - Part V, just select the answer that is really tru you and answer immediately.

1. A definite choice of vocations is important.

2. Helping the aged and the sick would be a source of satisfaction.

3. Many young people spend too much time in studying.

4. It is difficult to work with strangers.

5. Teachers are often unfair in awarding grades.

6. Working alone rather than with others is preferable.

7. Many people deliberately try to embarrass you.

8. Those in positions of authority too often abuse their employees.

9. Stressful situations leave one weak and exhausted.

10. An ideal job would be one where continuous learning was expected.

1 (A) (D)
2 (A) (D)
3 (A) (D)
4 (A) (D)
5 (A) (D)
6 (A) (D)
7 (A) (D)
8 (A) (D)
9 (A) (D)
10 (A) (D)

WHY specimen questions? Questions which will NOT be found in the Examination. The purpose of the specimen que is to familiarize you with; (1) the format of the Examination; (2) the directions you will be given for completing each part Examination; (3) the type of questions to which you will be asked to respond; (4) the content areas measured by the test e.g., word-meaning, arithmetic, spelling, judgment, science, etc.; (5) how to record your answers on the answer sheet. Do too concerned if you do not immediately know the answers to the specimen questions. YOUR important reaction is concerned enough to do some review study using various, readily available, sources of answer information such as books (very useful), the dictionary, 8th grade arithmetic textbooks, high school science textbooks, etc. You could have supplied with the answers to the specimen questions, but that would defeat one of the real values, for YOU, of the spec questions . . . study (finding out), learning (understanding), review (acquiring knowledge -- reinforcing learned material).

TEST-TAKING "TIPS"

1. Listen very carefully to the oral directions which are given to you.
2. Read the "General Instructions" carefully and follow them.
3. Be aware of the time allotted for each of the five parts of the Examination.
4. While the test questions are arranged in order of difficulty, you may find some earlier questions more difficult for you th some later ones. Do not waste time puzzling over a difficult question.
5. Indiscriminate guessing does not "pay off". An "educated", reasoned guess may be worthwhile.
6. If you change an answer to a question, be sure the change is justified.
7. Lack of adequate rest "the night before" will affect test-taking efficiency.
8. Try to relax - too much worry and anxiety is not helpful - have a positive attitude.
9. Take care of personal needs prior to the test-taking time.
10. REPORT illness, excessive fatigue, and other handicapping conditions or disabilities.

HOW TO TAKE A TEST

You have studied hard, long, and conscientiously.

With your official admission card in hand, and your heart pounding, you have been admitted to the examination room.

You note that there are several hundred other applicants in the examination room waiting to take the same test.

They all appear to be equally well prepared.

You know that nothing but your best effort will suffice. The "moment of truth" is at hand: you now have to demonstrate objectively, in writing, your knowledge of content and your understanding of subject matter.

You are fighting the most important battle of your life—to pass and/or score high on an examination which will determine your career and provide the economic basis for your livelihood.

What extra, special things should you know and should you do in taking the examination?

BEFORE THE TEST

YOUR PHYSICAL CONDITION IS IMPORTANT

If you are not well, you can't do your best work on tests. If you are half asleep, you can't do your best either. Here are some tips:

1. Get about the same amount of sleep you usually get. Don't stay up all night before the test, either partying or worrying—DON'T DO IT.

2. If you wear glasses, be sure to wear them when you go to take the test. This goes for hearing aids, too.

3. If you have any physical problems that may keep you from doing your best, be sure to tell the person giving the test. If you are sick or in poor health, you really cannot do your best on any test. You can always come back and take the test some other time.

AT THE TEST

EXAMINATION TECHNIQUES

1. Read the *general* instructions carefully. These are usually printed on the first page of the examination booklet. As a rule, these instructions refer to the timing of the examination; the fact that you should not start work until the signal and must stop work at a signal, etc. If there are any *special* instructions, such as a choice of questions to be answered, make sure that you note this instruction carefully.

2. When you are ready to start work on the examination, that is as soon as the signal has been given, read the instructions to each question booklet, underline any key words or phrases, such as *least, best, outline, describe,* and the like. In this way you will tend to answer as requested rather than discover on reviewing your paper that you *listed without describing,* that you selected the *worst* choice rather than the *best* choice, etc.

3. If the examination is of the objective or so-called multiple-choice type, that is, each question will also give a series of possible answers: A, B, C, or D, and you are called upon to select the best answer and write the letter next to that answer on your answer paper, it is advisable to start answering each question in turn. There may be anywhere from 50 to 100 such questions in the three or four hours allotted and you can see how much time would be taken if you read through all the questions before beginning to answer any. Furthermore, if you come across a question or a group of questions which you know would be difficult to answer, it would undoubtedly affect your handling of all the other questions.

4. If the examination is of the essay-type and contains but a few questions, it is a moot point as to whether you should read all the questions before starting to answer any one. Of course if you are given a choice, say five out of seven and the like, then it is essential to read all the questions so you can eliminate the two which are most difficult. If, however, you are asked to answer all the questions, there may be danger in trying to answer the easiest one first because you may find that you will spend too much time on it. The best technique is to answer the first question, then proceed to the second, etc.

5. Time your answers. Before the examination begins, write down the time it started, then add the time allowed for the examination and write down the time it must be completed, then divide the time available somewhat as follows:

   a. If 3½ hours are allowed, that would be 210 minutes. If you have 80 objective-type questions, that would be an average of about 2½ minutes per question. Allow yourself no more than 2 minutes per question, or a total of 160 minutes, which will permit about 50 minutes to review.

   b. If for the time allotment of 210 minutes, there are 7 essay questions to answer, that would average about 30 minutes a question. Give yourself only 25 minutes per question so that you have about 35 minutes to review.

6. The most important instruction is *to read each question* and make sure you know what is wanted. The second most important instruction is to *time yourself properly* so that you answer every question. The third most important instruction is to *answer every question*. Guess if you have to but include something for each question, Remember that you will receive no credit for a blank and will probably receive some credit if you write something in answer to an essay question. If you guess a letter, say "B" for a multiple-choice question, you may have guessed right. If you leave a blank as the answer to a multiple-choice question, the examiners may respect your feelings but it will not add a point to your score. Some exams may penalize you for wrong answers, so in such cases *only*, you may not want to guess unless you have some basis for your answer.

7. Suggestions

   a. Objective-Type Questions

   (1) Examine the question booklet for proper sequence of pages and questions.

   (2) Read all instructions carefully.

   (3) Skip any question which seems too difficult; return to it after all other questions have been answered.

   (4) Apportion your time properly; do not spend too much time on any single question or group of questions.

   (5) Note and underline key words — *all, most, fewest, least, best, worst, same, opposite.*

   (6) Pay particular attention to negatives.

   (7) Note unusual option, e.g., unduly long, short, complex, different or similar in content to the body of the question.

   (8) Observe the use of "hedging" words — *probably, may, most likely, etc.*

   (9) Make sure that your answer is put next to the same number as the question.

   (10) Do not second guess unless you have good reason to believe the second answer is definitely more correct.

   (11) Cross out original answer if you decide another answer is more accurate; do not erase, *until* you are ready to hand your paper in.

   (12) Answer all questions; guess unless instructed otherwise.

   (13) Leave time for review.

b. Essay-Type Questions

   (1) Read each question carefully.

   (2) Determine exactly what is wanted. Underline key words or phrases.

   (3) Decide on outline or paragraph answer.

   (4) Include many different points and elements unless asked to develop any one or two points or elements.

   (5) Show impartiality by giving pros and cons unless directed to select one side only.

   (6) Make and write down any assumptions you find necessary to answer the question.

   (7) Watch your English, grammar, punctuation, choice of words.

   (8) Time your answers; don't crowd material.

8. Answering the Essay Question

Most essay questions can be answered by framing the specific response around several key words or ideas. Here are a few such key words or ideas:

M's: manpower, materials, methods, money, management

P's: purpose, program, policy, plan, procedure, practice, problems, pitfalls, personnel, public relations

a. Six basic steps in handling problems:

   (1) preliminary plan and background development

   (2) collect information, data and facts

   (3) analyze and interpret information, data and facts

   (4) analyze and develop solutions as well as make recommendations

   (5) prepare report and sell recommendations

   (6) install recommendations and follow up effectiveness

b. Pitfalls to Avoid

   (1) *Taking Things for Granted*
   A statement of the situation does not necessarily imply that each of the elements is necessarily true; for example, a complaint may be invalid and biased so that all that can be taken for granted is that a complaint has been registered

   (2) *Considering only one side of a situation*
   Wherever possible, indicate several alternatives and then point out the reasons you selected the best one.

   (3) *Failing to indicate follow up*
   Whenever your answer indicates action on your part, make certain that you will take proper follow-up action to see how successful your recommendations, procedures, or actions turn out to be.

   (4) *Taking too long in answering any single question*
   Remember to time your answers properly.

EXAMINATION SECTION

COMMENTARY

No matter what the level of the examination tested for, be it for trainee or administrator, whether a specific substantive examination is drawn up *ad hoc* for the position announced or whether a brief, simple qualifying test is given, keen analysis of current testing practices reveals that the type of question indicative of general or mental ability or aptitude, or "intelligence," is an inevitable component and/or element of most examinations.

In other words, the examiners assume that all candidates must possess, or show, a certain level of understanding or "good sense" in matters or situations that may be considered common or general to all. This, then, is the purpose of the general-or-mental-type question: it seems to delimn, in objective terms, the basic, clearly definable, mental or intellectual status of the examinee, no matter what his education or his training or his experience or his present position or reputation.

In some cases, and for certain whole fields of job positions, tests of general and mental ability have even supplanted the specialized subject-area or position-information examination.

Moreoever, even in the latter type of examination, e.g., the specific position-type, it will be found that questions testing general qualities stud the examination at point after point.

This section should be of inestimable value to the candidate as he prepares not only for the job-examination, but also for any other examination that he may take at this time or in the future.

Now the candidate should "take" the tests of general and mental ability that follow, because of this special importance. These, particularly, portray the extended and rounded examination of general and/or mental ability.

The "Tests" that follow also serve to focus the candidate's attention on the variety and types of questions to be encountered, and to familiarize him with answer-patterns-and-nuances.

EXAMINATION SECTION

DIRECTIONS FOR THIS SECTION:
Each question or incomplete statement is followed by several suggested answers or completions. Select the one that *BEST* answers the question or completes the statement. *PRINT THE LETTER OF THE CORRECT ANSWER IN THE SPACE AT THE RIGHT.*

TEST 1

1. The *opposite* of despair is   1. ...
     A. hate   B. shame   C. despondent   D. hope   E. loyal
2. The *opposite* of constant is   2. ...
     A. feeble   B. fickle   C. sober   D. thorough   E. standing
3. A person *always* has   3. ...
     A. teeth   B. nerves   C. money   D. children   E. house
4. A mare is *always* _____ than her colt.   4. ...
     A. bigger   B. faster   C. stronger   D. older   E. slower
5. A sculptor is to a statue as a writer is to a   5. ...
     A. book   B. clay   C. human   D. pencil   E. library

1

6. If the words below are rearranged to make a good sentence, 6. ...
   with what letter would the *last* word of the sentence *begin*?
   always   are   on   hung   walls   pictures
   A. h   B. w   C. p   D. o   E. a

7. An event which might happen is said to be _____. 7. ...
   A. probably B. possible C. obvious D. fixed E. planned

8. The wind is to a sailboat as _____ is to a locomotive. 8. ...
   A. water   B. steam   C. a siren D. a sail E. a track

9. The *opposite* of victory is 9. ...
   A. prosperity B. outcome C. defeat D. glory E. chagrin

10. Gold is *more* costly than silver because it is 10. ...
    A. attractive B. scarcer C. stylish D. colorful E. heavier

11. The *opposite* of rough is 11. ...
    A. quiet   B. kindly   C. robust D. docile E. gentle

12. The idea that the earth is flat is 12. ...
    A. ridiculous B. improbable C. deceitful D. evil E. unjust

13. The two words *pertinent* and *permanent* mean _____. 13. ...
    A. the opposite   B. the same
    C. *neither* the same *nor* the opposite
    D. *both* the same *and* the opposite
    E. *all* of the above or *none* of the above

14. Darkness is related to sunlight in the same way as quiet 14. ...
    is related to
    A. dungeon B. sound C. din D. clamor E. tranquility

15. One number is *wrong* in the following series. *Which one?* 15. ...
    A. 5   B. 6   C. 7   D. 9   E. 9

16. A seed is related to a plant as a(n) _____ is related to 16. ...
    a bird.
    A. worm   B. shell   C. tree   D. root   E. egg

17. The air is to an airplane as a _____ is to an automobile. 17. ...
    A. driver B. road C. mechanic D. tire E. gas station

18. A boat race *always* has 18. ...
    A. wind B. swimmers C. trophy D. contestants E. masts

19. *Which one* of the five things below is *MOST* like these 19. ...
    three: giraffe, lizard, eagle?
    A. Leg   B. Wing   C. Bird   D. Mouth   E. Tail

20. Temperature is related to thermometer as time is related 20. ...
    to
    A. day   B. month   C. spring D. year   E. clock

21. *Which one* of the five words following is *MOST* unlike the 21. ...
    other four?
    A. Violent B. Evil   C. Pretty D. Good   E. Went

22. *Which* of the following is a trait of character? 22. ...
    A. Affluent B. Famous C. Lavish D. Unreliable E. Tough

23. *Which* word means the *opposite* of pride? 23. ...
    A. Happiness   B. Humility   C. Fickleness
    D. Comical   E. Loyalty

24. *What* is related to physiology as stars is to astronomy? 24. ...
    A. Veins   B. Corpuscles C. Blood D. Food E. Color

25. Write the letter that *precedes* the letter M in the alpha- 25. ...
    bet.
    A. N   B. O   C. P   D. L   E. J

2

TEST 2

1. Which word is spelled the *same* backwards and forward?   1. ...
   A. SOON   B. POOR   C. SEWER   D. MOO   E. SEES
2. Evolution is to revolution as crawl is to   2. ...
   A. floor   B. infant   C. totter   D. run   E. stand
3. A debate *always* involves   3. ...
   A. people   B. a meeting place   E. a trophy
   D. a controversy   E. an opinion
4. Order is to confusion as _____ is to war.   4. ...
   A. bombs   B. peace   C. planes   D. army   E. generals
5. *What* is related to ordinary as few is to less?   5. ...
   A. More   B. Several   C. Alone   D. Exceptional   E. Plain
6. Of the things following, four are alike in a certain way.   6. ...
   Which one is *NOT* like these four?
   A. Milk   B. Soot   C. Snow   D. Cotton   E. Ivory
7. To insist that stones have thoughts is   7. ...
   A. nonsense   B. psychological   C. evil   D. rumor   E. futile
8. Wood is to table as brick is to a(n) _____.   8. ...
   A. color   B. oven   C. seat   D. wall   E. bricklayer
9. *Which* of these grouped numbers is *equal to* 5?   9. ...
   A. 11-5   B. 6-2   C. 13-8   D. 9-5   E. 13-9
10. If one finds a kind of flower that was never seen before,   10. ...
    one has made a(n)
    A. gem   B. idea   C. fixation   D. style   E. discovery
11. A city *always* has _____.   11. ...
    A. tall buildings   B. restaurants   C. motels
    D. people   E. parks
12. Find the letter which in this sentence itself appears a   12. ...
    second time NEAREST the beginning.
    A. F   B. I   C. N   D. T   E. E
13. A person who pretends to be anything other than what he   13. ...
    is, is said to be
    A. honest   B. insincere   C. loyal   D. sorry   E. kind
14. If an act conforms to recognized principles or standards,   14. ...
    it is said to be
    A. impartial   B. punitive   C. lawful
    D. recognized   E. accepted
15. A general is to an army as a _____ is to a state.   15. ...
    A. city   B. mayor   C. governor   D. parks   E. laws
16. *Which one* of the five words below is *MOST* unlike the   16. ...
    other four?
    A. Agile   B. Fast   C. Speedy   D. Run   E. Alert
17. A man who acquires the property of others by deceit is   17. ...
    called a
    A. liar   B. swindler   C. convict   D. bailiff   E. counterfeiter
18. Feathers are to a bluebird as fur is to a _____.   18. ...
    A. coat   B. duck   C. leopard   D. stole   E. store
19. The *opposite* of joy is   19. ...
    A. sneer   B. wishful   C. affluent   D. happy   E. sorrow
20. If the first two statements following are true, the   20. ...
    third is _____.
    All members of this club are Progressives. John is not
    a Progressive. John is a member of this club.
    A. true   B. false   C. not certain
    D. not enough information given   E. indeterminable

3

21. If the first two statements following are true, the   21. ...
third is _____.
Some of Albert's friends are Mormons. Some of Albert's
friends are lawyers. Some of Albert's friends are Mormon
lawyers.
    A. true   B. false   C. not certain
    D. not enough information given   E. indeterminable
22. If the first two statements following are true, the third 22. ...
is _____.
It takes perfect motor coordination to become a good
fighter. Peter has perfect motor coordination. Peter
will become a fighter.
    A. true   B. false   C. not certain
    D. not enough information given   E. indeterminable
23. A gulf is to an ocean as a peninsula is to a _____.   23. ...
    A. pond   B. pool C. continent D. cape E. fortress
24. A coin or bill made by dishonest people to deceive the   24. ...
public and pass for real money is said to be _____.
    A. a token   B. counterfeit   C. a reproduction
    C. foreign   E. larceny
25. Today is to yesterday as modern is to   25. ...
    A. the next day   B. current   C. modernistic
    D. ancient   E. today

TEST 3

1. A person who is confident he can complete a task is said 1. ...
to be _____.
    A. courageous B. sure C. bright D. successful E. alert
2. Do what this mixed-up sentence tells you to do.   2. ...
total seven Write four the one and of _____.
    A. 8   B. 12   C. 11   D. 5   E. 7
3. If a child sleeping peacefully is awakened by a sudden   3. ...
cry, he is *likely* to be
    A. ill B. uncomfortable C. startled D. hungry E. morbid
4. A bank is to money as a _____ is to books.   4. ...
    A. authors B. building C. library D. librarian E. teacher
5. The *SHORTEST* distance between two points is a(n)   5. ...
    A. cross-section   B. straight line   C. angle
    D. drawing   E. circle
6. "No time was set for the conference." The word below that 6. ...
BEST describes this fact is
    A. indefinite B. decisive C. ignored D. powerful E. irrational
7. *What* is related to accident as sanitation is related to 7. ...
disease?
    A. Nurse B. Hospital C. Ambulance D. Medication E. Caution
8. A person who is influenced in making a decision by pre- 8. ...
conceived opinions is said to be
    A. subjective B. obstinate C. hateful D. ignorant E. objective
9. The *opposite* of extravagant is _____.   9. ...
    A. affluent B. costly C. frugal D. cheap E. heavier
10. A dinner *always* involves   10. ...
    A. service B. waitress C. cloth D. food E. forks

11. *Which* word is the *OPPOSITE* of rotund?   11. ...
    A. Tremendous B. Muscular C. Strong D. Skinny E. Elongated
12. A person who works hard and strives to achieve success   12. ...
    is said to be _____.
    A. ambitious B. lucky C. patient D. clever E. strong
13. A person who says things he knows to be wrong is said to   13. ...
    be
    A. hateful B. deliberate C. kind D. craven E. lying
14. The *opposite* of abolish is _____.   14. ...
    A. announce B. nullify C. continue D. refresh E. expunge
15. *Which one* of these five things is *most* unlike the other   15. ...
    four?
    A. Cucumber B. Fig C. Rose D. Tomato E. Cherry
16. A home *always* has a   16. ...
    A. radio   B. television   C. relationship
    D. parent   E. dining room
17. Which word makes the *truest* sentence?   17. ...
    Parents are _____ wiser than their children.
    A. usually B. rarely C. always D. exceedingly E. never
18. Of the five items listed below, four are alike in a cer-   18. ...
    tain way. *Which one* is *NOT* like the other four?
    A. Misery B. Love C. Sorrow D. Despondent E. Despair
19. A grandmother is always _____ than her grandchild.   19. ...
    A. good   B. generous C. older D. kinder E. wiser
20. *Which one* of the five words below tells *BEST* what a   20. ...
    weapon is?
    A. Knife   B. Target C. Aim   D. Bullet E. Gangster
21. A cat does not *always* have   21. ...
    A. a tail B. a collar C. whiskers D. eyes E. paws
22. A horse *cannot*   22. ...
    A. talk   B. run   C. neigh   D. kick   E. trot
23. *Which* group is *NOT* in sequence?   23. ...
    A. abcde   B. fghij   C. kmnop   D. rstuv   E. xyzab
24. The father of *my* mother is *my*   24. ...
    A. cousin B. nephew C. uncle D. grandfather E. godfather
25. One number is *wrong* in the following series. *Which one?*   25. ...
        1, 3, 9, 27, 82, 243....
    A. 1   B. 3   C. 27   D. 82   E. 243

KEYS (CORRECT ANSWERS)

TEST 1				TEST 2				TEST 3			
1.	D	11.	E	1.	E	11.	D	1.	B	11.	D
2.	B	12.	B	2.	D	12.	E	2.	B	12.	A
3.	B	13.	C	3.	D	13.	B	3.	C	13.	E
4.	D	14.	D	4.	B	14.	C	4.	C	14.	C
5.	A	15.	D	5.	E	15.	C	5.	B	15.	C
6.	B	16.	E	6.	B	16.	D	6.	A	16.	C
7.	B	17.	B	7.	A	17.	B	7.	E	17.	A
8.	B	18.	D	8.	D	18.	C	8.	A	18.	B
9.	C	19.	C	9.	C	19.	E	9.	C	19.	C
10.	B	20.	E	10.	E	20.	B	10.	D	20.	A
	21.	E			21.	C			21.	B	
	22.	D			22.	C			22.	A	
	23.	B			23.	C			23.	C	
	24.	C			24.	B			24.	D	
	25.	D			25.	D			25.	D	

EXAMINATION SECTION
TEST 1

DIRECTIONS: Each question or incomplete statement is followed by several suggested answers or completions. Select the one that BEST answers the question or completes the statement. *PRINT THE CORRECT ANSWER IN THE SPACE AT THE RIGHT.*

1. Add: 37.10
               .006
          300.105
          16.02
       7341.
         72.50

1.____

2. Add: 25 7/8
          31 3/4
          72 1/8
          96 1/2
          89 3/8

2.____

3. Multiply: .18902
               .018

3.____

4. Divide: .063$\overline{).6048}$

4.____

5. To OSCILLATE means to
  A. quiver   B. freeze
  C. swing back and forth   D. hate
  E. rebound

5.____

6. *A New York broker who studied in Scotland during his younger years took a keen interest in the game of golf as it was played there. When he returned to the United States back in the seventies, he introduced the game over here by reproducing one of England's most famous courses.*
According to the above paragraph, which one of the following statements is TRUE?
  A. Golf originated in the United States.
  B. The first golf course was built in England seventy years ago.
  C. Golf was introduced in the United States in the seventies.
  D. Golf was formerly played only by students.

6.____

7. CAT is to FELINE as COW is to
  A. quadruped   B. pedigreed   C. canine
  D. bovine   E. equine

7.____

8. BILL is to PAPER as COIN is to
   A. money   B. heavy   C. shiny   D. metal   E. round

   8.___

9. WATER is to FLUID as IRON is to
   A. metal   B. rusty   C. solid   D. rails   E. mines

   9.___

10. OVER is to UNDER as TRESTLE is to
    A. tunnel   B. bridge   C. trains
    D. skeleton   E. river

    10.___

11. VAGUE means MOST NEARLY
    A. style   B. definite   C. not clear
    D. silly   E. tired

    11.___

12. To AGGRAVATE is to
    A. indulge   B. counsel   C. inflate
    D. help   E. make worse

    12.___

13. PRECISION means MOST NEARLY
    A. cutting   B. exactness   C. risky
    D. measurement   E. training

    13.___

14. A TERSE statement is
    A. long   B. condensed   C. rude
    D. wild   E. exact

    14.___

15. A car will go 3/8 of a given distance in one hour.
    What part will it cover in 5/8 of an hour?

    15.___

16. An incubator was set with 120 eggs.
    If 18 eggs failed to hatch, what percent hatched?

    16.___

17. At $2.00 a case, what fraction of a case can be bought
    for 7/8 of a dollar?

    17.___

18. A earns $3.50 a day. B earns 1/4 more a day than A does.
    How many days will it take B to earn the same amount that
    A earns in 10 days?

    18.___

19. What is the postage on a package weighing 12 lbs., if
    the rate is 8 cents for the first pound and 4 cents for
    each additional pound?

    19.___

20. *Money orders may be cashed without gain or profit by any
    post office having surplus money order funds.*
    What one word in the above sentence is synonymous to
    excess?

    20.___

21. The jury AKWITED the prisoner.
    The word in capitals is misspelled. Write it correctly
    at the right.

    21.___

22. Dogs are SUGAYSHUS animals.
The word in capitals is misspelled. Write it correctly
at the right.

22.____

23. The parade caused a TRAFIK jam.
The word in capitals is misspelled. Write it correctly
at the right.

23.____

24. The soldiers were ready to drop with FATEEG.
The word in capitals is misspelled. Write it correctly
at the right.

24.____

25. To TOLERATE is to
   A. prohibit   B. spoil   C. endure
   D. liberate   E. rejoice

25.____

———

KEY (CORRECT ANSWERS)

1. 7766.731
2. 315 5/8
3. .00340236
4. 9.6
5. C

6. C
7. D
8. D
9. C
10. A

11. C
12. E
13. B
14. B
15. 15/64

16. 85%
17. 7/16
18. 8
19. 52¢
20. surplus

21. acquitted
22. sagacious
23. traffic
24. fatigue
25. C

———

TEST 2

DIRECTIONS: Each question or incomplete statement is followed by
several suggested answers or completions. Select the
one that BEST answers the question or completes the
statement. *PRINT THE CORRECT ANSWER IN THE SPACE AT
THE RIGHT*.

1. To CONCUR means to   1.__
    A. gather   B. repeat   C. assent
    D. cause   E. put together

2. *The world never knows its great men until it buries them*   2.__
    means MOST NEARLY
    A. worry kills more men than work
    B. when a thing is lost, its worth is known
    C. every shoe fits not every foot
    D. no man really lives who is buried in conceit

3. *The Congress of the United States provided for the coopera-*   3.__
    tion of the federal government with the states in the
    construction of rural roads all over the country and was
    a powerful force in the development of highways.
    Judging from the above paragraph, which one of the follow-
    ing statements is TRUE?
    A. Each state builds its highways and rural post roads
       unaided.
    B. Congress builds all highways in the United States.
    C. The states receive federal cooperation in the
       building of all roads.
    D. The federal government assists in the building of
       post roads.

4. LAKE is to LAND as ISLAND is to   4.__
    A. separated   B. land   C. lonely
    D. water   E. large

5. NOVELIST is to FICTION as HISTORIAN is to   5.__
    A. war   B. fact   C. books
    D. school   E. primitive

6. Four men agreed to dig a ditch in 20 days. After 10 days,   6.__
    only one-fourth of the ditch was completed.
    How many more men must be engaged to finish on time?

7. *Let a man be true to his intentions and his efforts to*   7.__
    fulfill them, and the point is gained, whether he succeed
    or not.
    The above statement states that
    A. a man cannot succeed unless he makes an effort to be
       true to his intentions
    B. he may be satisfied with himself if he makes an effort
       to be true to his intentions

C. every point is gained whether a man succeeds or fails.

D. no special effort is necessary for success

E. a certain amount of accomplishment always attends conscientious effort

8. MASS is to the WHOLE as ATOM is to
   A. physics   B. weight   C. solids
   D. part   E. theory

8.___

9. DIME is to CENT as DOLLAR is to
   A. silver   B. dime   C. nickel   D. paper   E. coin

9.___

10. WISE is to FOOLISH as KNOWLEDGE is to
    A. simple   B. ignorance   C. books
    D. learned   E. intolerance

10.___

11. REPUBLIC is to PRESIDENT as MONARCHY is to
    A. communists   B. ruler   C. constitution
    D. elections   E. emperor

11.___

12. The distance from A to C is 423 miles. Tourists left A at 7 A.M. and traveled 225 miles at 45 miles an hour, then stopped 30 minutes for lunch. The remainder of the trip was made at 36 miles an hour.
    At what time did they arrive at C?

12.___

13. The TRANSHENT population is quite large.
    The word in capitals is misspelled. Write it correctly at the right.

13.___

14. The LYOOTENANT wore a new uniform.
    The word in capitals is misspelled. Write it correctly at the right.

14.___

15. He stepped on the AKSELURAYTER.
    The word in capitals is misspelled. Write it correctly at the right.

15.___

16. Paper is easily PUNGKTYOORD.
    The word in capitals is misspelled. Write it correctly at the right.

16.___

17. Even in hot weather, the water supply is ADEKWAYT.
    The word in capitals is misspelled. Write it correctly at the right.

17.___

18. PLAUSIBLE explanations are
    A. ample   B. untrue
    C. courageous   D. apparently right
    E. impossible

18.___

19. Which one of the following words may be applied to   19.__
    OPTION but not to PURCHASE or SALE?
       A. Legal   B. Document   C. Permanent
       D. Abstract   E. Temporary   F. Concession

20. ATTENTUATE means to   20.__
       A. wire   B. flatter   C. heed
       D. lessen   E. be present   F. extend

21. GIVING is to LENDING as TAKING is to   21.__
       A. alms   B. prison   C. thieves
       D. stealing   E. kindness   F. borrowing

22. A and B together earned $180.00 on piece work. B worked   22.__
    only 2/3 as fast as A, but he worked 6 days more and
    received $90.00.
    How many days did A work?

23. CHEAP is to ABUNDANT as COSTLY is to   23.__
       A. plenty   B. inexpensive   C. high priced
       D. scarce   E. frugal

24. *Two-thirds of all American fires are home fires, and the*   24.__
    preponderant cause is carelessness. This source of
    economic waste and human suffering can be checked only as
    we exercise greater care to eliminate such fire hazards
    as the accumulation of inflammable rubbish, careless
    smoking habits, overheated stoves, etc. Remember this,
    that even though you have no fire loss, you share in the
    loss of every fire in the country.
    According to the above paragraph, which one of the follow-
    ing statements is TRUE?
       A. There are fewer fires in homes than in industrial
          plants.
       B. Fires are no loss when they are covered by insurance.
       C. This economic waste can be overcome only as we
          exercise greater care.
       D. Waste is the preponderant cause of home fires.
       E. Carelessness in the accumulation of rubbish causes
          fires.

25. If a stock of 500 rugs is divided into two parts, one of   25.__
    which contains 2/3 as many as the other, how many rugs
    are there in the smaller part?

KEY (CORRECT ANSWERS)

1. C
2. B
3. D
4. D
5. B

6. 8
7. E
8. D
9. B
10. B

11. E
12. 6:00 P.M.
13. transient
14. lieutenant
15. accelerator

16. accumulated
17. adequate
18. D
19. E
20. D

21. F
22. 12
23. D
24. C
25. 200

———

TEST 3

DIRECTIONS: Each question or incomplete statement is followed by several suggested answers or completions. Select the one that BEST answers the question or completes the statement. *PRINT THE CORRECT ANSWER IN THE SPACE AT THE RIGHT.*

1. John travels a mile in 1/3 of an hour. Ben travels a mile in 3/10 of an hour.
How many minutes does Ben finish before John, each traveling 12 miles?   1.__

2. KITTEN is to CAT as COLT is to   2.__
   A. young   B. pasture   C. horse
   D. donkey   E. cattle

3. WOLF is to HOWL as DOG is to   3.__
   A. bite   B. pet   C. bark
   D. pedigree   E. whine

4. DYNAMYT is used for blasting.
   The word in capitals is misspelled. Write it correctly
   at the right.   4.__

5. The champion's OPOHNENT won the boxing match.
   The word in capitals is misspelled. Write it correctly
   at the right.   5.__

6. The hungry man's appetite was APEEZD.
   The word in capitals is misspelled. Write it correctly
   at the right.   6.__

7. WHEN is to WHERE as TIME is to   7.__
   A. hour   B. place   C. clock   D. here   E. work

8. ATLANTIC is to OCEAN as BRAZIL is to   8.__
   A. South America   B. country   C. river
   D. large   E. small

9. REGIMENT is to ARMY as SHIP is to   9.__
   A. marines   B. wars   C. navy
   D. submarine   E. commerce

10. *Substitute or temporary clerks shall be paid at the rate   10.__
    of 75 cents an hour for each hour or part hour after
    6:00 P.M.*
    What one word in the above quotation is synonymous to
    a fixed value?

11. *The United States leads the world in the amount of sugar consumed per capita, more than a hundred pounds annually for every person in the nation. The rest of the world is just as fond of sugar but not so able to buy it.*
Judging from the above paragraph, which one of the following statements is TRUE?
    A. The United States leads in sugar production.
    B. Europeans pay more for sugar.
    C. Each person in the United States consumes a pound of sugar each week.
    D. The per capita consumption of sugar in the United States is the largest in the world.
    E. Americans are not so able to buy sugar as the rest of the world.
    F. More sugar is consumed in the United States than in the rest of the world.

11.____

12. HABITUAL means MOST NEARLY
    A. healthy   B. customary   C. clothing
    D. harness   E. deadly

12.____

13. A COMPETENT man is one who is
    A. capable   B. clever   C. idle
    D. ambitious   E. punctual

13.____

14. To ADHERE is to
    A. hate   B. tape   C. degrade
    D. cling to   E. listen

14.____

15. To CALCULATE is to
    A. number   B. compute   C. whitewash
    D. tell tales   E. think

15.____

16. Which one of the following terms may be applied to MOTOR-CYCLE and AIRPLANE but not to BICYCLE?
    A. High speed   B. Padded seats   C. Metal
    D. Rubber tires   E. Two wheels

16.____

17. *He can who believes he can.*
The above quotation means MOST NEARLY
    A. to believe a thing impossible is the way to make it so
    B. we are able when we feel so
    C. the man who believes is the man who achieves
    D. we walk by faith, not by sight
    E. nothing is impossible to him who tries

17.____

18. *Have many acquaintances, but few friends.*
The above quotation means MOST NEARLY
    A. be courteous to all, but intimate with few
    B. a true friend is forever a friend
    C. friends in distress make trouble less
    D. the only way to have a friend is to be one
    E. make friends of all you meet

18.____

19. *A man of many trades begs his bread on Sunday.*   19.__
    The above quotation means MOST NEARLY
    A. with too many irons in the fire some will burn
    B. doing everything is doing nothing
    C. one cannot do many things profitably at the same time
    D. an intense hour will do more than two dreamy years
    E. a man without a trade will beg his bread

20. *Caution is the parent of safety.*   20.__
    The above quotation means MOST NEARLY
    A. all things belong to the prudent
    B. better a mistake avoided than two corrected
    C. look before you leap
    D. better go around than jump and fall short

———

KEY (CORRECT ANSWERS)

1.	24 min.	11.	D
2.	C	12.	B
3.	C	13.	A
4.	dynamite	14.	D
5.	opponent	15.	B
6.	appeased	16.	A
7.	B	17.	C
8.	B	18.	A
9.	C	19.	C
10.	rate	20.	D

———

VERBAL ABILITIES TEST

FORM A

DIRECTIONS AND SAMPLE QUESTIONS

Study the sample questions carefully. Each question has four suggested answers. Decide which one is the best answer. Find the question number on the Sample Answer Sheet. Show your answer to the question by darkening completely the space corresponding to the letter that is the same as the letter of your answer. Keep your mark within the space. If you have to erase a mark, be sure to erase it completely. Mark only one answer for each question. Do NOT mark space E for any question.

SAMPLE VERBAL QUESTIONS

I. *Previous* means most nearly
   A) abandoned   C) timely
   B) former   D) younger

II. (*Reading*) "Just as the procedure of a collection department must be clear cut and definite, the steps being taken with the sureness of a skilled chess player, so the various paragraphs of a collection letter must show clear organization, giving evidence of a mind that, from the beginning, has had a specific end in view."

   The quotation best supports the statement that a collection letter should always
   A) show a spirit of sportsmanship
   B) be divided into several paragraphs
   C) be brief, but courteous
   D) be carefully planned

Decide which sentence is preferable with respect to grammar and usage suitable for a formal letter or report.

III. A) They do not ordinarily present these kind of reports in detail like this.
    B) A report of this kind is not hardly ever given in such detail as this one.
    C) This report is more detailed than what such reports ordinarily are.
    D) A report of this kind is not ordinarily presented in as much detail as this one is.

Find the correct spelling of the word and darken the proper answer space. If no suggested spelling is correct, darken space D.

IV. A) athalete   C) athlete
    B) athelete   D) none of these

V. SPEEDOMETER is related to POINTER as WATCH is related to
   A) case   C) dial
   B) hands   D) numerals

	SAMPLE ANSWER SHEET				
	A	B	C	D	E
I					
II					
III					
IV					
V					

	CORRECT ANSWERS TO SAMPLE QUESTIONS				
	A	B	C	D	E
I		■			
II				■	
III				■	
IV			■		
V		■			

EXAMINATION SECTION

Read each question carefully. Select the best answer and darken the proper space on the answer sheet.

1. *Flexible* means most nearly
   A) breakable   C) pliable
   B) flammable   D) weak

2. *Option* means most nearly
   A) use   C) value
   B) choice   D) blame

3. To *verify* means most nearly to
   A) examine   C) confirm
   B) explain   D) guarantee

4. *Indolent* means most nearly
   A) moderate   C) selfish
   B) hopeless   D) lazy

5. *Respiration* means most nearly
   A) recovery   C) pulsation
   B) breathing   D) sweating

6. PLUMBER is related to WRENCH as PAINTER is related to
   A) brush   C) shop
   B) pipe   D) hammer

7. LETTER is related to MESSAGE as PACKAGE is related to
   A) sender   C) insurance
   B) merchandise   D) business

8. FOOD is related to HUNGER as SLEEP is related to
   A) night   C) weariness
   B) dream   D) rest

9. KEY is related to TYPEWRITER as DIAL is related to
   A) sun   C) circle
   B) number   D) telephone

Grammar

10. A) I think that they will promote whoever has the best record.
    B) The firm would have liked to have promoted all employees with good records.
    C) Such of them that have the best records have excellent prospects of promotion.
    D) I feel sure they will give the promotion to whomever has the best record.

11. A) The receptionist must answer courteously the questions of all them callers.
    B) The receptionist must answer courteously the questions what are asked by the callers.
    C) There would have been no trouble if the receptionist had have always answered courteously.
    D) The receptionist should answer courteously the questions of all callers.

Spelling

12. A) collapsible   C) collapseble
    B) collapseable   D) none of these

13. A) ambigeuous   C) ambiguous
    B) ambigeous   D) none of these

14. A) predesessor   C) predecesser
    B) predecesar   D) none of these

15. A) sanctioned   C) sanctionned
    B) sancktioned   D) none of these

Reading

16. "The secretarial profession is a very old one and has increased in importance with the passage of time. In modern times, the vast expansion of business and industry has greatly increased the need and opportunities for secretaries, and for the first time in history their number has become large."

    The quotation best supports the statement that the secretarial profession
    A) is older than business and industry
    B) did not exist in ancient times
    C) has greatly increased in size
    D) demands higher training than it did formerly

17. "Civilization started to move ahead more rapidly when man freed himself of the shackles that restricted his search for the truth."

    The quotation best supports the statement that the progress of civilization
    A) came as a result of man's dislike for obstacles
    B) did not begin until restrictions on learning were removed
    C) has been aided by man's efforts to find the truth
    D) is based on continually increasing efforts

GO ON TO SIMILAR QUESTIONS ON NEXT PAGE.

2

18. *Vigilant* means most nearly
    A) sensible   C) suspicious
    B) watchful   D) restless

19. *Incidental* means most nearly
    A) independent   C) infrequent
    B) needless   D) casual

20. *Conciliatory* means most nearly
    A) pacific   C) obligatory
    B) contentious   D) offensive

21. *Altercation* means most nearly
    A) defeat   C) controversy
    B) concurrence   D) vexation

22. *Irresolute* means most nearly
    A) wavering   C) impudent
    B) insubordinate   D) unobservant

23. DARKNESS is related to SUNLIGHT as
    STILLNESS is related to
    A) quiet   C) sound
    B) moonlight   D) dark

24. DESIGNED is related to INTENTION as
    ACCIDENTAL is related to
    A) purpose   C) damage
    B) caution   D) chance

25. ERROR is related to PRACTICE as
    SOUND is related to
    A) deafness   C) muffler
    B) noise   D) horn

26. RESEARCH is related to FINDINGS as
    TRAINING is related to
    A) skill   C) supervision
    B) tests   D) teaching

27. A) If properly addressed, the letter will
       reach my mother and I.
    B) The letter had been addressed to myself
       and my mother.
    C) I believe the letter was addressed to
       either my mother or I.
    D) My mother's name, as well as mine, was
       on the letter.

28. A) The supervisor reprimanded the typist,
       whom she believed had made careless
       errors.
    B) The typist would have corrected the
       errors had she of known that the super-
       visor would see the report.
    C) The errors in the typed report were so
       numerous that they could hardly be
       overlooked.
    D) Many errors were found in the report
       which she typed and could not disregard
       them.

29. A) minieture   C) mineature
    B) minneature   D) none of these

30. A) extemporaneous   C) extemperaneous
    B) extempuraneus   D) none of these

31. A) problemmatical   C) problematicle
    B) problematical   D) none of these

32. A) descendant   C) desendant
    B) decendant   D) none of these

33. "The likelihood of America's exhausting
    her natural resources seems to be growing
    less. All kinds of waste are being re-
    worked and new uses are constantly being
    found for almost everything. We are get-
    ting more use out of our goods and are mak-
    ing many new byproducts out of what was
    formerly thrown away."
    *The quotation best supports the statement
    that* we seem to be in less danger of ex-
    hausting our resources because
    A) economy is found to lie in the use of
       substitutes
    B) more service is obtained from a given
       amount of material
    C) we are allowing time for nature to re-
       store them
    D) supply and demand are better controlled

34. "Telegrams should be clear, concise, and
    brief. Omit all unnecessary words. The
    parts of speech most often used in tele-
    grams are nouns, verbs, adjectives, and
    adverbs. If possible, do without pronouns,
    prepositions, articles, and copulative verbs.
    Use simple sentences, rather than complex
    or compound ones."
    *The quotation best supports the statement
    that* in writing telegrams one should always
    use
    A) common and simple words
    B) only nouns, verbs, adjectives, and
       adverbs
    C) incomplete sentences
    D) only the words essential to the meaning

GO ON TO SIMILAR QUESTIONS ON NEXT PAGE.

3

35. To *counteract* means most nearly to
   A) undermine   C) preserve
   B) censure   D) neutralize

36. *Deferred* means most nearly
   A) reversed   C) considered
   B) delayed   D) forbidden

37. *Feasible* means most nearly
   A) capable   C) practicable
   B) justifiable   D) beneficial

38. To *encounter* means most nearly to
   A) meet   C) overcome
   B) recall   D) retreat

39. *Innate* means most nearly
   A) eternal   C) native
   B) well-developed   D) prospective

40. STUDENT is related to TEACHER as DISCIPLE is related to
   A) follower   C) principal
   B) master   D) pupil

41. LECTURE is related to AUDITORIUM as EXPERIMENT is related to
   A) scientist   C) laboratory
   B) chemistry   D) discovery

42. BODY is related to FOOD as ENGINE is related to
   A) wheels   C) motion
   B) fuel   D) smoke

43. SCHOOL is related to EDUCATION as THEATER is related to
   A) management   C) recreation
   B) stage   D) preparation

44. A) Most all these statements have been supported by persons who are reliable and can be depended upon.
   B) The persons which have guaranteed these statements are reliable.
   C) Reliable persons guarantee the facts with regards to the truth of these statements.
   D) These statements can be depended on, for their truth has been guaranteed by reliable persons.

45. A) The success of the book pleased both his publisher and he.
   B) Both his publisher and he was pleased with the success of the book.
   C) Neither he or his publisher was disappointed with the success of the book.
   D) His publisher was as pleased as he with the success of the book.

46. A) extercate   C) extricate
   B) extracate   D) none of these

47. A) hereditory   C) hereditairy
   B) hereditary   D) none of these

48. A) auspiceous   C) auspicious
   B) auspiseous   D) none of these

49. A) sequance   C) sequense
   B) sequence   D) none of these

50. "The prevention of accidents makes it necessary not only that safety devices be used to guard exposed machinery but also that mechanics be instructed in safety rules which they must follow for their own protection, and that the lighting in the plant be adequate."

   The quotation best supports the statement that industrial accidents
   A) may be due to ignorance
   B) are always avoidable
   C) usually result from inadequate machinery
   D) cannot be entirely overcome

51. "The English language is peculiarly rich in synonyms, and there is scarcely a language spoken among men that has not some representative in English speech. The spirit of the Anglo-Saxon race has subjugated these various elements to one idiom, making not a patchwork, but a composite language."

   The quotation best supports the statement that the English language
   A) has few idiomatic expressions
   B) is difficult to translate
   C) is used universally
   D) has absorbed words from other languages

GO ON TO SIMILAR QUESTIONS ON NEXT PAGE.

52. To *acquiesce* means most nearly to
   A) assent
   B) acquire
   C) complete
   D) participate

53. *Unanimity* means most nearly
   A) emphasis
   B) namelessness
   C) harmony
   D) impartiality

54. *Precedent* means most nearly
   A) example
   B) theory
   C) law
   D) conformity

55. *Versatile* means most nearly
   A) broad-minded
   B) well-known
   C) up-to-date
   D) many-sided

56. *Authentic* means most nearly
   A) detailed
   B) reliable
   C) valuable
   D) practical

57. BIOGRAPHY is related to FACT as NOVEL is related to
   A) fiction
   B) literature
   C) narration
   D) book

58. COPY is related to CARBON PAPER as MOTION PICTURE is related to
   A) theater
   B) film
   C) duplicate
   D) television

59. EFFICIENCY is related to REWARD as CARELESSNESS is related to
   A) improvement
   B) disobedience
   C) reprimand
   D) repetition

60. ABUNDANT is related to CHEAP as SCARCE is related to
   A) ample
   B) costly
   C) inexpensive
   D) unobtainable

61. A) Brown's & Company employees have recently received increases in salary.
   B) Brown & Company recently increased the salaries of all its employees.
   C) Recently Brown & Company has increased their employees' salaries.
   D) Brown & Company have recently increased the salaries of all its employees.

62. A) In reviewing the typists' work reports, the job analyst found records of unusual typing speeds.
   B) It says in the job analyst's report that some employees type with great speed.
   C) The job analyst found that, in reviewing the typists' work reports, that some unusual typing speeds had been made.
   D) In the reports of typists' speeds, the job analyst found some records that are kind of unusual.

63. A) oblitorate
   B) oblitterat
   C) obbliterate
   D) none of these

64. A) diagnoesis
   B) diagnossis
   C) diagnosis
   D) none of these

65. A) contenance
   B) countenance
   C) countinance
   D) none of these

66. A) conceivably
   B) concieveably
   C) conceiveably
   D) none of these

67. "Through advertising, manufacturers exercise a high degree of control over consumers' desires. However, the manufacturer assumes enormous risks in attempting to predict what consumers will want and in producing goods in quantity and distributing them in advance of final selection by the consumers."

   The quotation best supports the statement that manufacturers
   A) can eliminate the risk of overproduction by advertising
   B) distribute goods directly to the consumers
   C) must depend upon the final consumers for the success of their undertakings
   D) can predict with great accuracy the success of any product they put on the market

68. "In the relations of man to nature, the procuring of food and shelter is fundamental. With the migration of man to various climates, ever new adjustments to the food supply and to the climate became necessary."

   The quotation best supports the statement that the means by which man supplies his material needs are
   A) accidental
   B) varied
   C) limited
   D) inadequate

GO ON TO SIMILAR QUESTIONS ON NEXT PAGE.

5

69. *Strident* means most nearly
   A) swaggering   C) angry
   B) domineering   D) harsh

70. To *confine* means most nearly to
   A) hide   C) eliminate
   B) restrict   D) punish

71. To *accentuate* means most nearly to
   A) modify   C) sustain
   B) hasten   D) intensify

72. *Banal* means most nearly
   A) commonplace   C) tranquil
   B) forceful   D) indifferent

73. *Incorrigible* means most nearly
   A) intolerable   C) irreformable
   B) retarded   D) brazen

74. POLICEMAN is related to ORDER as DOCTOR is related to
   A) physician   C) sickness
   B) hospital   D) health

75. ARTIST is related to EASEL as WEAVER is related to
   A) loom   C) threads
   B) cloth   D) spinner

76. CROWD is related to PERSONS as FLEET is related to
   A) expedition   C) navy
   B) officers   D) ships

77. CALENDAR is related to DATE as MAP is related to
   A) geography   C) mileage
   B) trip   D) vacation

78. A) Since the report lacked the needed information, it was of no use to him.
   B) This report was useless to him because there were no needed information in it.
   C) Since the report did not contain the needed information, it was not real useful to him.
   D) Being that the report lacked the needed information, he could not use it.

79. A) The company had hardly declared the dividend till the notices were prepared for mailing.
   B) They had no sooner declared the dividend when they sent the notices to the stockholders.
   C) No sooner had the dividend been declared than the notices were prepared for mailing.
   D) Scarcely had the dividend been declared than the notices were sent out.

80. A) compitition   C) competetion
    B) competition   D) none of these

81. A) occassion   C) ocassion
    B) occasion   D) none of these

82. A) knowlege   C) knowledge
    B) knolledge   D) none of these

83. A) deliborate   C) delibrate
    B) deliberate   D) none of these

84. "What constitutes skill in any line of work is not always easy to determine; economy of time must be carefully distinguished from economy of energy, as the quickest method may require the greatest expenditure of muscular effort, and may not be essential or at all desirable."

The quotation best supports the statement that
   A) the most efficiently executed task is not always the one done in the shortest time
   B) energy and time cannot both be conserved in performing a single task
   C) a task is well done when it is performed in the shortest time
   D) skill in performing a task should not be acquired at the expense of time

85. "It is difficult to distinguish between bookkeeping and accounting. In attempts to do so, bookkeeping is called the art, and accounting the science, of recording business transactions. Bookkeeping gives the history of the business in a systematic manner; and accounting classifies, analyzes, and interprets the facts thus recorded."

The quotation best supports the statement that
   A) accounting is less systematic than bookkeeping
   B) accounting and bookkeeping are closely related
   C) bookkeeping and accounting cannot be distinguished from one another
   D) bookkeeping has been superseded by accounting

FORM A
KEY (CORRECT ANSWERS)

If the competitor marked more than one answer to any question, draw a line through the answer boxes for the question. To make a stencil, punch out the answers on this page or on a separate answer sheet. Place this punched key over a competitor's sheet. Count the right answers. **DO NOT GIVE CREDIT FOR DOUBLE ANSWERS.**

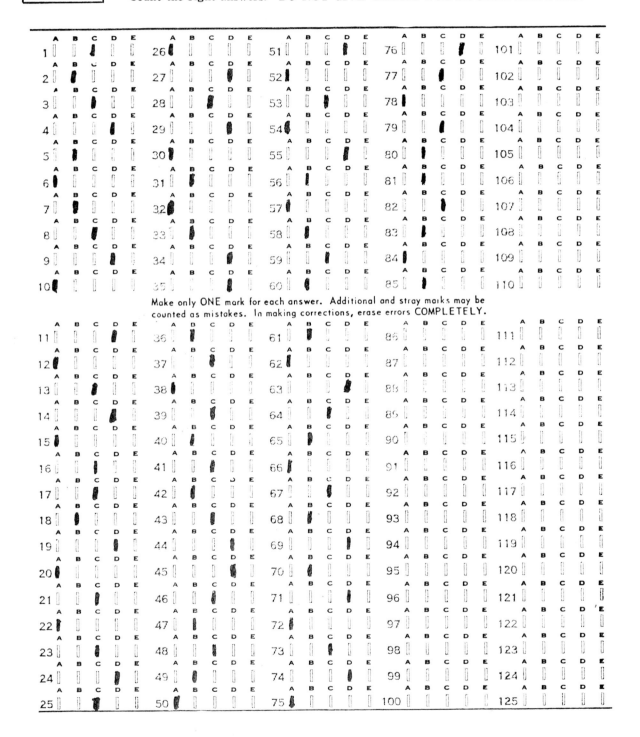

Make only ONE mark for each answer. Additional and stray marks may be counted as mistakes. In making corrections, erase errors COMPLETELY.

VERBAL ABILITIES TEST

FORM B

DIRECTIONS AND SAMPLE QUESTIONS

The time allowed both for the sample questions and for the test proper will be announced. Do not turn to page 9 until the signal to do so is given, even though you finish the sample questions.

Use the SPECIAL PENCIL furnished you by the examiner. Fill in the blanks at the top of the ANSWER SHEET. Place no other identifying marks on it. You are to record your answers on the separate answer sheet. For each question, select the best one of the suggested answers. Find the number on the answer sheet that is the same as the number of the question. Then, on the ANSWER SHEET, make a SOLID BLACK MARK in the space between the dotted lines just below the letter that is the same as the letter of your answer. Go over the mark two or three times because your answer sheet will be scored by an electric machine. If you wish to change your answer to a question, be sure to erase your first mark completely (do not merely cross it out) before making another. Make no unnecessary marks on your answer sheet. Keep it on a smooth hard surface.

The questions need not be taken up in order. You may answer first those questions that you are able to answer most readily and then use the remainder of the time for the questions you have omitted.

The sample questions below are similar to the questions in the test proper. Study the sample questions and answer them on the Sample Answer Sheet on the lower right-hand side of this page. Then compare your answers with the Correct Answers for Sample Questions.

SAMPLE QUESTIONS

In each question like samples I and II, select the one of the five suggested answers that means most nearly the same as the word or the group of words that is in italics. Mark the space on the Sample Answer Sheet under the letter that is the same as the letter of the answer you have selected.

I. To say that information is *authentic* means most nearly that it is
   A) detailed   D) valuable
   B) technical   E) practical
   C) reliable

    The space under C is marked for this question because *reliable* is the one of the five suggested answers that means most nearly the same as *authentic*.

II. *Previous* means most nearly
   A) abandoned   D) successive
   B) former   E) younger
   C) timely

III. (*Reading*) "Just as the procedure of a collection department must be clear-cut and definite, the steps being taken with the sureness of a skilled chess player, so the various paragraphs of a collection letter must show clear organization, giving evidence of a mind that, from the beginning, has had a specific end in view."

The quotation best supports the statement that a collection letter should always
   A) show a spirit of sportsmanship
   B) be divided into several paragraphs
   C) express confidence in the debtor
   D) be brief, but courteous
   E) be carefully planned

In each question like the following, find the correct spelling of the word and blacken the proper space on your answer sheet. If no suggested spelling is correct, blacken space D on your answer sheet.

IV. A) athalete   C) athlete
    B) athelete   D) none of these

    The correct spelling of the word is *athlete*. Since the C spelling is correct, the space under C is marked for this question.

Select the sentence that is preferable with respect to grammar and usage such as would be suitable in a formal letter or report. Then blacken the proper space on the answer sheet.

V. A) They don't ordinarily present these kind of reports in detail like this.
   B) Reports like this is not generally given in such great detail.
   C) A report of this kind isn't hardly ever given in such detail as this one.
   D) This report is more detailed than what such reports ordinarily are.
   E) A report of this kind is not ordinarily presented in such detail as this one.

SAMPLE ANSWER SHEET						CORRECT ANSWERS FOR SAMPLE QUESTIONS				
	A	B	C	D	E	A	B	C	D	E
I			■					■		
II							■			
III										■
IV			■					■		
V										■

8

EXAMINATION SECTION

Read each question carefully. Select the best answer and blacken the proper space on the answer sheet.

1. *Option* means most nearly
   A) use
   B) choice
   C) value
   D) blame
   E) mistake

2. *Irresolute* means most nearly
   A) wavering
   B) insubordinate
   C) impudent
   D) determined
   E) unobservant

3. *Flexible* means most nearly
   A) breakable
   B) inflammable
   C) pliable
   D) weak
   E) impervious

4. To *counteract* means most nearly to
   A) undermine
   B) censure
   C) preserve
   D) sustain
   E) neutralize

5. To *verify* means most nearly to
   A) justify
   B) explain
   C) confirm
   D) guarantee
   E) examine

6. *Indolent* means most nearly
   A) moderate
   B) relentless
   C) selfish
   D) lazy
   E) hopeless

7. To say that an action is *deferred* means most nearly that it is
   A) delayed
   B) reversed
   C) considered
   D) forbidden
   E) followed

8. To *encounter* means most nearly to
   A) meet
   B) recall
   C) overcome
   D) weaken
   E) retreat

9. *Feasible* means most nearly
   A) capable
   B) practicable
   C) justifiable
   D) beneficial
   E) reliable

10. *Respiration* means most nearly
    A) dehydration
    B) breathing
    C) pulsation
    D) sweating
    E) recovery

11. *Vigilant* means most nearly
    A) sensible
    B) ambitious
    C) watchful
    D) suspicious
    E) restless

12. To say that an action is taken *before the proper time* means most nearly that it is taken
    A) prematurely
    B) furtively
    C) temporarily
    D) punctually
    E) presently

13. *Innate* means most nearly
    A) eternal
    B) learned
    C) native
    D) prospective
    E) well-developed

14. *Precedent* means most nearly
    A) duplicate
    B) theory
    C) law
    D) conformity
    E) example

15. To say that the flow of work into an office is *incessant* means most nearly that it is
    A) more than can be handled
    B) uninterrupted
    C) scanty
    D) decreasing in volume
    E) orderly

16. *Unanimity* means most nearly
    A) emphasis
    B) namelessness
    C) disagreement
    D) harmony
    E) impartiality

17. *Incidental* means most nearly
    A) independent
    B) needless
    C) infrequent
    D) necessary
    E) casual

18. *Versatile* means most nearly
    A) broad-minded
    B) well-known
    C) old-fashioned
    D) many-sided
    E) up-to-date

19. *Conciliatory* means most nearly
    A) pacific
    B) contentious
    C) disorderly
    D) obligatory
    E) offensive

20. *Altercation* means most nearly
    A) defeat
    B) concurrence
    C) controversy
    D) consensus
    E) vexation

21. (*Reading*) "The secretarial profession is a very old one and has increased in importance with the passage of time. In modern times, the vast expansion of business and industry has greatly increased the need and opportunities for secretaries, and for the first time in history their number has become large."

    The quotation best supports the statement that the secretarial profession
    A) is older than business and industry
    B) did not exist in ancient times
    C) has greatly increased in size
    D) demands higher training than it did formerly
    E) has always had many members

9

22. (*Reading*) "The modern system of production unites various kinds of workers into a well-organized body in which each has a definite place."

The quotation best supports the statement that the modern system of production
A) increases production
B) trains workers
C) simplifies tasks
D) combines and places workers
E) combines the various plants

23. (*Reading*) "The prevention of accidents makes it necessary not only that safety devices be used to guard exposed machinery but also that mechanics be instructed in safety rules which they must follow for their own protection, and that the lighting in the plant be adequate."

The quotation best supports the statement that industrial accidents
A) may be due to ignorance
B) are always avoidable
C) usually result from inadequate machinery
D) cannot be entirely overcome
E) result in damage to machinery

24. (*Reading*) "It is wise to choose a duplicating machine that will do the work required with the greatest efficiency and at the least cost. Users with a large volume of business need speedy machines that cost little to operate and are well made."

The quotation best supports the statement that
A) most users of duplicating machines prefer low operating cost to efficiency
B) a well-built machine will outlast a cheap one
C) a duplicating machine is not efficient unless it is sturdy
D) a duplicating machine should be both efficient and economical
E) in duplicating machines speed is more usual than low operating cost

25. (*Reading*) "The likelihood of America's exhausting her natural resources seems to be growing less. All kinds of waste are being reworked and new uses are constantly being found for almost everything. We are getting more use out of our goods and are making many new byproducts out of what was formerly thrown away."

The quotation best supports the statement that we seem to be in less danger of exhausting our resources because
A) economy is found to lie in the use of substitutes
B) more service is obtained from a given amount of material
C) more raw materials are being produced
D) supply and demand are better controlled
E) we are allowing time for nature to restore them

26. (*Reading*) "Probably few people realize, as they drive on a concrete road, that steel is used to keep the surface flat and even, in spite of the weight of busses and trucks. Steel bars, deeply imbedded in the concrete, provide sinews to take the stresses so that they cannot crack the slab or make it wavy."

The quotation best supports the statement that a concrete road
A) is expensive to build
B) usually cracks under heavy weights
C) looks like any other road
D) is used exclusively for heavy traffic
E) is reinforced with other material

27. (*Reading*) "Through advertising, manufacturers exercise a high degree of control over consumers' desires. However, the manufacturer assumes enormous risks in attempting to predict what consumers will want and in producing goods in quantity and distributing them in advance of final selection by the consumers."

The quotation best supports the statement that manufacturers
A) can eliminate the risk of overproduction by advertising
B) completely control buyers' needs and desires
C) must depend upon the final consumers for the success of their undertakings
D) distribute goods directly to the consumers
E) can predict with great accuracy the success of any product they put on the market

28. (*Reading*) "Success in shorthand, like success in any other study, depends upon the interest the student takes in it. In writing shorthand it is not sufficient to know how to write a word correctly; one must also be able to write it quickly."

The quotation best supports the statement that
A) one must be able to read shorthand as well as to write it
B) shorthand requires much study
C) if a student can write correctly, he can also write quickly
D) proficiency in shorthand requires both speed and accuracy
E) interest in shorthand makes study unnecessary

GO ON TO THE NEXT PAGE

29. (*Reading*) "The countries in the Western Hemisphere were settled by people who were ready each day for new adventure. . The peoples of North and South America have retained, in addition to expectant and forward-looking attitudes, the ability and the willingness that they have often shown in the past to adapt themselves to new conditions."

The quotation best supports the statement that the peoples in the Western Hemisphere
A) no longer have fresh adventures daily
B) are capable of making changes as new situations arise
C) are no more forward-looking than the peoples of other regions
D) tend to resist regulations
E) differ considerably among themselves

30. (*Reading*) "Civilization started to move ahead more rapidly when man freed himself of the shackles that restricted his search for the truth."

The quotation best supports the statement that the progress of civilization
A) came as a result of man's dislike for obstacles
B) did not begin until restrictions on learning were removed
C) has been aided by man's efforts to find the truth
D) is based on continually increasing efforts
E) continues at a constantly increasing rate

31. (*Reading*) "It is difficult to distinguish between bookkeeping and accounting. In attempts to do so, bookkeeping is called the art, and accounting the science, of recording business transactions. Bookkeeping gives the history of the business in a systematic manner, and accounting classifies, analyzes, and interprets the facts thus recorded."

The quotation best supports the statement that
A) accounting is less systematic than bookkeeping
B) accounting and bookkeeping are closely related
C) bookkeeping and accounting cannot be distinguished from one another
D) bookkeeping has been superseded by accounting
E) the facts recorded by bookkeeping may be interpreted in many ways

32. (*Reading*) "Some specialists are willing to give their services to the Government entirely free of charge; some feel that a nominal salary, such as will cover traveling expenses, is sufficient for a position that is recognized as being somewhat honorary in nature; many other specialists value their time so highly that they will not devote any of it to public service that does not repay them at a rate commensurate with the fees that they can obtain from a good private clientele."

The quotation best supports the statement that the use of specialists by the Government
A) is rare because of the high cost of securing such persons
B) may be influenced by the willingness of specialists to serve
C) enables them to secure higher salaries in private fields
D) has become increasingly common during the past few years
E) always conflicts with private demands for their services

33. (*Reading*) "The leader of an industrial enterprise has two principal functions. He must manufacture and distribute a product at a profit, and he must keep individuals and groups of individuals working effectively together."

The quotation best supports the statement that an industrial leader should be able to
A) increase the distribution of his plant's product
B) introduce large-scale production methods
C) coordinate the activities of his employees
D) profit by the experience of other leaders
E) expand the business rapidly

34. (*Reading*) "The coloration of textile fabrics composed of cotton and wool generally requires two processes, as the process used in dyeing wool is seldom capable of fixing the color upon cotton. The usual method is to immerse the fabric in the requisite baths to dye the wool and then to treat the partially dyed material in the manner found suitable for cotton."

The quotation best supports the statement that the dyeing of textile fabrics composed of cotton and wool
A) is less complicated than the dyeing of wool alone
B) is more successful when the material contains more cotton than wool
C) is not satisfactory when solid colors are desired
D) is restricted to two colors for any one fabric
E) is usually based upon the methods required for dyeing the different materials

35. (*Reading*) "The fact must not be overlooked that only about one-half of the international trade of the world crosses the oceans. The other half is merely exchanges of merchandise between countries lying alongside each other or at least within the same continent."

The quotation best supports the statement that
A) the most important part of any country's trade is transoceanic
B) domestic trade is insignificant when compared with foreign trade
C) the exchange of goods between neighboring countries is not considered international trade
D) foreign commerce is not necessarily carried on by water
E) about one-half of the trade of the world is international

36. (*Reading*) "In the relations of man to nature, the procuring of food and shelter is fundamental. With the migration of man to various climates, ever new adjustments to the food supply and to the climate became necessary."

The quotation best supports the statement that the means by which man supplies his material needs are
A) accidental   D) uniform
B) varied   E) inadequate
C) limited

37. (*Reading*) "Every language has its peculiar word associations that have no basis in logic and cannot therefore be reasoned about. These idiomatic expressions are ordinarily acquired only by much reading and conversation although questions about such matters may sometimes be answered by the dictionary. Dictionaries large enough to include quotations from standard authors are especially serviceable in determining questions of idiom."

The quotation best supports the statement that idiomatic expressions
A) give rise to meaningless arguments because they have no logical basis
B) are widely used by recognized authors.
C) are explained in most dictionaries
D) are more common in some languages than in others
E) are best learned by observation of the language as actually used

38. (*Reading*) "Individual differences in mental traits assume importance in fitting workers to jobs because such personal characteristics are persistent and are relatively little influenced by training and experience."

The quotation best supports the statement that training and experience
A) are limited in their effectiveness in fitting workers to jobs
B) do not increase a worker's fitness for a job
C) have no effect upon a person's mental traits
D) have relatively little effect upon the individual's chances for success
E) should be based on the mental traits of an individual

39. (*Reading*) "The telegraph networks of the country now constitute wonderfully operated institutions, affording for ordinary use of modern business an important means of communication. The transmission of messages by electricity has reached the goal for which the postal service has long been striving, namely, the elimination of distance as an effective barrier of communication."

The quotation best supports the statement that
A) a new standard of communication has been attained
B) in the telegraph service, messages seldom go astray
C) it is the distance between the parties which creates the need for communication
D) modern business relies more upon the telegraph than upon the mails
E) the telegraph is a form of postal service

40. (*Reading*) "The competition of buyers tends to keep prices up, the competition of sellers to send them down. Normally the pressure of competition among sellers is stronger than that among buyers since the seller has his article to sell and must get rid of it, whereas the buyer is not committed to anything."

The quotation best supports the statement that low prices are caused by
A) buyer competition
B) competition of buyers with sellers
C) fluctuations in demand
D) greater competition among sellers than among buyers
E) more sellers than buyers

GO ON TO THE NEXT PAGE

In each question from 41 through 60, find the CORRECT spelling of the word, and blacken the proper space on your answer sheet. Sometimes there is no correct spelling; if none of the suggested spellings is correct, blacken space D on your answer sheet.

41. A) compitition C) competetion
  B) competition D) none of these

42. A) diagnoesis C) diagnosis
  B) diagnossis D) none of these

43. A) contenance C) countinance
  B) countenance D) none of these

44. A) deliborate C) delibrate
  B) deliberate D) none of these

45. A) knowlege C) knowledge
  B) knolledge D) none of these

46. A) occassion C) ocassion
  B) occasion D) none of these

47. A) sanctioned C) sanctionned
  B) sancktioned D) none of these

48. A) predesessor C) predecesser
  B) predecesar D) none of these

49. A) problemmatical C) problematicle
  B) problematical D) none of these

50. A) descendant C) desendant
  B) decendant D) none of these

51. A) collapsible C) collapseble
  B) collapseable D) none of these

52. A) sequance C) sequense
  B) sequence D) none of these

53. A) oblitorate C) obbliterate
  B) oblitterat D) none of these

54. A) ambigeuous C) ambiguous
  B) ambigeous D) none of these

55. A) minieture C) mineature
  B) minneature D) none of these

56. A) extemporaneous C) extemperaneous
  B) extempuraneus D) none of these

57. A) hereditory C) hereditairy
  B) hereditary D) none of these

58. A) conceivably C) conceiveably
  B) concieveably D) none of these

59. A) extercate C) extricate
  B) extracate D) none of these

60. A) auspiceous C) auspicious
  B) auspiseous D) none of these

Select the sentence that is preferable with respect to grammar and usage such as would be suitable in a formal letter or report. Then blacken the proper space on the answer sheet.

61. A) The receptionist must answer courteously the questions of all them callers.
  B) The questions of all callers had ought to be answered courteously.
  C) The receptionist must answer courteously the questions what are asked by the callers.
  D) There would have been no trouble if the receptionist had have always answered courteously.
  E) The receptionist should answer courteously the questions of all callers.

62. A) I had to learn a great number of rules, causing me to dislike the course.
  B) I disliked that study because it required the learning of numerous rules.
  C) I disliked that course very much, caused by the numerous rules I had to memorize.
  D) The cause of my dislike was on account of the numerous rules I had to learn in that course.
  E) The reason I disliked this study was because there were numerous rules that had to be learned.

63. A) If properly addressed, the letter will reach my mother and I.
  B) The letter had been addressed to myself and mother.
  C) I believe the letter was addressed to either my mother or I.
  D) My mother's name, as well as mine, was on the letter.
  E) If properly addressed, the letter it will reach either my mother or me.

64. A) A knowledge of commercial subjects and a mastery of English are essential if one wishes to be a good secretary.
  B) Two things necessary to a good secretary are that she should speak good English and to know commercial subjects.
  C) One cannot be a good secretary without she knows commercial subjects and English grammar.
  D) Having had good training in commercial subjects, the rules of English grammar should also be followed.
  E) A secretary seldom or ever succeeds without training in English as well as in commercial subjects.

65. A) He suspicions that the service is not so satisfactory as it should be.
    B) He believes that we should try and find whether the service is satisfactory.
    C) He raises the objection that the way which the service is given is not satisfactory.
    D) He believes that the quality of our services are poor.
    E) He believes that the service that we are giving is unsatisfactory.

66. A) Most all these statements have been supported by persons who are reliable and can be depended upon.
    B) The persons which have guaranteed these statements are reliable.
    C) Reliable persons guarantee the facts with regards to the truth of these statements.
    D) These statements can be depended on, for their truth has been guaranteed by reliable persons.
    E) Persons as reliable as what these are can be depended upon to make accurate statements.

67. A) Brown's & Company's employees have all been given increases in salary.
    B) Brown & Company recently increased the salaries of all its employees.
    C) Recently Brown & Company has increased their employees' salaries.
    D) Brown's & Company employees have recently received increases in salary.
    E) Brown & Company have recently increased the salaries of all its employees.

68. A) The personnel office has charge of employment, dismissals, and employee's welfare.
    B) Employment, together with dismissals and employees' welfare, are handled by the personnel department.
    C) The personnel office takes charge of employment, dismissals, and etc.
    D) The personnel office hires and dismisses employees, and their welfare is also its responsibility.
    E) The personnel office is responsible for the employment, dismissal, and welfare of employees.

69. A) This kind of pen is some better than that kind.
    B) I prefer having these pens than any other.
    C) This kind of pen is the most satisfactory for my use.
    D) In comparison with that kind of pen, this kind is more preferable.
    E) If I were to select between them all, I should pick this pen.

70. A) He could not make use of the report, as it was lacking of the needed information.
    B) This report was useless to him because there were no needed information in it.
    C) Since the report lacked the needed information, it was of no use to him.
    D) Being that the report lacked the needed information, he could not use it.
    E) Since the report did not contain the needed information, it was not real useful to him.

71. A) The paper we use for this purpose must be light, glossy, and stand hard usage as well.
    B) Only a light and a glossy, but durable, paper must be used for this purpose.
    C) For this purpose, we want a paper that is light, glossy, but that will stand hard wear.
    D) For this purpose, paper that is light, glossy, and durable is essential.
    E) Light and glossy paper, as well as standing hard usage, is necessary for this purpose.

72. A) The company had hardly declared the dividend till the notices were prepared for mailing.
    B) They had no sooner declared the dividend when they sent the notices to the stockholders.
    C) No sooner had the dividend been declared than the notices were prepared for mailing.
    D) Scarcely had the dividend been declared than the notices were sent out.
    E) The dividend had not scarcely been declared when the notices were ready for mailing.

GO ON TO THE NEXT PAGE.

14

73. A) Of all the employees, he spends the most time at the office.
    B) He spends more time at the office than that of his employees.
    C) His working hours are longer or at least equal to those of the other employees.
    D) He devotes as much, if not more, time to his work than the rest of the employees.
    E) He works the longest of any other employee in the office.

74. A) In the reports of typists' speeds, the job analyst found some records that are kind of unusual.
    B) It says in the job analyst's report that some employees type with great speed.
    C) The job analyst found that, in reviewing the typists' work reports, that some unusual typing speeds had been made.
    D) Work reports showing typing speeds include some typists who are unusual.
    E) In reviewing the typists' work reports, the job analyst found records of unusual typing speeds.

75. A) It is quite possible that we shall reemploy anyone whose training fits them to do the work.
    B) It is probable that we shall reemploy those who have been trained to do the work.
    C) Such of our personnel that have been trained to do the work will be again employed.
    D) We expect to reemploy the ones who have had training enough that they can do the work.
    E) Some of these people have been trained good and that will determine our reemploying them.

76. A) He as well as his publisher were pleased with the success of the book.
    B) The success of the book pleased both his publisher and he.
    C) Both his publisher and he was pleased with the success of the book.
    D) Neither he or his publisher was disappointed with the success of the book.
    E) His publisher was as pleased as he with the success of the book.

77. A) You have got to get rid of some of these people if you expect to have the quality of the work improve.
    B) The quality of the work would improve if they would leave fewer people do it.
    C) I believe it would be desirable to have fewer persons doing this work.
    D) If you had planned on employing fewer people than this to do the work, this situation would not have arose.
    E) Seeing how you have all those people on that work, it is not surprising that you have a great deal of confusion.

78. A) She made lots of errors in her typed report, and which caused her to be reprimanded.
    B) The supervisor reprimanded the typist, whom she believed had made careless errors.
    C) Many errors were found in the report which she typed and could not disregard them.
    D) The typist would have corrected the errors, had she of known that the supervisor would see the report.
    E) The errors in the typed report were so numerous that they could hardly be overlooked.

79. A) This kind of a worker achieves success through patience.
    B) Success does not often come to men of this type except they who are patient.
    C) Because they are patient, these sort of workers usually achieve success.
    D) This worker has more patience than any man in his office.
    E) This kind of worker achieves success through patience.

80. A) I think that they will promote whoever has the best record.
    B) The firm would have liked to have promoted all employees with good records.
    C) Such of them that have the best records have excellent prospects of promotion.
    D) I feel sure they will give the promotion to whomever has the best record.
    E) Whoever they find to have the best record will, I think, be promoted.

KEY (CORRECT ANSWERS)

Verbal Test

If the competitor marked more than one answer to any question, draw a line through the answer boxes for the question. To make a stencil, punch out the answers on this page or on a separate answer sheet. Place this punched key over a competitor's sheet. Count the right answers. DO NOT GIVE CREDIT FOR DOUBLE ANSWERS.

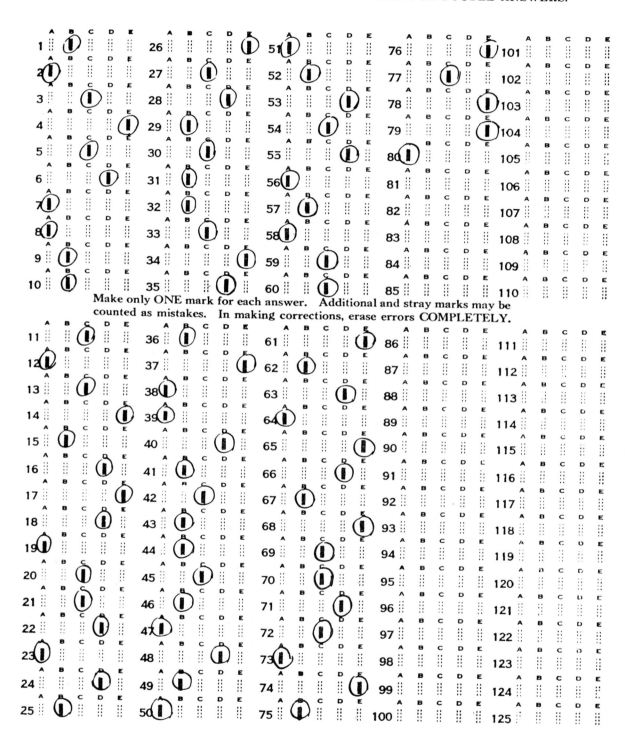

Make only ONE mark for each answer. Additional and stray marks may be counted as mistakes. In making corrections, erase errors COMPLETELY.

SPELLING

COMMENTARY

Spelling forms an integral part of tests of academic aptitude and achievement and of general and mental ability. Moreover, the spelling question is a staple of verbal and clerical tests in civil service entrance and promotional examinations.

Perhaps, the most rewarding way to learn to spell successfully is the direct, functional approach of learning to spell correctly, both orally and in writing, all words as they appear, both singly and in context.

In accordance with this positive method, the spelling question is presented here in "test" form, as it might appear on an actual examination.

The spelling question may appear on examinations in the following format:

> Five words are listed in each question. These are lettered A, B, C, D, and E. The examinee is to select one of the five (lettered) choices which is misspelled.

SAMPLE QUESTIONS

The directions for this part are approximately as follows:

> DIRECTIONS: Mark the space corresponding to the one MISSPELLED word in each of the following groups of words.

SAMPLE O

A. pitiful
B. latter
C. ommitted
D. agreement
E. reconcile

Since "ommitted" has been misspelled (correct spelling, omitted), C would be marked on the answer sheet.

SAMPLE OO

A. concept
B. notible
C. scrutiny
D. superlative
E. flexible

Since "notible" has been misspelled (correct spelling, notable), B would be marked on the answer sheet.

SPELLING
EXAMINATION SECTION
TEST 1

DIRECTIONS: Each question or incomplete statement is followed by
several suggested answers or completions. Select the
one that BEST answers the question or completes the
statement. *PRINT THE LETTER OF THE CORRECT ANSWER IN
THE SPACE AT THE RIGHT.*

Questions 1-5.

DIRECTIONS: Questions 1 through 5 consist of four words. Indicate
the letter of the word that is CORRECTLY spelled.

1. A. harassment   B. harrasment   1.____
    C. harasment   D. harrassment

2. A. maintainance   B. maintenence   2.____
    C. maintainence   D. maintenance

3. A. comparable   B. comprable   3.____
    C. comparible   D. commparable

4. A. suficient   B. sufficiant   4.____
    C. sufficient   D. suficiant

5. A. fairly   B. fairley   C. farely   D. fairlie

Questions 6-10.

DIRECTIONS: Questions 6 through 10 consist of four words. Indicate
the letter of the word that is INCORRECTLY spelled.

6. A. pallor   B. ballid   C. ballet   D. pallid   6.____

7. A. urbane   B. surburbane   7.____
    C. interurban   D. urban

8. A. facial   B. physical   C. fiscle   D. muscle   8.____

9. A. interceed   B. benefited   9.____
    C. analogous   D. altogether

10. A. seizure   B. irrelevant   10.____
    C. inordinate   D. dissapproved

KEY (CORRECT ANSWERS)

1. A		6. B	
2. D		7. B	
3. A		8. C	
4. C		9. A	
5. A		10. D	

TEST 2

DIRECTIONS: Each of Questions 1 through 15 consists of two words preceded by the letters A and B. In each question, one of the words may be spelled INCORRECTLY or both words may be spelled CORRECTLY. If one of the words in a question is spelled INCORRECTLY, print in the space at the right the capital letter preceding the INCORRECTLY spelled word. If both words are spelled CORRECTLY, print the letter C.

1.	A. easely	B. readily	1._
2.	A. pursue	B. decend	2._
3.	A. measure	B. laboratory	3._
4.	A. exausted	B. traffic	4._
5.	A. discussion	B. unpleasant	5._
6.	A. campaign	B. murmer	6._
7.	A. guarantee	B. sanatary	7._
8.	A. communication	B. safty	8._
9.	A. numerus	B. celebration	9._
10.	A. nourish	B. begining	10._
11.	A. courious	B. witness	11._
12.	A. undoubtedly	B. thoroughly	12._
13.	A. accessible	B. artifical	13._
14.	A. feild	B. arranged	14._
15.	A. admittence	B. hastily	15._

KEY (CORRECT ANSWERS)

1. A	6. B	11. A
2. B	7. B	12. C
3. C	8. B	13. B
4. A	9. A	14. A
5. C	10. B	15. A

TEST 3

DIRECTIONS: In each of the following sentences, one word is misspelled. Following each sentence is a list of four words taken from the sentence. Indicate the letter of the word which is MISSPELLED in the sentence. *PRINT THE LETTER OF THE CORRECT ANSWER IN THE SPACE AT THE RIGHT.*

1. The placing of any inflammable substance in any building, or the placing of any device or contrivence capable of producing fire, for the purpose of causing a fire is an attempt to burn.
   A. inflammable   B. substance
   C. device   D. contrivence
   1.____

2. The word *break* also means obtaining an entrance into a building by any artifice used for that purpose, or by colussion with any person therein.
   A. obtaining   B. entrance
   C. artifice   D. colussion
   2.____

3. Any person who with intent to provoke a breech of the peace causes a disturbance or is offensive to others may be deemed to have committed disorderly conduct.
   A. breech   B. disturbance
   C. offensive   D. committed
   3.____

4. When the offender inflicts a grevious harm upon the person from whose possession, or in whose presence, property is taken, he is guilty of robbery.
   A. offender   B. grevious
   C. possession   D. presence
   4.____

5. A person who willfully encourages or advises another person in attempting to take the latter's life is guilty of a felony.
   A. willfully   B. encourages
   C. advises   D. attempting
   5.____

6. He maliciously demurred to an ajournment of the proceedings.
   A. maliciously   B. demurred
   C. ajournment   D. proceedings
   6.____

7. His innocence at that time is irrelevant in view of his more recent villianous demeanor.
   A. innocence   B. irrelevant
   C. villianous   D. demeanor
   7.____

8. The mischievous boys aggrevated the annoyance of their neighbor.
   A. mischievous   B. aggrevated
   C. annoyance   D. neighbor
   8.____

9. While his perseverence was commendable, his judgment was   9.__
   debatable.
   A. perseverence   B. commendable
   C. judgment   D. debatable

10. He was hoping the appeal would facilitate his aquittal.   10.__
    A. hoping   B. appeal
    C. facilitate   D. aquittal

11. It would be preferable for them to persue separate courses. 11.__
    A. preferable   B. persue
    C. separate   D. courses

12. The litigant was complimented on his persistance and   12.__
    achievement.
    A. litigant   B. complimented
    C. persistance   D. achievement

13. Ocassionally there are discrepancies in the descriptions   13.__
    of miscellaneous items.
    A. ocassionally   B. discrepancies
    C. descriptions   D. miscellaneous

14. The councilmanic seargent-at-arms enforced the prohibition. 14.__
    A. councilmanic   B. seargent-at-arms
    C. enforced   D. prohibition

15. The teacher had an ingenious device for maintaning atten-   15.__
    dance.
    A. ingenious   B. device
    C. maintaning   D. attendance

16. A worrysome situation has developed as a result of the   16.__
    assessment that absenteeism is increasing despite our
    conscientious efforts.
    A. worrysome   B. assessment
    C. absenteeism   D. conscientious

17. I concurred with the credit manager that it was practicable 17.__
    to charge purchases on a biennial basis, and the company
    agreed to adhear to this policy.
    A. concurred   B. practicable
    C. biennial   D. adhear

18. The pastor was chagrined and embarassed by the irreverent   18.__
    conduct of one of his parishioners.
    A. chagrined   B. embarassed
    C. irreverent   D. parishioners

19. His inate seriousness was belied by his flippant demeanor. 19.__
    A. inate   B. belied
    C. flippant   D. demeanor

20. It was exceedingly regrettable that the excessive number   20.____
     of challanges in the court delayed the start of the trial.
    A. exceedingly   B. regrettable
    C. excessive   D. challanges

_____

KEY (CORRECT ANSWERS)

1. D		11. B	
2. D		12. C	
3. A		13. A	
4. B		14. B	
5. A		15. C	
6. C		16. A	
7. C		17. D	
8. B		18. B	
9. A		19. A	
10. D		20. D	

_____

TEST 4

Questions 1-11.

DIRECTIONS: Each question consists of three words. In each question
one of the words may be spelled incorrectly or all three
may be spelled correctly. For each question, if one of
the words is spelled INCORRECTLY, write the letter of
the incorrect word in the space at the right. If all
three words are spelled CORRECTLY, write the letter D
in the space at the right.

        SAMPLE I: (A) guide   (B) departmint   (C) stranger
                                    (B)
        SAMPLE II: (A) comply   (B) valuable   (C) window

In Sample I, departmint is incorrect. It should be
spelled department. Therefore, B is the answer.

In Sample II, all three words are spelled correctly.
Therefore, D is the answer.

1.	A. argument	B. reciept	C. complain	1.__
2.	A. sufficient	B. postpone	C. visible	2.__
3.	A. expirience	B. dissatisfy	C. alternate	3.__
4.	A. occurred	B. noticable	C. appendix	4.__
5.	A. anxious	B. guarantee	C. calender	5.__
6.	A. sincerely	B. affectionately	C. truly	6.__
7.	A. excellant	B. verify	C. important	7.__
8.	A. error	B. quality	C. enviroment	8.__
9.	A. exercise	B. advance	C. pressure	9.__
10.	A. citizen	B. expence	C. memory	10.__
11.	A. flexable	B. focus	C. forward	

Questions 12-15.

DIRECTIONS: Each of Questions 12 through 15 consists of a group of
four words. Examine each group carefully; then in the
space at the right, indicate
    A - if only one word in the group is spelled correctly
    B - if two words in the group are spelled correctly
    C - if three words in the group are spelled correctly
    D - if all four words in the group are spelled correct

12. Wendsday, particular, similar, hunderd   12.____

13. realize, judgment, opportunities, consistent   13.____

14. equel, principle, assistense, commitee   14.____

15. simultaneous, privilege, advise, ocassionaly   15.____

———

KEY (CORRECT ANSWERS)

1. B	6. D	11. A
2. D	7. A	12. B
3. A	8. C	13. D
4. B	9. D	14. A
5. C	10. B	15. C

———

TEST 5

DIRECTIONS: Each of Questions 1 through 15 consists of two words preceded by the letters A and B. In each item, one of the words may be spelled INCORRECTLY or both words may be spelled CORRECTLY. If one of the words in a question is spelled INCORRECTLY, print in the space at the right the letter preceding the INCORRECTLY spelled word. If both words are spelled CORRECTLY, print the letter C.

1. A. justified   B. offering
2. A. predjudice   B. license
3. A. label   B. pamphlet
4. A. bulletin   B. physical
5. A. assure   B. exceed
6. A. advantagous   B. evident
7. A. benefit   B. occured
8. A. acquire   B. graditude
9. A. amenable   B. boundry
10. A. deceive   B. voluntary
11. A. imunity   B. conciliate
12. A. acknoledge   B. presume
13. A. substitute   B. prespiration
14. A. reputible   B. announce
15. A. luncheon   B. wretched

EXAMINATION SECTION

1. C	6. A	11. A
2. A	7. B	12. A
3. C	8. B	13. B
4. C	9. B	14. A
5. C	10. C	15. C

TEST 6

DIRECTIONS: Questions 1 through 15 contain lists of words, one of which is misspelled. Indicate the MISSPELLED word in each group. *PRINT THE LETTER OF THE CORRECT ANSWER IN THE SPACE AT THE RIGHT.*

1. A. felony   B. lacerate   1.____
    C. cancellation   D. seperate

2. A. batallion   B. beneficial   2.____
    C. miscellaneous   D. secretary

3. A. camouflage   B. changeable   C. embarass   D. inoculate   3.____

4. A. beneficial   B. disasterous   4.____
    C. incredible   D. miniature

5. A. auxilliary   B. hypocrisy   C. phlegm   D. vengeance   5.____

6. A. aisle   B. cemetary   6.____
    C. courtesy   D. extraordinary

7. A. crystallize   B. innoculate   7.____
    C. eminent   D. symmetrical

8. A. judgment   B. maintainance   8.____
    C. bouillon   D. eery

9. A. isosceles   B. ukulele   C. mayonaise   D. iridescent   9.____

10. A. remembrance   B. occurence   10.____
    C. correspondence   D. countenance

11. A. corpuscles   B. mischievous   11.____
    C. batchelor   D. bulletin

12. A. terrace   B. banister   C. concrete   D. masonery   12.____

13. A. balluster   B. gutter   C. latch   D. bridging   13.____

14. A. personnell   B. navel   C. therefor   D. emigrant   14.____

15. A. committee   B. submiting   15.____
    C. amendment   D. electorate

KEY (CORRECT ANSWERS)

1. D	6. B	11. C
2. A	7. B	12. D
3. C	8. B	13. A
4. B	9. C	14. A
5. A	10. B	15. B

TEST 7

Questions 1-5.

DIRECTIONS: Questions 1 through 5 consist of groups of four words.
              Select answer:
              A if only ONE word is spelled correctly in a group
              B if TWO words are spelled correctly in a group
              C if THREE words are spelled correctly in a group
              D if all FOUR words are spelled correctly in a group

1. counterfeit, embarass, panicky, supercede   1._

2. benefited, personnel, questionnaire, unparalelled   2._

3. bankruptcy, describable, proceed, vacuum   3._

4. handicapped, mispell, offerred, pilgrimmage   4._

5. corduroy, interfere, privilege, separator   5._

Questions 6-10.

DIRECTIONS: Questions 6 through 10 consist of four pairs of words
              each. Some of the words are spelled correctly; others
              are spelled incorrectly. For each question, indicate
              in the space at the right the letter preceding that
              pair of words in which BOTH words are spelled CORRECTLY.

6.   A. hygienic, inviegle   B. omniscience, pittance   6._
     C. plagarize, nullify   D. seargent, perilous

7.   A. auxilary, existence   B. pronounciation, accordance 7._
     C. ignominy, indegence   D. suable, baccalaureate

8.   A. discreet, inaudible   B. hypocrisy, currupt   8._
     C. liquidate, maintainance   D. transparancy, onerous

9.   A. facility, stimulent   B. frugel, sanitary   9._
     C. monetary, prefatory   D. punctileous, credentials

10. A. bankruptsy, perceptible   B. disuade, resilient   10._
     C. exhilerate, expectancy   D. panegyric, disparate

Questions 11-15.

DIRECTIONS: Each question or incomplete statement is followed by
              several suggested answers or completions. Select the
              one that BEST answers the question or completes the
              statement. *PRINT THE LETTER OF THE CORRECT ANSWER IN
              THE SPACE AT THE RIGHT.*

11. The silent *e* must be retained when the suffix -*able* is   11.___
     added to the word
        A. argue   B. love   C. move   D. notice

12. The CORRECTLY spelled word in the choices below is   12.___
        A. kindergarden   B. zylophone
        C. hemorrhage   D. mayonaise

13. Of the following words, the one spelled CORRECTLY is   13.___
        A. begger   B. cemetary
        C. embarassed   D. coyote

14. Of the following words, the one spelled CORRECTLY is   14.___
        A. dandilion B. wiry   C. sieze   D. rythmic

15. Of the following words, the one spelled CORRECTLY is   15.___
        A. beligerent   B. anihilation
        C. facetious   D. adversery

                              _____

KEY (CORRECT ANSWERS)

1. B	6. B	11. D
2. C	7. D	12. C
3. D	8. A	13. D
4. A	9. C	14. B
5. D	10. D	15. C

                              _____

TEST 8

1. If the administrator attempts to withold information, there is a good likelihood that there will be serious repercussions.
    A. administrator   B. withold
    C. likelihood   D. repercussions

2. He condescended to apologize, but we felt that a beligerent person should not occupy an influential position.
    A. condescended   B. apologize
    C. beligerent   D. influential

3. Despite the sporadic delinquent payments of his indebtedness, Mr. Johnson has been an exemplery customer.
    A. sporadic   B. delinquent
    C. indebtedness   D. exemplery

4. He was appreciative of the support he consistantly acquired, but he felt that he had waited an inordinate length of time for it.
    A. appreciative   B. consistantly
    C. acquired   D. inordinate

5. Undeniably they benefited from the establishment of a receivership, but the question of statutary limitations remained unresolved.
    A. undeniably   B. benefited
    C. receivership   D. statutary

6. Mr. Smith profered his hand as an indication that he considered it a viable contract, but Mr. Nelson alluded to the fact that his colleagues had not been consulted.
    A. profered   B. viable
    C. alluded   D. colleagues

7. The treatments were beneficial according to the optomotrists, and the consensus was that minimal improvement could be expected.
    A. beneficial   B. optomotrists
    C. consensus   D. minimal

8. Her frivalous manner was unbecoming because the air of   8.____
   solemnity at the cemetery was pervasive.
      A. frivalous   B. solemnity
      C. cemetery   D. pervasive

9. The clandestine meetings were designed to make the two   9.____
   adversaries more amicable, but they served only to
   intensify their emnity.
      A. clandestine   B. adversaries
      C. amicable   D. emnity

10. Do you think that his innovative ideas and financial   10.____
    acumen will help stabalize the fluctuations of the
    stock market?
      A. innovative   B. acumen
      C. stabalize   D. fluctuations

11. In order to keep a perpetual inventory, you will have to   11.____
    keep an uninterrupted surveillance of all the
    miscellanious stock.
      A. perpetual   B. uninterrupted
      C. surveillance   D. miscellanious

12. She used the art of pursuasion on the children because   12.____
    she found that caustic remarks had no perceptible effect
    on their behavior.
      A. pursuasion   B. caustic
      C. perceptible   D. effect

13. His sacreligious outbursts offended his constituents,   13.____
    and he was summarily removed from office by the City
    Council.
      A. sacreligious   B. constituents
      C. summarily   D. Council

14. They exhorted the contestants to greater efforts, but the   14.____
    exhorbitant costs in terms of energy expended resulted
    in a feeling of lethargy.
      A. exhorted   B. contestants
      C. exhorbitant   D. lethargy

15. Since he was knowledgable about illicit drugs, he was   15.____
    served with a subpoena to appear for the prosecution.
      A. knowledgable   B. illicit
      C. subpoena   D. prosecution

16. In spite of his lucid statements, they denigrated his   16.____
    report and decided it should be succintly paraphrased.
      A. lucid   B. denigrated
      C. succintly   D. paraphrased

17. The discussion was not germane to the contraversy, but   17.____
    the indicted man's insistence on further talk was allowed.
      A. germane   B. contraversy
      C. indicted   D. insistence

18. The legislators were enervated by the distances they had   18
    traveled during the election year to fullfil their
    speaking engagements.
    A. legislators   B. enervated
    C. traveled   D. fullfil

19. The plaintiffs' attornies charged the defendant in the   19
    case with felonious assault.
    A. plaintiffs'   B. attornies
    C. defendant   D. felonious

20. It is symptomatic of the times that we try to placate all, 20
    but a proposal for new forms of disciplinery action was
    promulgated by the staff.
    A. symptomatic   B. placate
    C. disciplinery   D. promulgated

―――――

KEY (CORRECT ANSWERS)

1. B	11. D
2. C	12. A
3. D	13. A
4. B	14. C
5. D	15. A
6. A	16. C
7. B	17. B
8. A	18. D
9. D	19. B
10. C	20. C

―――――

TEST 9

DIRECTIONS: Each of Questions 1 through 15 consists of a single word which is spelled either correctly or incorrectly. If the word is spelled CORRECTLY, you are to print the letter C (Correct) in the space at the right. If the word is spelled INCORRECTLY, you are to print the letter W (Wrong).

1. pospone

2. diffrent

3. height

4. carefully

5. ability

6. temper

7. deslike

8. seldem

9. alcohol

10. expense

11. vegatable

12. dispensary

13. specemin

14. allowance

15. exersise

1. ____
2. ____
3. ____
4. ____
5. ____
6. ____
7. ____
8. ____
9. ____
10. ____
11. ____
12. ____
13. ____
14. ____
15. ____

EXAMINATION SECTION

1. W	6. C	11. W
2. W	7. W	12. C
3. C	8. W	13. W
4. C	9. C	14. C
5. C	10. C	15. W

TEST 10

DIRECTIONS: Each of Questions 1 through 10 consists of four words, one of which may be spelled incorrectly or all four words may be spelled correctly. If one of the words in a question is spelled incorrectly, print in the space at the right the capital letter preceding the word which is spelled INCORRECTLY. If all four words are spelled CORRECTLY, print the letter E.

1. A. dismissal   B. collateral   1.
    C. leisure   D. proffession

2. A. subsidary   B. outrageous   C. liaison   D. assessed   2.

3. A. already   B. changeable   C. mischevous   D. cylinder   3.

4. A. supersede   B. deceit   C. dissension   D. imminent   4.

5. A. arguing   B. contagious   C. comparitive D. accessible 5.

6. A. indelible   B. existance   6.
    C. presumptuous   D. mileage

7. A. extention   B. aggregate   C. sustenance   D. gratuitous 7.

8. A. interrogate   B. exaggeration   8.
    C. vacillate   D. moreover

9. A. parallel   B. derogatory   C. admissable   D. appellate   9.

10. A. safety   B. cumalative   C. disappear   D. usable   10.

KEY (CORRECT ANSWERS)

1. D	6. B
2. A	7. A
3. C	8. E
4. E	9. C
5. C	10. B

TEST 11

DIRECTIONS: Each of Questions 1 through 10 consists of four words, one of which may be spelled incorrectly or all four words may be spelled correctly. If one of the words in a question is spelled INCORRECTLY, print in the space at the right the capital letter preceding the word which is spelled incorrectly. If all four words are spelled CORRECTLY, print the letter E.

1. A. vehicular   B. gesticulate   1.___
    C. manageable   D. fullfil

2. A. inovation   B. onerous   2.___
    C. chastise   D. irresistible

3. A. familiarize   B. dissolution   3.___
    C. oscillate   D. superflous

4. A. census   B. defender   4.___
    C. adherence   D. inconceivable

5. A. voluminous   B. liberalize   5.___
    C. bankrupcy   D. conversion

6. A. justifiable   B. executor   6.___
    C. perpatrate   D. dispelled

7. A. boycott   B. abeyence   C. enterprise   D. circular   7.___

8. A. spontaineous   B. dubious   8.___
    C. analyze   D. premonition

9. A. intelligible   B. apparently   9.___
    C. genuine   D. crucial

10. A. plentiful   B. ascertain   10.___
    C. carreer   D. preliminary

KEY (CORRECT ANSWERS)

1.	D	6.	C
2.	A	7.	B
3.	D	8.	A
4.	E	9.	E
5.	C	10.	C

TEST 12

DIRECTIONS: Questions 1 through 25 consist of four words each, of which one of the words may be spelled incorrectly or all four words may be spelled correctly. If one of the words in a question is spelled INCORRECTLY, print in the space at the right the capital letter preceding the word which is spelled incorrectly. If all four words are spelled CORRECTLY, print the letter E.

1. A. temporary   B. existance   1.__
    C. complimentary   D. altogether

2. A. privilege   B. changeable   C. jeopardize   D. commitment   2.__

3. A. grievous   B. alloted   C. outrageous   D. mortgage   3.__

4. A. tempermental   B. accommodating   4.__
    C. bookkeeping   D. panicky

5. A. auxiliary   B. indispensable   5.__
    C. ecstasy   D. fiery

6. A. dissappear B. buoyant   C. imminent   D. parallel   6.__

7. A. loosly   B. medicine   C. schedule   D. defendant   7.__

8. A. endeavor   B. persuade   8.__
    C. retroactive   D. desparate

9. A. usage   B. servicable   9.__
    C. disadvantageous   D. remittance

10. A. beneficary B. receipt   C. excitable   D. implement   10.__

11. A. accompanying   B. intangible   11.__
    C. offered   D. movable

12. A. controlling   B. seize   12.__
    C. repetitious   D. miscellaneous

13. A. installation   B. accommodation   13.__
    C. consistant   D. illuminate

14. A. incidentaly   B. privilege   14.__
    C. apparent   D. chargeable

15. A. prevalent   B. serial   15.__
    C. briefly   D. disatisfied

16. A. reciprocal   B. concurrence   16.__
    C. persistence   D. withold

17. A. deferred   B. suing   C. fulfilled   D. pursuant   17.___

18. A. questionnable   B. omission   18.___
     C. acknowledgment   D. insistent

19. A. guarantee   B. committment   19.___
     C. mitigate   D. publicly

20. A. prerogative   B. apprise   20.___
     C. extrordinary   D. continual

21. A. arrogant   B. handicapped   21.___
     C. judicious   D. perennial

22. A. permissable   B. deceive   22.___
     C. innumerable   D. retrieve

23. A. notable   B. allegiance   C. reimburse   D. illegal   23.___

24. A. wholly   B. disbursement   24.___
     C. hindrance   D. conciliatory

25. A. guidance   B. condemn   C. publically   D. coercion   25.___

KEY (CORRECT ANSWERS)

1. B		11. C	
2. E		12. E	
3. B		13. C	
4. A		14. A	
5. E		15. D	
6. A		16. D	
7. A		17. E	
8. D		18. A	
9. B		19. B	
10. A		20. C	

21. E
22. A
23. E
24. E
25. C

SPELLING
EXAMINATION SECTION
TEST 1

DIRECTIONS: In each of the following tests in this part, select the letter of the one MISSPELLED word in each of the following groups of words. *PRINT THE LETTER OF THE CORRECT ANSWER IN THE SPACE AT THE RIGHT.*

1. A. grateful   B. fundimental   C. census   D. analysis   1.____

2. A. installment   B. retrieve   C. concede   D. dissapear   2.____

3. A. accidentaly   B. dismissal   C. conscientious   D. indelible   3.____

4. A. perceive   B. carreer   C. anticipate   D. acquire   4.____

5. A. facillity   B. reimburse   C. assortment   D. guidance   5.____

6. A. plentiful   B. across   C. advantagous   D. similar   6.____

7. A. omission   B. pamphlet   C. guarrantee   D. repel   7.____

8. A. maintenance   B. always   C. liable   D. anouncement   8.____

9. A. exaggerate   B. sieze   C. condemn   D. commit   9.____

10. A. pospone   B. altogether   C. grievance   D. excessive   10.____

11. A. banana   B. trafic   C. spectacle   D. boundary   11.____

12. A. commentator   B. abbreviation   C. battaries   D. monastery   12.____

13. A. practically   B. advise   C. pursuade   D. laboratory   13.____

14. A. fatigueing   B. invincible   C. strenuous   D. ceiling   14.____

15. A. propeller   B. reverence   C. piecemeal   D. underneth   15.____

16. A. annonymous   B. envelope   C. transit   D. variable   16.____

17. A. petroleum   B. bigoted   C. meager   D. resistence   17.____

18. A. permissible   B. indictment   C. fundemental   D. nowadays   18.____

19. A. thief   B. bargin   C. nuisance   D. vacant   19.__

20. A. technique   B. vengeance   C. aquatic   D. heighth   20.__

TEST 2

1.   A. apparent   B. superintendent   1.__
     C. releive   D. calendar

2.   A. foreign   B. negotiate   C. typical   D. disipline   2.__

3.   A. posponed   B. argument   3.__
     C. susceptible   D. deficit

4.   A. preferred   B. column   C. peculiar   D. equiped   4.__

5.   A. exaggerate   B. disatisfied   5.__
     C. repetition   D. already

6.   A. livelihood   B. physician   C. obsticle   D. strategy   6.__

7.   A. courageous   B. ommission   C. ridiculous D. awkward   7.__

8.   A. sincerely   B. abundance   C. negligable D. elementary   8.__

9.   A. obsolete   B. mischievous   9.__
     C. enumerate   D. atheletic

10. A. fiscel   B. beneficiary   10.__
     C. concede   D. translate

11. A. segregate   B. excessivly C. territory   D. obstacle   11.__

12. A. unnecessary   B. monopolys   12.__
     C. harmonious   D. privilege

13. A. sinthetic   B. intellectual   13.__
     C. gracious   D. archaic

14. A. beneficial   B. fulfill   C. sarcastic   D. disolve   14.__

15. A. umbrella   B. sentimental   15.__
     C. inefficent   D. psychiatrist

16. A. noticable   B. knapsack   C. librarian   D. meant   16.__

17. A. conference   B. upheaval   C. vulger   D. odor   17.__

18. A. surmount   B. pentagon   C. calorie   D. inumerable 18.__

19. A. classifiable   B. moisturize   19.__
     C. monitor   D. assesment

20. A. thermastat   B. corrupting C. approach   D. thinness   20.__

TEST 3

1.	A. typical	B. descend	C. summarize	D. continuel	1.___
2.	A. courageous	B. recomend	C. omission	D. eliminate	2.___
3.	A. compliment C. auxilary		B. illuminate D. installation		3.___
4.	A. preliminary C. syllable		B. aquainted D. analysis		4.___
5.	A. accustomed	B. negligible	C. interupted	D. bulletin	5.___
6.	A. summoned	B. managment	C. mechanism	D. sequence	6.___
7.	A. commitee	B. surprise	C. noticeable	D. emphasize	7.___
8.	A. occurrance	B. likely	C. accumulate	D. grievance	8.___
9.	A. obstacle C. baggage		B. particuliar D. fascinating		9.___
10.	A. innumerable C. applicant		B. seize D. dictionery		10.___
11.	A. monkeys	B. rigid	C. unnatural	D. roomate	11.___
12.	A. surveying	B. figurative	C. famous	D. curiosety	12.___
13.	A. rodeo C. calendar		B. inconcievable D. magnificence		13.___
14.	A. handicaped	B. glacier	C. defiance	D. emperor	14.___
15.	A. schedule	B. scrawl	C. seclusion	D. sissors	15.___
16.	A. tissues	B. tomatos	C. tyrants	D. tragedies	16.___
17.	A. casette	B. graceful	C. penicillin	D. probably	17.___
18.	A. gnawed	B. microphone	C. clinicle	D. batch	18.___
19.	A. amateur	B. altitude	C. laborer	D. expence	19.___
20.	A. mandate	B. flexable	C. despise	D. verify	20.___

TEST 4

1.	A. primery	B. mechanic	C. referred	D. admissible	1.___
2.	A. cessation	B. beleif	C. aggressive	D. allowance	2.___
3.	A. leisure C. familiar		B. authentic D. contemptable		3.___

3

4. A. volume   B. forty   C. dilemma   D. seldum   4.__

5. A. discrepancy   B. aquisition   5.__
    C. exorbitant   D. lenient

6. A. simultanous   B. penetrate   6.__
    C. revision   D. conspicuous

7. A. ilegible   B. gracious   C. profitable   D. obedience   7.__

8. A. manufacturer   B. authorize   8.__
    C. compelling   D. pecular

9. A. anxious   B. rehearsal   C. handicaped   D. tendency   9.__

10. A. meticulous   B. accompaning   10.__
    C. initiative   D. shelves

11. A. hammaring   B. insecticide   11.__
    C. capacity   D. illogical

12. A. budget   B. luminous   C. aviation   D. lunchon   12.__

13. A. moniter   B. bachelor   13.__
    C. pleasurable   D. omitted

14. A. monstrous   B. transistor   C. narrative   D. anziety   14.__

15. A. engagement   B. judical   C. pasteurize   D. tried   15.

16. A. fundimental   B. innovation   16.__
    C. perpendicular   D. extravagant

17. A. bookkeeper   B. brutality   C. gymnaseum   D. cemetery   17.__

18. A. sturdily   B. pretentious   18.__
    C. gourmet   D. enterance

19. A. resturant   B. tyranny   19.__
    C. kindergarten   D. ancestry

20. A. benefit   B. possess   C. speciman   D. noticing   20.__

TEST 5

1. A. arguing   B. correspondance   1.__
    C. forfeit   D. dissension

2. A. occasion   B. description   2.__
    C. prejudice   D. elegible

3. A. accomodate   B. initiative   C. changeable   D. enroll   3.__

4.	A. temporary	B. insistent	C. benificial	D. separate	4.____
5.	A. achieve C. unanimous		B. dissappoint D. judgment		5.____
6.	A. procede	B. publicly	C. sincerity	D. successful	6.____
7.	A. deceive	B. goverment	C. preferable	D. repetitive	7.____
8.	A. emphasis	B. skillful	C. advisible	D. optimistic	8.____
9.	A. tendency	B. rescind	C. crucial	D. noticable	9.____
10.	A. privelege	B. abbreviate	C. simplify	D. divisible	10.____
11.	A. irresistible C. mutual		B. varius D. refrigerator		11.____
12.	A. amateur C. rehearsal		B. distinguish D. poision		12.____
13.	A. biased	B. ommission	C. precious	D. coordinate	13.____
14.	A. calculated	B. enthusiasm	C. sincerely	D. parashute	14.____
15.	A. sentry	B. materials	C. incredable	D. budget	15.____
16.	A. chocolate	B. instrument	C. volcanoe	D. shoulder	16.____
17.	A. ancestry	B. obscure	C. intention	D. ninty	17.____
18.	A. artical	B. bracelet	C. beggar	D. hopeful	18.____
19.	A. tournament C. perpendiclar		B. sponsor D. dissolve		19.____
20.	A. yeild	B. physician	C. greasiest	D. admitting	20.____

TEST 6

1.	A. achievment C. questionnaire		B. maintenance D. all are correct	1.____
2.	A. prevelant C. separate		B. pronunciation D. all are correct	2.____
3.	A. permissible C. seize		B. relevant D. all are correct	3.____
4.	A. corroborate C. eighth		B. desparate D. all are correct	4.____

5. A. exceed   B. feasibility   5.__
    C. psycological   D. all are correct

6. A. parallel   B. aluminum   C. calendar   D. eigty   6.__

7. A. microbe   B. ancient   C. autograph   D. existance   7.__

8. A. plentiful   B. skillful   C. amoung   D. capsule   8.__

9. A. erupt   B. quanity   C. opinion   D. competent   9.__

10. A. excitement   B. discipline   C. luncheon   D. regreting   10.__

11. A. magazine   B. expository   C. imitation   D. permenent   11.__

12. A. ferosious   B. machinery   12.__
    C. precise   D. magnificent

13. A. conceive   B. narritive   C. separation   D. management   13.__

14. A. muscular   B. witholding   C. pickle   D. glacier   14.__

15. A. vehicel   B. mismanage   15.__
    C. correspondence   D. dissatisfy

16. A. sentince   B. bulletin   C. notice   D. definition   16.__

17. A. appointment   B. exactly   17.__
    C. typest   D. light

18. A. penalty   B. suparvise   C. consider   D. division   18.__

19. A. schedule   B. accurate   C. corect   D. simple   19.__

20. A. suggestion   B. installed   C. proper   D. agincy   20.__

TEST 7

1. A. symtom   B. serum   C. antiseptic   D. aromatic   1.__

2. A. register   B. registrar   C. purser   D. burser   2.__

3. A. athletic   B. tragedy   C. batallion   D. sophomore   3.__

4. A. latent   B. godess   C. aisle   D. whose   4.__

5. A. rhyme   B. rhythm   C. thime   D. thine   5.__

6. A. eighth   B. exaggerate   C. electorial   D. villain   6.__

7. A. statute   B. superintendent   7.__
    C. iresistible   D. colleague

8.	A. sieze	B. therefor	C. auxiliary	D. changeable	8.____
9.	A. siege	B. knowledge	C. lieutenent	D. weird	9.____
10.	A. acquitted	B. polititian	C. professor	D. conqueror	10.____
11.	A. changeable	B. chargeable	C. salable	D. useable	11.____
12.	A. promissory	B. prisoner	C. excellent	D. tyrany	12.____

13. A. conspicuous   B. essance   13.____
    C. comparative   D. brilliant

14.	A. notefying	B. accentuate	C. adhesive	D. primarily	14.____
15.	A. exercise	B. sublime	C. stuborn	D. shameful	15.____
16.	A. presume	B. transcript	C. strech	D. wizard	16.____

17. A. specify   B. regional   17.____
    C. arbitrary   D. segragation

18. A. requirement   B. happiness   18.____
    C. achievement   D. gentlely

| 19. | A. endurance | B. fusion | C. balloon | D. enormus | 19.____ |
| 20. | A. luckily | B. schedule | C. simplicity | D. sanwich | 20.____ |

TEST 8

1. A. maintain   B. maintainance   1.____
   C. sustain   D. sustenance

2. A. portend   B. portentious   2.____
   C. pretend   D. pretentious

3. A. prophesize   B. prophesies   3.____
   C. farinaceous   D. spaceous

| 4. | A. choose | B. chose | C. choosen | D. chasten | 4.____ |

5. A. censure   B. censorious   5.____
   C. pleasure   D. pleasurible

6.	A. cover	B. coverage	C. adder	D. adege	6.____
7.	A. balloon	B. diregible	C. direct	D. descent	7.____
8.	A. whemsy	B. crazy	C. flimsy	D. lazy	8.____
9.	A. derision	B. pretention	C. sustention	D. contention	9.____

10. A. question   B. questionaire   10.__
     C. legion   D. legionary

11. A. chattle   B. cattle   C. dismantle   D. kindle   11.__

12. A. canal   B. cannel   C. chanel   D. colonel   12.__

13. A. hemorrage B. storage   C. manage   D. foliage   13.__

14. A. surgeon   B. sturgeon C. luncheon   D. stancheon 14.__

15. A. diploma   B. commission C. dependent D. luminious 15.__

16. A. likelihood B. blizzard C. machanical D. suppress   16.__

17. A. commercial B. releif   C. disposal   D. endeavor   17.__

18. A. operate   B. bronco   C. excaping   D. grammar   18.__

19. A. orchard   B. collar   C. embarass   D. distant   19.__

20. A. sincerly B. possessive C. weighed   D. waist   20.__

TEST 9

1.   A. statute   B. stationary   1.__
     C. staturesque   D. stature

2.   A. practicible   B. practical   2.__
     C. particle   D. reticule

3.   A. plague   B. plaque   C. ague   D. aigrete   3.__

4.   A. theology B. idealogy C. psychology D. philology 4.__

5.   A. dilema   B. stamina   C. feminine   D. strychnine 5.__

6.   A. deceit   B. benefit   C. grieve   D. hienous   6.__

7.   A. commensurable   B. measurable   7.__
     C. duteable   D. salable

8.   A. homogeneous   B. heterogeneous   8.__
     C. advantageous   D. religeous

9.   A. criticize B. dramatise C. exorcise   D. exercise   9.__

10. A. ridiculous B. comparable C. merciful   D. cotten   10.__

11. A. antebiotic B. stitches C. pitiful   D. sneaky   11.__

12. A. amendment   B. candadate   12.__
     C. accountable   D. recommendation

8

13. A. avocado   B. recruit   C. tripping   D. probally   13.____

14. A. calendar   B. desirable   C. familar   D. vacuum   14.____

15. A. deteriorate   B. elligible   15.____
     C. liable   D. missile

16. A. amateur   B. competent   16.____
     C. mischeivous   D. occasion

17. A. friendliness   B. saleries   17.____
     C. cruelty   D. ammunition

18. A. wholesome   B. cieling   C. stupidity   D. eligible   18.____

19. A. comptroller   B. traveled   19.____
     C. accede   D. procede

20. A. Britain   B. Brittainica   20.____
     C. conductor   D. vendor

_____

TEST 10

1.   A. lengthen   B. region   C. gases   D. inspecter   1.____

2.   A. imediately   B. forbidden   2.____
     C. complimentary   D. aeronautics

3.   A. continuous   B. paralel   C. opposite   D. definite   3.____

4.   A. Antarctic   B. Wednesday   C. Febuary   D. Hungary   4.____

5.   A. transmission   B. exposure   5.____
     C. pistol   D. customery

6.   A. juvinile   B. martyr   6.____
     C. deceive   D. collaborate

7.   A. unnecessary   B. repetitive   7.____
     C. cancellation   D. airey

8.   A. transit   B. availible   C. objection   D. galaxy   8.____

9.   A. ineffective   B. believeable   9.____
     C. arrangement   D. aggravate

10. A. possession   B. progress   C. reception   D. predjudice   10.____

11. A. congradulate   B. percolate   11.____
     C. major   D. leisure

12. A. convenience   B. privilige   12.____
     C. emerge   D. immerse

9

13. A. erasable   B. inflammable   13.__
     C. audable   D. laudable

14. A. final   B. fines   C. finis   D. Finish   14.__

15. A. emitted   B. representative   15.__
     C. discipline   D. insistance

16. A. diphthong   B. rarified   C. library   D. recommend   16.__

17. A. compel   B. belligerent   17.__
     C. successful   D. sargeant

18. A. dispatch   B. dispise   C. dispose   D. dispute   18.__

19. A. administrator   B. adviser   19.__
     C. diner   D. celluler

20. A. ignite   B. ignision   C. igneous   D. ignited   20.__

TEST 11

1. A. repellent   B. secession   C. sebaceous   D. saxaphone   1.__

2. A. navel   B. counteresolution   2.__
    C. marginalia   D. perceptible

3. A. Hammerskjold   B. Nehru   3.__
    C. U Thamt   D. Khrushchev

4. A. perculate   B. periwinkle   4.__
    C. perigee   D. retrogression

5. A. buccaneer   B. tobacco   C. Buffalo   D. oscilate   5.__

6. A. siege   B. wierd   C. seize   D. cemetery   6.__

7. A. equaled   B. bigoted   7.__
    C. benefited   D. kaleideoscope

8. A. blamable   B. bullrush   8.__
    C. questionnaire   D. irascible

9. A. tobagganed   B. acquiline   9.__
    C. capillary   D. cretonne

10. A. daguerrotype   B. elegiacal   10.__
    C. iridescent   D. inchoate

11. A. bayonet   B. braggadocio   11.__
    C. corollary   D. connoiseur

10

12. A. equinoctial   B. fusillade   12.____
     C. fricassee   D. potpouri

13. A. octameter   B. impressario   13.____
     C. hyetology   D. hieroglyphics

14. A. innanity   B. idyllic   C. fylfot   D. inimical   14.____

15. A. liquefy   B. rarefy   C. putrify   D. sapphire   15.____

16. A. canonical   B. stupified   16.____
     C. millennium   D. memorabilia

17. A. paraphenalia   B. odyssey   17.____
     C. onomatopoeia   D. osseous

18. A. peregrinate   B. pecadillo   18.____
     C. reptilian   D. uxorious

19. A. pharisaical   B. vicissitude   19.____
     C. puissance   D. wainright

20. A. holocaust   B. tesselate   C. scintilla   D. staccato   20.____

TEST 12

1. A. questionnaire   B. gondoleer   1.____
    C. chandelier   D. acquiescence

2. A. surveillence   B. surfeit   2.____
    C. vaccinate   D. belligerent

3. A. occassionally   B. recurrence   3.____
    C. silhouette   D. incessant

4. A. transferral   B. benefical   4.____
    C. descendent   D. dependent

5. A. separately   B. flouresence   5.____
    C. deterrent   D. parallel

6. A. acquittal   B. enforceable   6.____
    C. counterfeit   D. indispensible

7. A. susceptible   B. accelarate   7.____
    C. exhilarate   D. accommodation

8. A. impedimenta   B. collateral   8.____
    C. liason   D. epistolary

9. A. inveigle   B. panegyric   C. reservoir   D. manuver   9.____

11

10. A. synopsis   B. parephernalia   10.__
     C. affidavit   D. subpoena

11. 'A. grosgrain   B. vermilion   C. abbatoir   D. connoiseur   11.__

12. A. gabardine   B. camoflage   C. hemorrhage D. contraband   12.__

13. A. opprobrious   B. defalcate   13.__
     C. fiduciery   D. recommendations

14. A. nebulous   B. necessitate   14.__
     C. impricate   D. discrepancy

15. A. discrete   B. condesension   15.__
     C. condign   D. condiment

16. A. cavalier   B. effigy   16.__
     C. legitimatly   D. misalliance

17. A. rheumatism   B. vaporous   17.__
     C. cannister   D. hallucinations

18. A. paleonthology   B. octogenarian   18.__
     C. gradient   D. impingement

19. A. fusilade   B. fusilage   C. ensilage   D. desiccate   19.__

20. A. rationale B. raspberry   C. reprobate D. varigated   20.__

KEY (CORRECT ANSWERS)

TEST 1

1. B. fundamental
2. D. disappear
3. A. accidentally
4. B. career
5. A. facility

6. C. advantageous
7. C. guarantee
8. D. announcement
9. B. seize
10. A. postpone

11. B. traffic
12. C. batteries
13. C. persuade
14. A. fatiguing
15. D. underneath

16. A. anonymous
17. D. resistance
18. C. fundamental
19. B. bargain
20. D. height

TEST 2

1. C. relieve
2. D. discipline
3. A. postponed
4. D. equipped
5. B. dissatisfied

6. C. obstacle
7. B. omission
8. C. negligible
9. D. athletic
10. A. fiscal

11. B. excessively
12. B. monopolies
13. A. synthetic
14. D. dissolve
15. C. inefficient

16. A. noticeable
17. C. vulgar
18. D. innumerable
19. D. assessment
20. A. thermostat

TEST 3

1. D. continual
2. B. recommend
3. C. auxiliary
4. B. acquainted
5. C. interrupted

6. B. management
7. A. committee
8. A. occurrence
9. B. particular
10. D. dictionary

11. D. roommate
12. D. curiosity
13. B. inconceivable
14. A. handicapped
15. D. scissors

16. B. tomatoes
17. A. cassette
18. C. clinical
19. D. expense
20. B. flexible

TEST 4

1. A. primary
2. B. belief
3. D. contemptible
4. D. seldom
5. B. acquisition

6. A. simultaneous
7. A. illegible
8. D. peculiar
9. C. handicapped
10. B. accompanying

11. A. hammering
12. D. luncheon
13. A. monitor
14. D. anxiety
15. B. judicial

16. A. fundamental
17. C. gymnasium
18. D. entrance
19. A. restaurant
20. C. specimen

TEST 5

1. B. correspondence
2. D. eligible
3. A. accommodate
4. C. beneficial
5. B. disappoint

6. A. proceed
7. B. government
8. C. advisable
9. D. noticeable
10. A. privilege

11. B. various
12. D. poison
13. B. omission
14. D. parachute
15. C. incredible

16. C. volcano
17. D. ninety
18. A. article
19. C. perpendicular
20. A. yield

TEST 6

1. A. achievement
2. A. prevalent
3. D. all are correct
4. B. desperate
5. C. psychological

6. D. eighty
7. D. existence
8. C. among
9. B. quantity
10. D. regretting

11. D. permanent
12. A. ferocious
13. B. narrative
14. B. withholding
15. A. vehicle

16. A. sentence
17. C. typist
18. B. supervise
19. C. correct
20. D. agency

TEST 7

1. A. symptom
2. D. bursar
3. C. battalion
4. B. goddess
5. C. thyme

6. C. electoral
7. C. irresistible
8. A. seize
9. C. lieutenant
10. B. politician

11. D. usable
12. D. tyrany
13. B. essence
14. A. notifying
15. C. stubborn

16. C. stretch
17. D. segregation
18. D. gently
19. D. enormous
20. D. sandwich

TEST 8

1. B. maintenance
2. B. portentous
3. D. spacious
4. C. chosen
5. D. pleasurable

6. D. adage
7. B. dirigible
8. A. whimsy
9. B. pretension
10. B. questionnaire

11. A. chattel
12. C. channel
13. A. hemorrhage
14. D. stanchion
15. D. luminous

16. C. mechanical
17. B. relief
18. C. escaping
19. C. embarrass
20. A. sincerely

TEST 9

1. C. statuesque
2. A. practicable
3. D. aigrette
4. B. ideology
5. A. dilemma

6. D. heinous
7. C. dutiable
8. D. religious
9. B. dramatize
10. D. cotton

11. A. antibiotic
12. B. candidate
13. D. probably
14. C. familiar
15. B. eligible

16. C. mischievous
17. B. salaries
18. B. ceiling
19. D. proceed
20. B. Brittanica

TEST 10

1. D. inspector
2. A. immediately
3. B. parallel
4. C. February
5. D. customary

6. A. juvenile
7. D. airy
8. B. available
9. B. believable
10. D. prejudice

11. A. congratulate
12. B. privilege
13. C. audible
14. D. Finnish
15. D. insistence

16. B. rarefied
17. D. sergeant
18. B. despise
19. D. cellular
20. B. ignition

TEST 11

1. D. saxophone
2. B. counterresolution
3. C. U Thant
4. A. percolate
5. D. oscillate

6. B. weird
7. D. kaleidoscope
8. B. bulrush
9. B. aquiline
10. A. daguerreotype

11. D. connoisseur
12. D. potpourri
13. B. impresario
14. A. inanity
15. C. putrefy

16. B. stupefied
17. A. paraphernalia
18. B. peccadillo
19. D. wainwright
20. B. tessellate

TEST 12

1. B. gondolier
2. A. surveillance
3. A. occasionally
4. B. beneficial
5. B. fluorescence

6. D. indispensable
7. B. accelerate
8. C. liaison
9. D. maneuver
10. B. paraphernalia

11. D. connoisseur
12. B. camouflage
13. C. fiduciary
14. C. imprecate
15. B. condescension

16. C. legitimately
17. C. canister
18. A. paleontology
19. A. fusillade
20. D. variegated

WORD MEANING

COMMENTARY

DESCRIPTION OF THE TEST

On many examinations, you will have questions about the meaning of words, or vocabulary.

In this type of question, you have to state what a word or phrase means. (A phrase is a group of words.) This word or phrase is in CAPITAL letters in a sentence. You are also given for each question five other words or groups of words - lettered A, B, C, D, and E - as possible answers. One of these words or groups of words means the same as the word or group of words in CAPITAL letters. Only one is right. You are to pick out the one that is right and select the letter of your answer.

HINTS FOR ANSWERING WORD-MEANING QUESTIONS

Read each question carefully.

Choose the best answer of the five choices, even though it is not the word you might use yourself.

Answer first those that you know. Then do the others.

If you know that some of the suggested answers are not right, pay no more attention to them.

Be sure that you have selected an answer for every question, even if you have to guess.

———

SAMPLE QUESTIONS

DIRECTIONS: For the following questions, select the word or group of words lettered A, B, C, D, or E that means *MOST NEARLY* the same as the word in capital letters. Indicate the letter of the *CORRECT* answer for each question.

SAMPLE QUESTIONS 1 AND 2

1. The letter was SHORT. SHORT means *most nearly*
    A. tall   B. wide   C. brief   D. heavy   E. dark
    EXPLANATION
    SHORT is a word you have used to describe something that is small, or not long, or little, etc. Therefore, you would not have to spend much time figuring out the right answer. You would choose C. brief.
2. The young man is VIGOROUS. VIGOROUS means *most nearly*
    A. serious B. reliable C. courageous D. strong E. talented
    EXPLANATION
    VIGOROUS is a word that you have probably used yourself or read somewhere. It carries with it the idea of being active, full of pep, etc. Which one of the five choices comes closest to meaning that? Certainly not A. serious, B. reliable, or E. talented; C. courageous - maybe, D. strong - maybe. But between courageous or strong, you would have to agree that strong is the better choice. Therefore, you would choose D. strong.

———

EXAMINATION SECTION

DIRECTIONS FOR THIS SECTION:
    For the following questions, select the word or group of words lettered A, B, C, D, or E that means MOST NEARLY the same as the word in capital letters. *PRINT THE LETTER OF THE CORRECT ANSWER IN THE SPACE AT THE RIGHT.*

TEST 1

1. To IMPLY means *most nearly* to   1. ...
    A. agree to B. hint at C. laugh at D. mimic E. reduce
2. APPRAISAL means *most nearly*   2. ...
    A. allowance B. composition C. prohibition D. quantity E. valuation
3. To DISBURSE means *most nearly* to   3. ...
    A. approve B. expend C. prevent D. relay E. restrict
4. POSTERITY means *most nearly*   4. ...
    A. back payment   B. current procedure   C. final effort
    D. future generations E. rare specimen
5. PUNCTUAL means *most nearly*   5. ...
    A. clear B. honest C. polite D. prompt E. prudent
6. PRECARIOUS means *most nearly*   6. ...
    A. abundant B. alarmed C. cautious D. insecure E. placid
7. To FOSTER means *most nearly* to   7. ...
    A. delegate B. demote C. encourage D. plead E. surround
8. PINNACLE means *most nearly*   8. ...
    A. center B. crisis C. outcome D. peak E. personification
9. COMPONENT means *most nearly*   9. ...
    A. flattery B. opposite C. trend D. revision E. element
10. To SOLICIT means *most nearly* to   10. ...
    A. ask B. prohibit C. promise D. revoke E. surprise
11. LIAISON means *most nearly*   11. ...
    A. asset B. coordination C. difference D. policy E. procedure
12. To ALLEGE means *most nearly* to   12. ...
    A. assert B. break C. irritate D. reduce E. wait
13. INFILTRATION means *most nearly*   13. ...
    A. consumption B. disposal C. enforcement D. penetration E. seizure
14. To SALVAGE means *most nearly* to   14. ...
    A. announce B. combine C. prolong D. try E. save
15. MOTIVE means *most nearly*   15. ...
    A. attack B. favor C. incentive D. patience E. tribute
16. To PROVOKE means *most nearly* to   16. ...
    A. adjust B. incite C. leave D. obtain E. practice
17. To SURGE means *most nearly* to   17. ...
    A. branch B. contract C. revenge D. rush E. want
18. To MAGNIFY means *most nearly* to   18. ...
    A. attract B. demand C. generate D. increase E. puzzle
19. PREPONDERANCE means *most nearly*   19. ...
    A. decision B. judgment C. superiority D. submission E. warning
20. To ABATE means *most nearly* to   20. ...
    A. assist B. coerce C. diminish D. indulge E. trade

TEST 2

1. AVARICE means *most nearly*   1. ...
    A. flight B. greed C. pride D. thrift E. average
2. PREDATORY means *most nearly*   2. ...
    A. offensive B. plundering C. previous D. timeless E. perilous

3. To VINDICATE means *most nearly* to   3. ...
    A. clear B. conquer C. correct D. illustrate E. alleviate
4. INVETERATE means *most nearly*   4. ...
    A. backward B. erect C. habitual D. lucky E. gradual
5. To DISCERN means *most nearly* to   5. ...
    A. describe B. fabricate C. recognize D. seek E. dilute
6. COMPLACENT means *most nearly*   6. ...
    A. indulgent B. listless C. overjoyed D. satisfied E. pliant
7. ILLICIT means *most nearly*   7. ...
    A. insecure B. unclear C. eligible D. unlimited E. unlawful
8. To PROCRASTINATE means *most nearly* to   8. ...
    A. declare B. multiply C. postpone D. steal E. proclaim
9. IMPASSIVE means *most nearly*   9. ...
    A. calm B. frustrated C. thoughtful D. unhappy E. perturbed
10. AMICABLE means *most nearly*   10. ...
    A. cheerful B. flexible C. friendly D. poised E. amorous
11. FEASIBLE means *most nearly*   11. ...
    A. breakable B. easy C. likeable D. practicable E. fearful
12. INNOCUOUS means *most nearly*   12. ...
    A. harmless B. insecure C. insincere D. unfavorable E. innate
13. OSTENSIBLE means *most nearly*   13. ...
    A. apparent B. hesitant C. reluctant D. showy E. concealed
14. INDOMITABLE means *most nearly*   14. ...
    A. excessive   B. unconquerable   C. unreasonable
    D. unthinkable   E. indubitable
15. CRAVEN means *most nearly*   15. ...
    A. carefree B. hidden C. miserly D. needed E. cowardly
16. To ALLAY means *most nearly* to   16. ...
    A. discuss B. quiet C. refine D. remove E. arrange
17. To ALLUDE means *most nearly* to   17. ...
    A. denounce B. refer C. state D. support E. align
18. NEGLIGENCE means *most nearly*   18. ...
    A. carelessness B. denial C. objection D. refusal E. eagerness
19. To AMEND means *most nearly* to   19. ...
    A. correct B. destroy C. end D. list E. dissent
20. RELEVANT means *most nearly*   20. ...
    A. conclusive B. careful C. obvious D. related E. incompetent

TEST 3

1. CONFIRM means *most nearly*   1. ...
    A. belong B. limit C. think over D. verify E. refine
2. PERILOUS means *most nearly*   2. ...
    A. dangerous B. mysterious C. tiring D. undesirable E. fickle
3. PROFICIENT means *most nearly*   3. ...
    A. likable B. obedient C. profitable D. profound E. skilled
4. IMPLICATE means *most nearly*   4. ...
    A. arrest B. confess C. involve D. question E. imply
5. ASSERT means *most nearly*   5. ...
    A. confide B. help C. state D. wish E. confirm
6. TEDIOUS means *most nearly*   6. ...
    A. boring B. easy C. educational D. difficult E. timorous
7. CONSEQUENCE means *most nearly*   7. ...
    A. punishment B. reason C. result D. tragedy E. basis
8. REPUTABLE means *most nearly*   8. ...
    A. durable B. effective C. powerful D. honorable E. tangible

9. REPROACH means *most nearly*   9. ...
   A. anger B. blame C. pardon D. trap E. repel
10. DIVERSE means *most nearly*   10. ...
    A. confused B. indistinct C. unacceptable D. destructive E. unlike
11. EVENTUAL means *most nearly*   11. ...
    A. complete B. exciting C. final D. important E. enticing
12. ACCESSORY means *most nearly*   12. ...
    A. accomplice B. dishonest C. fugitive D. planner E. perpetrator
13. ALLEVIATE means *most nearly*   13. ...
    A. enrage B. increase C. lessen D. omit E. lift up
14. RETICENT means *most nearly*   14. ...
    A. doubtful B. humorous C. intelligent D. reserved E. reliant
15. DILEMMA means *most nearly*   15. ...
    A. caution B. decision C. hope D. direction E. predicament
16. FLAUNT means *most nearly*   16. ...
    A. compliment B. display C. punish D. warn E. reserve
17. CONCUR means *most nearly*   17. ...
    A. agree B. capture C. rescue D. trust E. disagree
18. REPUDIATE means *most nearly*   18. ...
    A. plot B. reject C. revise D. strike E. attest
19. FRANTIC means *most nearly*   19. ...
    A. criminal B. desperate C. jealous D. indirect E. sanguine
20. PREMONITION means *most nearly*   20. ...
    A. certainty B. forewarning C. puzzle D. thinking E. promise

TEST 4

1. To CONTEND means *most nearly* to   1. ...
   A. claim B. defeat C. refuse D. penalize E. contest
2. EXPEDIENT means *most nearly*   2. ...
   A. fearless B. suitable C. dishonest C. convincing E. famous
3. PROPONENT means *most nearly*   3. ...
   A. basic truth   B. witness   C. driver
   D. supporter   E. antongist
4. DUBIOUS means *most nearly*   4. ...
   A. uneventful B. silly C. uncertain D. untrue E. firm
5. CONTRITE means *most nearly*   5. ...
   A. painful B. sorry C. guilty D. hopeful E. joyful
6. To CONCEDE means *most nearly* to   6. ...
   A. suggest B. decide C. admit D. trust E. consign
7. EQUITABLE means *most nearly*   7. ...
   A. peaceful B. insurable C. lenient D. just E. equine
8. To ALIGN means *most nearly* to   8. ...
   A. cheat B. slander C. misinform D. criticize E. malinger
9. To REPRIMAND means *most nearly* to   9. ...
   A. shout B. scold C. complain D. punish E. recommend
10. INFLEXIBLE means *most nearly*   10. ...
    A. powerful B. impartial C. unpopular D. unbending E. lax
11. INTACT means *most nearly*   11. ...
    A. considerate B. inside C. whole D. lasting E. incomplete
12. To DETER means *most nearly* to   12. ...
    A. strike B. prevent C. disagree D. loosen E. detract
13. PRUDENT means *most nearly*   13. ...
    A. prudish B. strict C. stingy D. shy E. cautious
14. REMISS MEANS *most nearly*   14. ...
    A. neglectful B. dishonest C. prevented D. evil E. deceived

3

15. APPREHENSIVE means *most nearly*
    A. dangerous B. harmful C. sad D. fearful E. approved
16. CONTRABAND means *most nearly*
    A. dissolved B. illegal C. fake D. unknown E. grouped
17. To DISSEMINATE means *most nearly* to
    A. spread B. mislead C. undermine D. disagree E. divert
18. CONTEMPT means *most nearly*
    A. pity B. hatred C. scorn D. brutality E. opinion
19. To HARASS means *most nearly* to
    A. retreat B. whip C. control D. torment E. harangue
20. OPAQUE means *most nearly*
    A. thick   B. invisible   C. lucid
    D. light colored   E. not transparent

15. ...
16. ...
17. ...
18. ...
19. ...
20. ...

KEYS (CORRECT ANSWERS)

TEST 1	TEST 2	TEST 3	TEST 4
1. B	1. B	1. D	1. A
2. E	2. B	2. A	2. B
3. B	3. A	3. E	3. D
4. D	4. C	4. C	4. C
5. D	5. C	5. C	5. B
6. D	6. D	6. A	6. C
7. C	7. E	7. C	7. D
8. D	8. C	8. D	8. B
9. E	9. A	9. B	9. B
10. A	10. C	10. E	10. D
11. B	11. D	11. C	11. C
12. A	12. A	12. A	12. B
13. D	13. A	13. C	13. E
14. E	14. B	14. D	14. A
15. C	15. E	15. E	15. D
16. B	16. B	16. B	16. B
17. D	17. B	17. A	17. A
18. D	18. A	18. B	18. C
19. C	19. A	19. B	19. D
20. C	20. D	20. B	20. E

4

WORD MEANING
EXAMINATION SECTION

DIRECTIONS: Each question or incomplete statement is followed by several suggested answers or completions. Select the one that BEST answers the question or completes the statement. *PRINT THE LETTER OF THE CORRECT ANSWER IN THE SPACE AT THE RIGHT.*

1. He implied that he would work overtime if necessary.   1.___
   In this sentence, the word *implied* means
   A. denied   B. explained
   C. guaranteed   D. hinted

2. The bag of the vacuum cleaner was inflated.   2.___
   In this sentence, the word *inflated* means
   A. blown up with air   B. filled with dirt
   C. loose   D. torn

3. Burning material during certain hours is prohibited.   3.___
   In this sentence, the word *prohibited* means
   A. allowed   B. forbidden   C. legal   D. required

4. He was rejected when he applied for the job.   4.___
   In this sentence, the word *rejected* means
   A. discouraged   B. put to work
   C. tested   D. turned down

5. The foreman was able to substantiate his need for extra   5.___
   supplies.
   In this sentence, the word *substantiate* means
   A. estimate   B. meet   C. prove   D. reduce

6. The new instructions supersede the old ones.   6.___
   In this sentence, the word *supersede* means
   A. explain   B. improve   C. include   D. replace

7. Shake the broom free of surplus water and hang it up to   7.___
   dry.
   In this sentence, the word *surplus* means
   A. dirty   B. extra   C. rinse   D. soapy

8. When a crack is filled, the asphalt must be tamped.   8.___
   In this sentence, the word *tamped* means
   A. cured   B. heated
   C. packed down   D. wet down

9. The apartment was left vacant.   9.___
   In this sentence, the word *vacant* means
   A. clean   B. empty   C. furnished   D. locked

10. The caretaker spent the whole day doing various repairs.   10.___
    In this sentence, the word *various* means
    A. different   B. necessary   C. small   D. special

11. He came back to assist his partner.
    In this sentence, the word *assist* means   11.__
       A. call   B. help   C. stop   D. question

12. A person who is biased cannot be a good foreman.   12.__
    In this sentence, the word *biased* means
       A. easy-going   B. prejudiced
       C. strict   D. uneducated

13. The lecture for the new employees was brief.   13.__
    In this sentence, the word *brief* means
       A. educational   B. free
       C. interesting   D. short

14. He was asked to clarify the order.   14.__
    In this sentence, the word *clarify* means
       A. follow out   B. make clear
       C. take back   D. write out

15. The employee was commended by his foreman.   15.__
    In this sentence, the word *commended* means
       A. assigned   B. blamed   C. picked   D. praised

16. Before the winter, the lawnmower engine was dismantled.   16.__
    In this sentence, the word *dismantled* means
       A. oiled   B. repaired
       C. stored away   D. taken apart

17. They excavated a big hole on the project lawn.   17.__
    In this sentence, the word *excavated* means
       A. cleaned out   B. discovered
       C. dug out   D. filled in

18. The new man was told to sweep the exterior area.   18.__
    In this sentence, the word *exterior* means
       A. asphalt   B. nearby   C. outside   D. whole

19. The officer refuted the statement of the driver.   19.__
    As used in this sentence, the word *refuted* means MOST
    NEARLY
       A. disproved   B. elaborated upon
       C. related   D. supported

20. The mechanism of the parking meter is not intricate.   20.__
    As used in this sentence, the word *intricate* means MOST
    NEARLY
       A. cheap   B. complicated
       C. foolproof   D. strong

21. The weight of each box fluctuates.   21.__
    As used in this sentence, the word *fluctuates* means MOST
    NEARLY
       A. always changes   B. decreases
       C. increases gradually   D. is similar

22. The person chosen to investigate the new procedure should   22.___
    be impartial.
    As used in this sentence, the word *impartial* means MOST
    NEARLY
       A. experienced   B. fair
       C. forward looking   D. important

23. Carelessness in the safekeeping of keys will not be   23.___
    tolerated.
    As used in this sentence, the word *tolerated* means MOST
    NEARLY
       A. forgotten   B. permitted
       C. punished lightly   D. understood

24. The traffic was easily diverted.   24.___
    As used in this sentence, the word *diverted* means MOST
    NEARLY
       A. controlled   B. speeded up
       B. stopped   D. turned aside

25. A transcript of the report was prepared in the office.   25.___
    As used in this sentence, the word *transcript* means MOST
    NEARLY
       A. brief   B. copy
       C. record   D. translation

26. The change was authorized by the supervisor.   26.___
    As used in this sentence, the word *authorized* means MOST
    NEARLY
       A. completed B. corrected C. ordered   D. permitted

27. The supervisor read the excerpt of the collector's report.   27.___
    According to this sentence, the supervisor read _____ the
    report.
       A. a passage from   B. a summary of
       C. the original of   D. the whole of

28. During the probation period, the worker proved to be   28.___
    inept.
    The word *inept* means MOST NEARLY
       A. incompetent   B. insubordinate
       C. satisfactory   D. uncooperative

29. The putative father was not living with the family.   29.___
    The word *putative* means MOST NEARLY
       A. reputed   B. unemployed
       C. concerned   D. indifferent

30. The adopted child researched various documents of vital   30.___
    statistics in an effort to discover the names of his
    natural parents.
    The words *vital statistics* mean MOST NEARLY statistics
    relating to
       A. human life   B. hospitals
       C. important facts   D. health and welfare

31. Despite many requests for them, there was a scant supply   31.__
of new blotters.
The word *scant* means MOST NEARLY
    A. adequate   B. abundant
    C. insufficient   D. expensive

32. Did they replenish the supply of forms in the cabinet?   32.__
The word *replenish* means MOST NEARLY
    A. straighten up   B. refill
    C. sort out   D. use

33. Employees may become bored if they are assigned diverse   33.__
duties.
The word *diverse* means MOST NEARLY
    A. interesting   B. different
    C. challenging   D. enjoyable

Questions 34-37.

DIRECTIONS: Each of Questions 34 through 37 consists of a
               capitalized word followed by four suggested meanings
               of the word. Select the word or phrase which means
               MOST NEARLY the same as the capitalized word.

34. PROFICIENCY   34.__
    A. vocation   B. competency
    C. repugnancy   D. prominence

35. BIBLIOGRAPHY   35.__
    A. description   B. stenography
    C. photograph   D. compilation of books

36. FIDELITY   36.__
    A. belief   B. treachery
    C. strength   D. loyalty

37. ACCELERATE   37.__
    A. adjust   B. press   C. quicken   D. strip

38. One of the machinists in your shop enjoys the reputation   38.__
of being a great equivocator.
This means MOST NEARLY that he
    A. takes pride and is happy in his work
    B. generally hedges and often gives misleading answers
    C. is a strong union man with great interest in his
       fellow workers' welfare
    D. is good at resolving disputes

39. When a person has the reputation of persistently making   39.__
foolish or silly remarks, it may be said that he is
    A. inane   B. meticulous
    C. a procrastinator   D. a prevaricator

40. When two mechanics, called A and B, make measurements of
    the same workpiece and find significant discrepancies in
    their measurements, it is MOST NEARLY correct to state
    that
    A. mechanic B made an erroneous reading
    B. mechanic A was careless in making his measurements
    C. both mechanics made their measurements correctly
    D. there was considerable difference in the two sets
       of measurements

40.____

41. A foreman who *expedites* a job,
    A. abolishes it   B. makes it bigger
    C. slows it down   D. speeds it up

41.____

42. If a man is working at a *uniform* speed, it means he is
    working at a speed which is
    A. changing   B. fast   C. slow   D. steady

42.____

43. To say that a caretaker is *obstinate* means that he is
    A. cooperative   B. patient
    C. stubborn   D. willing

43.____

44. To say that a caretaker is *negligent* means that he is
    A. careless   B. neat   C. nervous   D. late

44.____

45. To say that something is *absurd* means that it is
    A. definite   B. not clear
    C. ridiculous   D. unfair

45.____

46. To say that a foreman is *impartial* means that he is
    A. fair   B. improving C. in a hurry D. watchful

46.____

47. A man who is *lenient* is one who is
    A. careless   B. harsh
    C. inexperienced   D. mild

47.____

48. A man who is *punctual* is one who is
    A. able   B. polite   C. prompt   D. sincere

48.____

49. If you think one of your men is too *awkward* to do a job,
    it means you think he is too
    A. clumsy   B. lazy   C. old   D. weak

49.____

50. A person who is *seldom* late, is late
    A. always   B. never   C. often   D. rarely

50.____

KEY (CORRECT ANSWERS)

1. D	11. B	21. A	31. C	41. D
2. A	12. B	22. B	32. B	42. D
3. B	13. D	23. B	33. B	43. C
4. D	14. B	24. D	34. B	44. A
5. C	15. D	25. B	35. D	45. C
6. D	16. D	26. D	36. D	46. A
7. B	17. C	27. A	37. C	47. D
8. C	18. C	28. A	38. B	48. C
9. B	19. A	29. A	39. B	49. A
10. A	20. B	30. A	40. D	50. D

TEST 2

1. The Department of Health can certify that conditions in a   1.___
   housing accommodation are detrimental to life or health.
   As used in the above sentence, the word *detrimental* means
   MOST NEARLY
      A. injurious   B. serious
      C. satisfactory   D. necessary

2. The Administrator shall have the power to revoke any   2.___
   adjustment in rents granted either the landlord or the
   tenant.
   As used in the above sentence, the word *revoke* means
   MOST NEARLY
      A. increase   B. decrease   C. rescind   D. restore

Questions 3-5.

DIRECTIONS: Each of Questions 3 through 5 consists of a capitalized word followed by four suggested meanings of the word. Select the word which means MOST NEARLY the same as the capitalized word.

3. DOGMATISM   3.___
      A. dramatism   B. positiveness
      C. doubtful   D. tentativeness

4. ELECTRODE   4.___
      A. officer   B. electrolyte
      C. terminal   D. positive

5. EMIT   5.___
      A. return   B. enter   C. omit   D. discharge

6. The word *inflammable* means MOST NEARLY   6.___
      A. burnable   B. acid   C. poisonous   D. explosive

7. The word *disinfect* means MOST NEARLY   7.___
      A. deodorize   B. sterilize   C. bleach   D. dissolve

8. He wanted to ascertain the facts before arriving at a   8.___
   conclusion.
   The word *ascertain* means MOST NEARLY
      A. disprove   B. determine   C. convert   D. provide

9. Did the supervisor assent to her request for annual leave?   9.___
    The word *assent* means MOST NEARLY
      A. allude   B. protest   C. agree   D. refer

10. The new worker was fearful that the others would rebuff   10.___
    her.
    The word *rebuff* means MOST NEARLY
      A. ignore   B. forget   C. copy   D. snub

11. The supervisor of that office does not condone lateness.   11.___
    The word *condone* means MOST NEARLY
      A. mind   B. excuse   C. punish   D. remember

12. Each employee was instructed to be as concise as possible   12.___
    when preparing a report.
    The word *concise* means MOST NEARLY
      A. exact   B. sincere   C. flexible   D. brief

13. The shovelers should not distribute the asphalt faster   13.___
    than it can be properly handled by the rakers.
    As used above, *distribute* means MOST NEARLY
      A. dump   B. pick-up   C. spread   D. heat

14. Any defective places should be cut out.   14.___
    As used above, *defective* means MOST NEARLY
      A. low   B. hard   C. soft   D. faulty

15. *Sphere of authority* is called   15.___
      A. constituency   B. dictatorial
      C. jurisdiction   D. vassal

16. Rollers are made in several sizes.   16.___
    As used above, *several* means MOST NEARLY
      A. large   B. heavy   C. standard   D. different

17. Sometimes a roller is run over an old surface to detect   17.___
    weak spots.
    As used above, *detect* means MOST NEARLY
      A. compact   B. remove   C. find   D. strengthen

18. Reconstruction of the old base is sometimes required as   18.___
    a preliminary operation.
    As used above, *preliminary* means MOST NEARLY
      A. first   B. necessary   C. important   D. local

19. If a man makes an *absurd* remark, he makes one which is   19.___
    MOST NEARLY
      A. misleading   B. ridiculous
      C. unfair   D. wicked

20. A worker who is *adept* at his job is one who is MOST   20.___
    NEARLY
      A. cooperative   B. developed
      C. diligent   D. skilled

21. If a man states a condition is *general*, he means it is   21.___
    MOST NEARLY
        A. artificial   B. prevalent
        C. timely   D. transient

Questions 22-50.

DIRECTIONS: Each of Questions 22 through 50 consists of a sentence
              in which a word is italicized. Of the four words
              following each sentence, select the word whose meaning
              is MOST NEARLY the same as the meaning of the italicized
              word.

22. The agent's first *assignment* was to patrol on Hicks   22.___
    Avenue.
        A. test   B. sign   C. job   D. deadline

23. Agents get many *inquiries* from the public.   23.___
        A. complaints   B. suggestions
        C. compliments   D. questions

24. The names of all fifty states were written in *abbreviated* 24.___
    form.
        A. shortened   B. corrected
        C. eliminated   D. illegible

25. The meter was examined and found to be *defective*.   25.___
        A. small   B. operating C. destroyed D. faulty

26. Agent Roger's reports are *legible*, but Agent Baldwin's   26.___
    are not.
        A. similar   B. readable   C. incorrect D. late

27. The time allowed, as shown by the meter, had *expired*.   27.___
        A. started   B. broken   C. ended   D. violated

28. The busy *commercial* area is quiet in the evenings.   28.___
        A. deserted   B. growing   C. business   D. local

29. The district office *authorized* the giving of summonses   29.___
    to illegally parked trucks.
        A. suggested   B. approved
        C. prohibited   D. recorded

30. Department property must be used *exclusively* for official 30.___
    business.
        A. occasionally   B. frequently
        C. only   D. properly

31. The District Commander *banned* driving in the area.   31.___
        A. detoured   B. permitted
        C. encouraged   D. prohibited

32. Two copies of the summons are *retained* by the Enforcement   32.__
    Agent.
    A. kept   B. distributed
    C. submitted   D. signed

33. The Agent *detected* a parking violation.   33.__
    A. cancelled   B. discovered
    C. investigated   D. reported

34. *Pedestrians* may be given summonses for violating traffic   34.__
    regulations.
    A. Bicycle riders   B. Horsemen
    C. Motorcyclists   D. Walkers

35. Parked cars are not allowed to *obstruct* traffic.   35.__
    A. direct   B. lead   C. block   D. speed

36. It was *obvious* to the Agent that the traffic light was   36.__
    broken.
    A. uncertain   B. surprising
    C. possible   D. clear

37. The signs stated that parking in the area was *restricted*   37.__
    to vehicles of foreign diplomats.
    A. allowed   B. increased   C. desired   D. limited

38. Each violation carries an *appropriate* fine.   38.__
    A. suitable   B. extra   C. light   D. heavy

39. Strict enforcement of parking regulations helps to   39.__
    alleviate traffic congestion.
    A. extend   B. build   C. relieve   D. increase

40. The Bureau has a rule which states that an Agent shall   40.__
    speak and act *courteously* in any relationship with the
    public.
    A. respectfully   B. timidly
    C. strangely   D. intelligently

41. City traffic regulations prohibit parking at *jammed*   41.__
    meters.
    A. stuck   B. timed   C. open   D. installed

42. A *significant* error was made by the collector.   42.__
    A. doubtful   B. foolish   C. important   D. strange

43. It is better to *disperse* a crowd.   43.__
    A. hold back   B. quiet   C. scatter   D. talk to

44. Business groups wish to *expand* the program.   44.__
    A. advertise   B. defeat   C. enlarge   D. expose

45. The procedure was *altered* to assist the storekeepers.   45.__
    A. abolished   B. changed
    C. improved   D. made simpler

46. The collector was instructed to *survey* the damage to the   46.___
    parking meter.
       A. examine   B. give the reason for
       C. repair   D. report

47. It is *imperative* that a collector's report be turned in   47.___
    after each collection.
       A. desired   B. recommended
       C. requested   D. urgent

48. The collector was not able to *extricate* the key.   48.___
       A. find   B. free
       C. have a copy made of   D. turn

49. Parking meters have *alleviated* one of our major traffic   49.___
    problems.
       A. created   B. lightened
       C. removed   D. solved

50. Formerly drivers with learners' permits could drive only   50.___
    on *designated* streets.
       A. dead-end   B. not busy   C. one way   D. specified

                  _____

KEY (CORRECT ANSWERS)

1. A	11. B	21. B	31. D	41. A
2. C	12. D	22. C	32. A	42. C
3. B	13. C	23. D	33. B	43. C
4. C	14. D	24. A	34. D	44. C
5. D	15. C	25. D	35. C	45. B
6. A	16. D	26. B	36. D	46. A
7. B	17. C	27. C	37. D	47. D
8. B	18. A	28. C	38. A	48. B
9. C	19. B	29. B	39. C	49. B
10. D	20. D	30. C	40. A	50. D

                  _____

TEST 3

DIRECTIONS: Each question or incomplete statement is followed by several suggested answers or completions. Select the one that BEST answers the question or completes the statement. *PRINT THE LETTER OF THE CORRECT ANSWER IN THE SPACE AT THE RIGHT.*

1. Sprinkler systems in buildings can retard the spread of fires.
   As used in this sentence, the word *retard* means MOST NEARLY
      A. quench   B. slow   C. reveal   D. aggravate   1.__

2. Although there was widespread criticism, the director refused to curtail the program.
   As used in this sentence, the word *curtail* means MOST NEARLY
      A. change   B. discuss   C. shorten   D. expand   2.__

3. Argon is an inert gas.
   As used in this sentence, the word *inert* means MOST NEARLY
      A. unstable   B. uncommon   C. volatile   D. inactive   3.__

4. The firemen turned their hoses on the shed and the main building simultaneously.
   As used in this sentence, the word *simultaneously* means MOST NEARLY
      A. in turn   B. without hesitation   4.__
      C. with great haste   D. at the same time

5. The officer was rebuked for his failure to act promptly.
   As used in this sentence, the word *rebuked* means MOST NEARLY
      A. demoted   B. reprimanded   5.__
      C. discharged   D. reassigned

6. Parkways in the city may be used to facilitate responses to fire alarms.
   As used in this sentence, the word *facilitate* means MOST NEARLY
      A. reduce   B. alter   C. complete   D. ease   6.__

7. Fire extinguishers are most effective when the fire is incipient.
   As used in this sentence, the word *incipient* means MOST NEARLY
      A. accessible   B. beginning   7.__
      C. red hot   D. confined

8. It is important to convey to new members the fundamentals   8.___
   of the procedure.
   As used in this sentence, the words *convey to* means MOST
   NEARLY
       A. prove for   B. confirm for
       C. suggest to   D. impart to

9. The explosion was a graphic illustration of the effects   9.___
   of neglect and carelessness.
   As used in this sentence, the word *graphic* means MOST
   NEARLY
       A. terrible   B. typical   C. unique   D. vivid

10. The worker was assiduous in all things relating to his   10.___
    duties.
    As used in this sentence, the word *assiduous* means MOST
    NEARLY
        A. aggressive   B. careless
        C. persistent   D. cautious

11. A worker must be adept to be successful at his work.   11.___
    As used in this sentence, the word *adept* means MOST NEARLY
        A. ambitious B. strong   C. agile   D. skillful

12. The extinguisher must be inverted before it will operate.   12.___
    As used in this sentence, the word *inverted* means MOST
    NEARLY
        A. turned over   B. completely filled
        C. lightly shaken   D. unhooked

13. Assume that the bridge operator may at times be assigned   13.___
    to the task of coordinating the bridge crew for the
    various routine jobs.
    As used in this sentence, the word *coordinating* means
    MOST NEARLY
        A. ordering   B. testing
        C. scheduling   D. instructing

14. The worker made an insignificant error.   14.___
    As used in this sentence, the word *insignificant* means
    MOST NEARLY
        A. latent   B. serious
        C. accidental   D. minor

15. An Assistant Supervisor should be attentive.   15.___
    As used in this sentence, the word *attentive* means MOST
    NEARLY
        A. watchful   B. prompt   C. negligent D. willing

16. The Assistant Supervisor reported a cavity in the roadway.   16.___
    As used in this sentence, the word *cavity* means MOST
    NEARLY
        A. lump   B. wreck   C. hollow   D. oil-slick

17. Anyone working in traffic must be cautious.
    As used in this sentence, the word *cautious* means MOST
    NEARLY
        A. brave   B. careful   C. expert   D. fast   17.__

Questions 18-20.

DIRECTIONS: Each of Questions 18 through 20 consists of a capitalized
               word followed by four suggested meanings of the word.
               Select the word or phrase which means MOST NEARLY the
               same as the capitalized word.

18. OSMOSIS   18.__
        A. combining   B. diffusion
        C. ossification   D. incantation

19. COLLOIDAL   19.__
        A. mucinous   B. powdered   C. hairy   D. beautiful

20. PRETEXT   20.__
        A. ritual   B. fictitious reason
        C. sermon   D. truthful motive

21. *Easily broken or snapped* defines the word   21.__
        A. brittle   B. pliable   C. cohesive   D. volatile

22. *At right angles to a given line or surface* defines the   22.__
    word
        A. horizontal   B. oblique
        C. perpendicular   D. adjacent

23. *Tools with cutting edges for enlarging or shaping holes*   23.__
    are
        A. screwdrivers   B. pliers
        C. reamers   D. nippers

24. *An instrument used for measuring very small distances* is   24.__
    called a
        A. gage   B. compass
        C. slide ruler   D. micrometer

25. When the phrase *acrid smoke* is used, it refers to smoke   25.__
    that is
        A. irritating   B. dense
        C. black   D. very hot

26. The officer gave explicit directions on how the work was   26.__
    to be done.
    As used in this sentence, the word *explicit* means MOST
    NEARLY
        A. implied   B. clear   C. vague   D. brief

27. After the fire had been extinguished, the debris was
    taken outside and soaked.
    As used in this sentence, the word *debris* means MOST
    NEARLY
    A. wood   B. rubbish   C. couch   D. paper

27.___

28. The trapped man blanched when he saw the life net below
    him.
    As used in this sentence, the word *blanched* means MOST
    NEARLY
    A. turned pale   B. sprang forward
    C. flushed   D. fainted

28.___

29. The worker and his supervisor discussed the problem
    candidly.
    As used in this sentence, the word *candidly* means MOST
    NEARLY
    A. angrily   B. frankly
    C. tolerantly   D. understandingly

29.___

30. The truck came careening down the street.
    As used in this sentence, the word *careening* means MOST
    NEARLY
    A. with sirens screaming
    B. at a slow speed
    C. swaying from side to side
    D. out of control

30.___

31. The population of the province is fairly homogeneous.
    As used in this sentence, the word *homogeneous* means MOST
    NEARLY
    A. devoted to agricultural pursuits
    B. conservative in outlook
    C. essentially alike
    D. sophisticated

31.___

32. The reports of injuries during the past month are being
    tabulated.
    As used in this sentence, the word *tabulated* means MOST
    NEARLY
    A. analyzed
    B. placed in a file
    C. put in the form of a table
    D. verified

32.___

33. The terms offered were tantamount to surrender.
    As used in this sentence, the word *tantamount* means MOST
    NEARLY
    A. equivalent   B. opposite
    C. preferable   D. preliminary

33.___

34. The man's injuries were superficial.
    As used in this sentence, the word *superficial* means MOST
    NEARLY
    A. on the surface   B. not fatal
    C. free from infection   D. not painful

34.___

35. This experience warped his outlook on life.
As used in this sentence, the word *warped* means MOST NEARLY
    A. changed   B. improved
    C. strengthened   D. twisted

35.__

36. Hotel guests usually are transients.
As used in this sentence, the word *transients* means MOST NEARLY
    A. persons of considerable wealth
    B. staying for a short time
    C. visitors from other areas
    D. untrustworthy persons

36.__

37. The pupil's work specimen was considered unsatisfactory because of his failure to observe established tolerances.
As used in this sentence, the word *tolerances* means MOST NEARLY
    A. safety precautions
    B. regard for the rights of others
    C. allowable variations in dimensions
    D. amount of waste produced in an operation

37.__

38. Punishment was severe because the act was considered willful.
As used in this sentence, the word *willful* means MOST NEARLY
    A. brutal   B. criminal
    C. harmful   D. intentional

38.__

39. The malfunctioning of the system was traced to a defective thermostat.
As used in this sentence, the word *thermostat* means MOST NEARLY a device that reacts to changes in
    A. amperage   B. water pressure
    C. temperature   D. atmospheric pressure

39.__

40. His garden contained a profusion of flowers, shrubs, and bushes.
As used in this sentence, the word *profusion* means MOST NEARLY
    A. abundance   B. display
    C. representation   D. scarcity

40.__

41. The inspector would not approve the work because it was out of plumb.
As used in this sentence, the words *out of plumb* means MOST NEARLY not
    A. properly seasoned   B. of the required strength
    C. vertical   D. fireproof

41.__

42. The judge admonished the witness for his answer.
As used in this sentence, the word *admonished* means MOST NEARLY
    A. complimented   B. punished
    C. questioned   D. warned

42.__

43. A millimeter is a measure of length.
    The length represented by *one millimeter* is   43.___
       A. one-thousandth of a meter
       B. one thousand meters
       C. one-millionth of a meter
       D. one million meters

44. It is not possible to misconstrue his letter.   44.___
    As used in this sentence, the word *misconstrue* means
    MOST NEARLY
       A. decipher   B. forget
       C. ignore   D. misinterpret

45. The wire connecting the two terminals must be kept taut.   45.___
    As used in this sentence, the word *taut* means MOST NEARLY
    without
       A. defects   B. slack
       C. electrical charge   D. pressure

46. Reaching the summit appeared beyond the capacity of the   46.___
    hikers.
    As used in this sentence, the word *summit* means MOST NEARLY
       A. canyon   B. peak   C. plateau   D. ravine

47. The plot was thwarted by the quick action of the police.   47.___
    As used in this sentence, the word *thwarted* means MOST
    NEARLY
       A. blocked   B. discovered
       C. punished   D. solved

48. An abrasive was required by the machinist to complete his   48.___
    task.
    As used in this sentence, the word *abrasive* means a
    substance used for
       A. coating   B. lubricating
       C. measuring   D. polishing

49. The facades of the building were dirty and grimy.   49.___
    As used in this sentence, the word *facades* means MOST
    NEARLY
       A. cellars   B. fronts
       C. residents   D. surroundings

50. Several firemen were injured by the detonation.   50.___
    As used in this sentence, the word *detonation* means MOST
    NEARLY
       A. accident   B. collapse   C. collision   D. explosion

————

KEY (CORRECT ANSWERS)

1. B	11. D	21. A	31. C	41. C
2. C	12. A	22. C	32. C	42. D
3. D	13. C	23. C	33. A	43. A
4. D	14. D	24. D	34. A	44. D
5. B	15. A	25. A	35. D	45. B
6. D	16. C	26. B	36. B	46. B
7. B	17. B	27. B	37. C	47. A
8. D	18. B	28. A	38. D	48. D
9. D	19. A	29. B	39. C	49. B
10. C	20. B	30. C	40. A	50. D

EXAMINATION SECTION

TEST 1

DIRECTIONS: Each question or incomplete statement is followed by several suggested answers or completions. Select the one that BEST answers the question or completes the statement. *PRINT THE LETTER OF THE CORRECT ANSWER IN THE SPACE AT THE RIGHT.*

Questions 1-20.

DIRECTIONS: Column I below lists words used in medical practice. Column II lists phrases which describe the words in Column I. Opposite the number preceding each of the words in Column I, place the letter preceding the phrase in Column II which BEST describes the word in Column I.

COLUMN I

1. Abrasion
2. Aseptic
3. Cardiac
4. Catarrh
5. Contamination
6. Dermatology
7. Disinfectant
8. Dyspepsia
9. Epidemic
10. Epidermis
11. Incubation
12. Microscope
13. Pediatrics
14. Plasma
15. Prenatal
16. Retina
17. Syphilis

COLUMN II

A. A disturbance of digestion   1.___

B. Destroying the germs of disease   2.___

    3.___

C. A general poisoning of the blood   4.___

D. An instrument used for injecting fluids   5.___

    6.___

E. A scraping off of the skin   7.___

F. Free from disease germs

    8.___

G. An apparatus for viewing internal organs by means of x-rays   9.___

    10.___

H. An instrument for assisting the eye in observing minute objects   11.___

    12.___

I. An inoculable immunizing agent   13.___

J. The extensive prevalence in a community of a disease   14.___

    15.___

K. Chemical product of an organ   16.___

    17.___

L. Preceding birth

COLUMN I (cont'd)	COLUMN II (cont'd)	
18. Syringe	M. Fever	18.__
19. Toxemia	N. The branch of medical science that relates to the skin and its diseases	19.__
20. Vaccine		20.__
	O. Fluid part of the blood	
	P. The science of the hygienic care of children	
	Q. Infection by contact	
	R. Relating to the heart	
	S. Inner structure of the eye	
	T. Outer portion of the skin	
	U. Pertaining to the duct-less glands	
	V. An infectious venereal disease	
	W. The development of an infectious disease from the period of infection to that of the appearance of the first symptoms	
	X. Simple inflammation of a mucous membrane	
	Y. An instrument for measuring blood pressure	

Questions 21-25.

DIRECTIONS: Each of Questions 21 through 25 consists of four words.
Three of these words belong together. One word does
NOT belong with the other three. For each group of
words, you are to select the one word which does NOT
belong with the other three words.

21. A. conclude   B. terminate   C. initiate   D. end   21.__

22. A. deficient   B. inadequate   22.__
     C. excessive   D. insufficient

23. A. rare   B. unique   C. unusual   D. frequent   23.__

24. A. unquestionable   B. uncertain   24.___
    C. doubtful   D. indefinite

25. A. stretch   B. contract   C. extend   D. expand   25.___

KEY (CORRECT ANSWERS)

1. E
2. F
3. R
4. X
5. Q

6. N
7. B
8. A
9. J
10. T

11. W
12. H
13. P
14. O
15. L

16. S
17. V
18. D
19. C
20. I

21. C
22. C
23. D
24. A
25. B

TEST 2

DIRECTIONS: Each question or incomplete statement is followed by several suggested answers or completions. Select the one that BEST answers the question or completes the statement. *PRINT THE LETTER OF THE CORRECT ANSWER IN THE SPACE AT THE RIGHT.*

Questions 1-4.

DIRECTIONS: Questions 1 through 4 pertain to the meaning of terms which may be encountered in laboratory work. For each question, select the option whose meaning is MOST NEARLY the same as that of the numbered item.

1. Atrophied   1.__
   A. enlarged   B. relaxed
   C. strengthened   D. wasted

2. Leucocyte   2.__
   A. white cell   B. red cell
   C. epithelial cell   D. dermal cell

3. Permeable   3.__
   A. volatile   B. variable
   C. flexible   D. penetrable

4. Attenuate   4.__
   A. dilute   B. infect
   C. oxidize   D. strengthen

Questions 5-11.

DIRECTIONS: For Questions 5 through 11, select the letter preceding the word which means MOST NEARLY the same as the first word.

5. legible   5.__
   A. readable   B. eligible   C. learned   D. lawful

6. observe   6.__
   A. assist   B. watch   C. correct   D. oppose

7. habitual   7.__
   A. punctual   B. occasional
   C. usual   D. actual

8. chronological   8.__
   A. successive   B. earlier
   C. later   D. studious

9. arrest   9.___
    A. punish   B. run   C. threaten   D. stop

10. abstain   10.___
    A. refrain   B. indulge   C. discolor   D. spoil

11. toxic   11.___
    A. poisonous   B. decaying
    C. taxing   D. defective

12. The *initial* contact is of great importance in setting a   12.___
    pattern for future relations.
    The word *initial*, as used in this sentence, means MOST
    NEARLY
    A. first   B. written   C. direct   D. hidden

13. The doctor prescribed a diet which was *adequate* for the   13.___
    patient's needs.
    The word *adequate*, as used in this sentence, means MOST
    NEARLY
    A. insufficient   B. unusual
    C. required   D. enough

14. The child was reported to be suffering from a vitamin   14.___
    deficiency.
    The word *deficiency*, as used in this sentence, means MOST
    NEARLY
    A. surplus   B. infection   C. shortage   D. injury

15. In obtaining medical case data, a medical record librarian   15.___
    should discourage the patient from giving *irrelevant*
    information.
    The word *irrelevant*, as used in this sentence, means MOST
    NEARLY
    A. too detailed   B. pertaining to relatives
    C. insufficient   D. inappropriate

16. The doctor requested that a *tentative* appointment be made   16.___
    for the patient.
    The word *tentative*, as used in this sentence, means MOST
    NEARLY
    A. definite   B. subject to change
    C. later   D. of short duration

17. The black plague resulted in an usually high *mortality*   17.___
    rate in the population of Europe.
    The term *mortality rate*, as used in this sentence, means
    MOST NEARLY
    A. future immunity of the people
    B. death rate
    C. general weakening of the health of the people
    D. sickness rate

18. The public health assistant was asked to file a number   18.__
of *identical* reports on the case.
The word *identical*, as used in this sentence, means MOST
NEARLY
   A. accurate   B. detailed   C. same   D. different

19. The nurse assisted in the *biopsy* of the patient.   19.__
The word *biopsy*, as used in this sentence, means MOST
NEARLY
   A. autopsy
   B. excision and diagnostic study of tissue
   C. biography and health history
   D. administering of anesthesia

20. The assistant noted that the swelling on the patient's   20.__
face had *subsided*.
The word *subsided*, as used in this sentence, means MOST
NEARLY
   A. become aggravated   B. increased
   C. vanished   D. abated

21. The patient was given food *intravenously*.   21.__
The word *intravenously*, as used in this sentence, means
MOST NEARLY
   A. orally   B. against his will
   C. through the veins   D. without condiment

Questions 22-25.

DIRECTIONS: Each of Questions 22 through 25 consists of four words.
Three of these words belong together. One word does
NOT belong with the other three. For each group of
words, you are to select the one word which does NOT
belong with the other three words.

22. A. accelerate B. quicken   C. accept   D. hasten   22.__

23. A. sever   B. rupture   C. rectify   D. tear   23.__

24. A. innocuous B. injurious C. dangerous D. harmful 24.__

25. A. adulterate   B. contaminate   25.__
  C. taint   D. disinfect

KEY (CORRECT ANSWERS)

1. D	6. B	11. A	16. B	21. C
2. A	7. C	12. A	17. B	22. C
3. D	8. A	13. D	18. C	23. C
4. A	9. D	14. C	19. B	24. A
5. A	10. A	15. D	20. D	25. D

TEST 3

DIRECTIONS: Each question or incomplete statement is followed by several suggested answers or completions. Select the one that BEST answers the question or completes the statement. *PRINT THE LETTER OF THE CORRECT ANSWER IN THE SPACE AT THE RIGHT.*

Questions 1-25.

DIRECTIONS: Each of Questions 1 through 25 consists of a word, in capitals, followed by four suggested meanings of the word. For each question, indicate in the space at the right the letter preceding the word which means MOST NEARLY the same as the word in capitals.

1. TEMPORARY   1.____
    A. permanently   B. for a limited time
    C. at the same time   D. frequently

2. INQUIRE   2.____
    A. order   B. agree   C. ask   D. discharge

3. SUFFICIENT   3.____
    A. enough   B. inadequate
    C. thorough   D. capable

4. AMBULATORY   4.____
    A. bedridden   B. left-handed
    C. walking   D. laboratory

5. DILATE   5.____
    A. enlarge   B. contract   C. revise   D. restrict

6. NUTRITIOUS   6.____
    A. protective   B. healthful
    C. fattening   D. nourishing

7. CONGENITAL   7.____
    A. with pleasure   B. defective
    C. likeable   D. existing from birth

8. ISOLATION   8.____
    A. sanitation   B. quarantine
    C. rudeness   D. exposure

9. SPASM   9.____
    A. splash   B. twitch   C. space   D. blow

10. HEMORRHAGE   10.____
    A. bleeding   B. ulcer
    C. hereditary disease   D. lack of blood

11. NOXIOUS   11.__
    A. gaseous   B. harmful   C. soothing   D. repulsive

12. PYOGENIC   12.__
    A. disease producing   B. fever producing
    C. pus forming   D. water forming

13. RENAL   13.__
    A. brain   B. heart   C. kidney   D. stomach

14. ENDEMIC   14.__
    A. epidemic
    B. endermic
    C. endoblast
    D. peculiar to a particular people or locality, as a disease

15. MACULATION   15.__
    A. reticulation   B. inoculation
    C. maturation   D. defilement

16. TOLERATE   16.__
    A. fear   B. forgive   C. allow   D. despise

17. VENTILATE   17.__
    A. vacate   B. air   C. extricate   D. heat

18. SUPERIOR   18.__
    A. perfect   B. subordinate
    C. lower   D. higher

19. EXTREMITY   19.__
    A. extent   B. limb   C. illness   D. execution

20. DIVULGED   20.__
    A. unrefined   B. secreted   C. revealed   D. divided

21. SIPHON   21.__
    A. drain   B. drink   C. compute   D. discard

22. EXPIRATION   22.__
    A. trip   B. demonstration
    C. examination   D. end

23. AEROSOL   23.__
    A. a gas dispersed in a liquid
    B. a liquid dispersed in a gas
    C. a liquid dispersed in a solid
    D. a solid dispersed in a liquid

24. ETIOLOGY   24.__
    A. cause of a disease   B. method of cure
    C. method of diagnosis   D. study of insects

25.   IN VITRO   25.___
      A. in alkali   B. in the body
      C. in the test tube   D. in vacuum

———————

KEY (CORRECT ANSWERS)

1. B	11. B
2. C	12. C
3. A	13. C
4. C	14. D
5. A	15. D
6. D	16. C
7. D	17. B
8. B	18. D
9. B	19. B
10. A	20. C

21. A
22. D
23. B
24. A
25. C

———————

VERBAL ANALOGIES

The verbal-analogy type question is now a staple component of tests of general and mental ability, scholastic aptitude, professional qualification, and civil service examinations. This question-type is also being used for achievement testing.

The verbal analogy is considered an excellent measure for evaluating the ability of the student to reason with and in words. It is not, primarily, a test of vocabulary *per se,* for very rarely are the words that are used in this type of question difficult or abstruse in meaning (as they are, for example, in the same-opposite or sentence-completion type). Rather, they are everyday terms and phrases descriptive of materials and actions familiar to all of us.

The verbal analogy is a test of *word relationships* and *idea relationships,* involving a neat and algebraic-like arrangement in ratio (proportion) form not of numbers but of words. Some testers see in this type of question the development on the verbal (linguistic or qualitative) side of the same logical reasoning as occurs on the mathematical (numerical or quantitative) side in number problems. This type of question is ranked just after the reading-comprehension type in difficulty. However, it constitutes by far the most fascinating and challenging area in aptitude testing.

In general, three levels of ability are involved in answering the verbal analogy question.

First, and easiest in this connection, is the ability to understand the meanings of the words used in the question (understanding).

Second, and more difficult , is the ability to comprehend the relationship between the subject-, or question-, pair of words (the process of logical reasoning).

Third, and most difficult of all, is the ability to select from the five (pairs of) choices given, that choice which bears the same relationship to (within) itself as the subject words bear to one another. This involves analysis, comparison, and judgment (the process of evaluation).

In the verbal-analogy type of question, two important symbols are employed, which must be thoroughly understood beforehand. These are the colon(:), which is to be translated into words, when reading the question, in the same way as its mathematical equivalent, that is, "is to"; and the double colon (::), which is to be translated as "in the same way as." Thus, the analogy, BURGLAR: PRISON :: juvenile delinquent : reformatory, is to be read, <u>A burglar is to a prison in the same way as a juvenile delinquent is to a reformatory</u>. Or, reading for meaning, we could say instead, "A burglar is punished by being sent to a prison in the same way as a juvenile delinquent is punished by being sent to a reformatory."

SAMPLE QUESTIONS AND EXPLANATIONS

DIRECTIONS: Each question in this part consists of a pair of words in capital letters, which have a certain relationship to each other, followed *either* by a third word in capital letters and five lettered words in small letters (1 blank missing) OR by five lettered pairs of words in small letters (2 blanks missing). Choose *either* the letter of the word that is related to the third word in capital letters OR of the pair of words that are related to each other in the same way as the first two capitalized words are related to each other, and mark the appropriate space on your answer sheet.

1. EROSION : ROCKS :: DISSIPATION : _____
    A. character   B. temperance   C. penance   D. influence
    E. sincerity
2. MUNDANE : SPIRITUAL :: SECULAR : _____
    A. scientist   B. clerical   C. pecuniary   D. municipal
    E. teacher
3. ANARCHY : LAWLESSNESS :: _____ : _____
    A. autocracy : peace   B. disturbance : safety
    C. government : order   D. confusion : law
    E. democracy : dictatorship
4. UMBRELLA : RAIN :: _____ : _____
    A. roof : snow   B. screen : insects
    C. sewer : water   D. body : disease
    E. gong : dinner

EXPLANATION OF QUESTION 1

Item A, character, is correct.

Erosion is a geological development that wears away Rocks. This is an example of a cause-effect relationship -- a concrete relationship

Dissipation wears away character (Item A) in the same way --howeve this is an abstract relationship.

But the comparison is apt and appropriate. This is a usual, genera type of analogy whose difficulty is compounded by the fact that a concrete relationship is compared with an abstract one.

Item B, temperance (moderation), is merely one aspect of character.

Item C, penance (repentance), bears no relationship to dissipation in the sense of the subject words.

Item D, influence, and Item E, sincerity, may or may not be affecte by dissipation.

This question is an example of a one-blank analogy, that is, only o word is to be supplied in the answer (a subject pair and a third subje word being given in the question itself).

EXPLANATION OF QUESTION 2

Item B, clerical, is correct.

Mundane means worldly, earthly. The opposite of this word is spiritual -- unworldly, devout, eternal. This is a relationship of opposites.

Secular means worldly, earthly, temporal. It is a synonym for munda What is needed as the answer is an opposite equal in meaning to spirit

A. A scientist may or may not be worldly or spiritual. At any rate an adjective is needed as an answer, and scientist is a noun.

B. Clerical ("pertaining to the clergy") denotes, usually, apiritua or religious qualities. It is an adjective. This is the correct answer

C. Pecuniary refers to money, and may, therefore, be regarded as a synonym for secular.

D. Municipal refers to municipalities or cities, and has no standing here as an answer.

E. A teacher may or may not be worldly or spiritual. At any rate, just as for A. scientist, it is a noun and not an adjective, which is needed as an answer here.

EXPLANATION OF QUESTION 3
   Item C, <u>government : order</u>, is correct.
   <u>Anarchy</u>, or no government, is characterized by <u>lawlessness</u> while a <u>government</u> is characterized by <u>order</u>. This is an example of an <u>object (situation) : characteristic</u> relationship.
   Item A, <u>autocracy : peace</u>, is incorrect since very often autocracy (absolute monarchy or rule by an individual) is characterized by war.
   Item B, <u>disturbance : safety</u>, is manifestly untrue.
   Item D, <u>confusion : law</u>, is likewise untrue.
   Item E, <u>democracy : dictatorship</u>, bears no relationship to the meaning conveyed by the subject pair.
   This is an example of a two-blank analogy, that is, a pair of words is to be supplied. This is the more difficult type of analogy, and the one most frequently encountered on advanced-level examinations.

———

EXPLANATION OF QUESTION 4
   Item B, <u>screen : insects</u>, is correct.
   By means of an <u>umbrella</u>, one keeps the <u>rain</u> off his person just as a <u>screen</u> keeps <u>insects</u> out of the house. This is an example of an <u>object: assists</u> relationship.
   Item A, <u>roof : snow</u>, is not correct since a roof keeps out many other things as well, e.g., light, heat, rain, insects, etc.
   Item C, <u>sewer : water</u>, is incorrect since a sewer keeps water <u>in</u> or water flows through and in a sewer.
   Item D, <u>body : disease</u>, is incorrect since often disease enters and destroys the body.
   Item E, <u>gong : dinner</u>, is incorrect since the gong merely summons to dinner but does not keep anyone away.

———

   As can be discerned from the examples above, there are many possible relationships on which word analogies may be formed. Some of these will be listed and illustrated below. However, the important point is not to ponder over labels and attempt to peg the relationships thereby. This is as unnecessary as it is time-consuming. The real object, or the real method, is to examine and to fully comprehend the relationship expressed in the subject pair and *then* to select as the correct answer that item which *most approximately* is in greatest consonance with all or most of the aspects of the given relationship.

———

TYPES AND FORMS OF ANALOGY QUESTIONS

   Some or all of the following types of analogies or relationships are to be encountered on examinations.
1. PART : WHOLE
     Example: LEG : BODY :: wheel : car
2. CAUSE : EFFECT
     Example: RAIN : FLOOD :: disease : epidemic
3. CONCRETE : ABSTRACT
     Example: ROAD : VEHICLE :: life : person
4. WORD : SYNONYM
     Example: VACUOUS : EMPTY :: seemly : fit
5. WORD : ANTONYM
     Example: SLAVE : FREEMAN :: desolate : joyous

6. OBJECT : MATERIAL
     Example: COAT : WOOL :: dress : cotton
  7. OBJECT : DEFINITION
     Example: ASSEVERATE : AFFIRM :: segregate : separate
  8. OBJECT : SEX
     Example: COLT : MARE :: buck : doe
  9. TIME : TIME
     Example: DAY : NIGHT :: sunrise : sunset
 10. DEGREE : DEGREE
     Example: HAPPY : ECSTATIC :: warm : hot
 11. OBJECT : TOOL
     Example: STENCIL : TYPEWRITER :: thread : needle
 12. USER : TOOL
     Example: FARMER : HOE :: dentist : drill
 13. CREATOR : CREATION
     Example: ARTIST : PICTURE :: poet : poem
 14. CATEGORY : TYPE
     Example: RODENT : SQUIRREL :: fish : flounder
 15. PERSON (ANIMAL,ETC.) : CHARACTERISTIC
     Example: MONSTER : FEROCITY :: baby : helplessness
 16. OBJECT : CHARACTERISTIC
     Example: PICKLE : SOUR :: sugar : sweet
 17. PERSON : FUNCTION
     Example: TEACHER : EDUCATION :: doctor : health
 18. INSTRUMENT : FUNCTION
     Example: CAMERA : PHOTOGRAPHY :: ruler : measurement
 19. WORD : GRAMMATICAL FORM
     Example: WE : I :: they : he
 20. SYMBOL : ATTITUDE
     Example: SALUTE : PATRIOTISM :: prayer : religion
 21. REWARD : ACTION
     Example: MEDAL : BRAVERY :: trophy : championship
 22. OBJECT : ASSISTS
     Example: WATER : THIRST :: food : hunger
 23. OBJECT : HINDERS
     Example: NOISE : STUDY :: rut : car
 24. PERSON : RELATIONSHIP
     Example: FATHER : SON :: uncle : nephew
 25. OBJECT : LOCALE
     Example: SHIP : WATER :: airplane : air
 26. OBJECT : METHOD
     Example: DOOR : KEY :: safe : combination
 27. QUALITY : PROFUSION
     Example: WIND : TORNADO :: water : flood
 28. QUALITY : ABSENCE
     Example: FORTITUDE : COWARDICE :: carefully : casually
 29. SIZE : SIZE
     Example: BOAT : SHIP :: lake : sea
 30. GENUS : SPECIES
     Example: RODENT : RAT :: canine : wolf

   There are other relationships, but these will suffice to show some
of those more frequently occurring.

———

SUGGESTIONS FOR ANSWERING THE VERBAL ANALOGY QUESTION (APTITUDE)

1. Always keep in mind that a verbal analogy is a relationship of likeness between two things, consisting in the resemblances not, usually, of the things themselves but of two or more of their attributes, functions, circumstances, or effects. Therefore, in the one-blank or two-blank questions, you are not looking so much for similarity in structure (although this may prove to be a factor, too), as you are for a relationship in the <u>functioning</u> of the subject words.

2. How do we proceed to answer the verbal-analogy type question? *First,* discover for yourself in a meaningful way the exact relationship existing between the subject words. Whether you are able to label or tag this relationship is not so important (as we have said before) as to <u>understand</u> the relationship that exists. The logical *second* and *final* step is to examine the possible answers given and to ascertain which of these possibilities, on the basis of *meaning, order,* and *form,* bears a similar relationship to the subject pair.

3. For the analogy in question, the subject words (i.e., the question words given in the first part of the analogy) need not be of the same class, type, order, or species as the object words (i.e., the answer-words or fill-ins). For example, in the analogy, BUCCANEER:SAILOR :: fungus : plant, the subject words (in capital letters) are types of people, the object words (in small letters) refer to types of things. However, the analogy that exists is on the basis of a descriptive relationship between these two different sets of words. (The first word in each pair constitutes the depredatory or despoiling form of the second, which is the general category name.) Thus, it is actually the <u>total</u> effect of the *first pair* on each other that is being compared with the <u>total</u> effect of the *second pair* on each other: *this is what really counts,* and not the individual components of each pair.

4. The order of the object words must be in the same sequence as the order of the subject words. For example, the analogy, INAUGURATION : PRESIDENT :: ordination : priest, is correct. But, INAUGURATION : PRESIDENT :: priest : ordination, would be incorrect. Watch for this <u>reversal</u> of order in word sequence; it is a common source of entrapment for the uninitiated.

5. Likewise, it is necessary to check to see that the parts of speech used in the analogy are the same, and occur in the same sequence. For example, if the subject pair contains a noun and an adjective in that order, the object pair <u>must</u> contain a noun and an adjective in *that* order. Thus, MOTHER : GOOD :: murderer : bad, is correct. But, MOTHER : GOOD :: murderer : badly, is incorrect.

6. The best way to answer the analogy question -- one-blank or two-blanks -- is to study intensively the relationship contained in the given pair. Having fully comprehended this relationship and, perhaps, having "labeled" it, proceed to scan the possible answers, choosing the most likely one. This will save time, and avoid needless trial and error.

VERBAL ANALOGIES

EXAMINATION SECTION

TEST 1

DIRECTIONS: In Questions 1 to 10, the first two *italicized* words
have a relationship to each other. Determine that
relationship, and then match the third *italicized* word
with the one of the lettered choices with which it
has the same relationship as the words of the first
pair have to each other. *PRINT THE LETTER OF THE
CORRECT ANSWER IN THE SPACE AT THE RIGHT.*

In order to help you understand the procedure, a
sample question is given:

SAMPLE: *dog* is to *bark* as *cat* is to
        A. animal   B. small   C. meow
        D. pet   E. snarl

The relationship between *dog* and *bark* is that the
sound which a dog normally emits is a bark. In the
same way, the sound which a cat emits is a meow.
Thus, C is the CORRECT answer.

1. *Fine* is to *speeding* as *jail* is to   1._____
    A. bars   B. prisoner   C. warden
    D. confinement   E. steal

2. *Orchid* is to *rose* as *gold* is to   2._____
    A. watch   B. copper   C. mine   D. coin   E. mint

3. *Pistol* is to *machine gun* as *button* is to   3._____
    A. coat   B. bullet   C. zipper
    D. tailor   E. needle and thread

4. *Spontaneous* is to *unrehearsed* as *planned* is to   4._____
    A. completed   B. organized   C. restricted
    D. understood   E. informal

5. *Friendly* is to *hostile* as *loyalty* is to   5._____
    A. fealty   B. evil   C. devotion
    D. warlike   E. treachery

6. *Fear* is to *flight* as *bravery* is to   6._____
    A. courage   B. danger   C. resistance
    D. injury   E. unyielding

7. *Economical* is to *stingy* as *sufficient* is to   7._____
    A. abundant   B. adequate   C. expensive
    D. needy   E. greedy

8. *Astronomer* is to *observation* as *senator* is to   8._____
    A. caucus   B. election   C. convention
    D. legislation   E. patronage

9. *Hunger* is to *food* as *exhaustion* is to
   A. labor   B. play   C. illness
   D. debility   E. rest

9.___

10. *Entertainment* is to *boredom* as *efficiency* is to
    A. ignorance   B. government   C. waste
    D. expert   E. time and motion studies

10.___

KEY (CORRECT ANSWERS)

1.	E	6.	C
2.	B	7.	A
3.	C	8.	D
4.	B	9.	E
5.	E	10.	C

TEST 2

DIRECTIONS: In Questions 1 to 10, the first two *italicized* words have a relationship to each other. Determine that relationship, and then match the third *italicized* word with the one of the lettered choices with which it has the same relationship as the words of the first pair have to each other. *PRINT THE LETTER OF THE CORRECT ANSWER IN THE SPACE AT THE RIGHT.*

1. *Diamond* is to *glass* as *platinum* is to   1.____
   A. jewelry   B. metal   C. aluminum
   D. mine   E. white

2. *Water* is to *aqueduct* as *electricity* is to   2.____
   A. meter   B. battery   C. fuse   D. wire   E. solenoid

3. *Oratory* is to *filibuster* as *reign* is to   3.____
   A. tyrant   B. terror   C. government
   D. bluster   E. confusion

4. *Gravity* is to *gaiety* as *taunt* is to   4.____
   A. ridicule   B. console   C. avoid
   D. amuse   E. condone

5. *Electron* is to *atom* as *earth* is to   5.____
   A. sun   B. solar system   C. moon
   D. planet   E. center

6. *Flattery* is to *adulation* as *cruelty* is to   6.____
   A. pain   B. barbarity   C. censorious
   D. compassion   E. duality

7. *Rowboat* is to *oar* as *automobile* is to   7.____
   A. land   B. engine   C. driver
   D. passenger   E. piston

8. *Friction* is to *oil* as *war* is to   8.____
   A. conference   B. peace   C. munitions
   D. satellite   E. retaliation

9. *Disease* is to *infection* as *reaction* is to   9.____
   A. control   B. injury   C. relapse
   D. stipulation   E. sensation

10. *Persecution* is to *martyr* as *swindle* is to   10.____
    A. embezzler   B. refuge   C. confidence man
    D. bank   E. dupe

KEY (CORRECT ANSWERS)

1. C	6. B
2. D	7. B
3. E	8. A
4. B	9. E
5. B	10. E

TEST 3

DIRECTIONS: In Questions 1 to 10, the first two *italicized* words have a relationship to each other. Determine that relationship, and then match the third *italicized* word with the one of the lettered choices with which it has the same relationship as the words of the first pair have to each other. *PRINT THE LETTER OF THE CORRECT ANSWER IN THE SPACE AT THE RIGHT.*

1. *Woman* is to *man* as *Mary* is to   1.____
   A. woman   B. child   C. female   D. John   E. male

2. *Land* is to *ocean* as *soldier* is to   2.____
   A. river   B. sailor   C. shore   D. uniform   E. sailing

3. *Sugar* is to *candy* as *flour* is to   3.____
   A. eat   B. cook   C. candy   D. bread   E. sweet

4. *Sorrow* is to *joy* as *laugh* is to   4.____
   A. amuse   B. tears   C. fun   D. weep   E. cry

5. *Heat* is to *fire* as *pain* is to   5.____
   A. injury   B. wind   C. weather   D. cool   E. summer

6. *Grass* is to *cattle* as *milk* is to   6.____
   A. growing   B. lawn   C. baby   D. green   E. sun

7. *Winter* is to *spring* as *autumn* is to   7.____
   A. summer   B. winter   C. warm   D. cold   E. flower

8. *Rising* is to *falling* as *smile* is to   8.____
   A. climbing   B. baking   C. scolding
   D. frown   E. laughing

9. *Day* is to *night* as *succeed* is to   9.____
   A. fail   B. sunshine   C. evening
   D. afternoon   E. morning

10. *Apple* is to *fruit* as *corn* is to   10.____
    A. orange   B. eat   C. grain   D. cereal   E. food

_____

KEY (CORRECT ANSWERS)

1. D	6. C
2. B	7. B
3. D	8. D
4. E	9. A
5. A	10. C

TEST 4

DIRECTIONS: In Questions 1 to 10, the first two *italicized* words have a relationship to each other. Determine that relationship, and then match the third *italicized* word with the one of the lettered choices with which it has the same relationship as the words of the first pair have to each other. *PRINT THE LETTER OF THE CORRECT ANSWER IN THE SPACE AT THE RIGHT.*

1. *Robin* is to *feathers* as *cat* is to   1.____
     A. sing   B. fur   C. eat   D. bird   E. fly

2. *Late* is to *end* as *early* is to   2.____
     A. prompt   B. enter   C. begin   D. start   E. end

3. *Beginning* is to *end* as *horse* is to   3.____
     A. cart   B. automobile   C. wagon
     D. travel   E. ride

4. *Kitten* is to *cat* as *baby* is to   4.____
     A. rabbit   B. mother   C. dog   D. cow   E. lamb

5. *Little* is to *weak* as *big* is to   5.____
     A. boy   B. man   C. tall   D. baby   E. strong

6. *Arm* is to *hand* as *leg* is to   6.____
     A. knee   B. toe   C. elbow   D. foot   E. finger

7. *Alive* is to *dead* as *well* is to   7.____
     A. grow   B. sick   C. decay   D. sleep   E. play

8. *In* is to *out* as *bad* is to   8.____
     A. up   B. open   C. good   D. shut   E. on

9. *Dust* is to *dry* as *mud* is to   9.____
     A. wet   B. blow   C. splash   D. fly   E. settle

10. *Width* is to *wide* as *height* is to   10.____
     A. high   B. low   C. tall   D. brief   E. short

KEY (CORRECT ANSWERS)

1. B	6. D
2. C	7. B
3. A	8. C
4. B	9. A
5. E	10. C

TEST 5

DIRECTIONS: In Questions 1 to 10, the first two *italicized* words have a relationship to each other. Determine that relationship, and then match the third *italicized* word with the one of the lettered choices with which it has the same relationship as the words of the first pair have to each other. *PRINT THE LETTER OF THE CORRECT ANSWER IN THE SPACE AT THE RIGHT.*

1. *Above* is to *below* as *before* is to   1.__
   A. beyond   B. behind   C. beside   D. between   E. after

2. *Start* is to *stop* as *begin* is to   2.__
   A. go   B. run   C. wait   D. finish   E. work

3. *Everything* is to *nothing* as *always* is to   3.__
   A. forever   B. usually   C. never
   D. sometimes   E. something

4. *Search* is to *find* as *question* is to   4.__
   A. answer   B. reply   C. study
   D. problem   E. explain

5. *Top* is to *spin* as *spear* is to   5.__
   A. bottom   B. roll   C. throw   D. sharp   E. pin

6. *Scale* is to *weight* as *thermometer* is to   6.__
   A. weather   B. temperature   C. pounds
   D. spring   E. chronometer

7. *Congress* is to *senator* as *convention* is to   7.__
   A. election   B. chairman   C. delegate
   D. nominee   E. representative

8. *Dividend* is to *investor* as *wage* is to   8.__
   A. employee   B. salary   C. consumer
   D. price   E. employer

9. *Terminate* is to *commence* as *adjourn* is to   9.__
   A. enact   B. convene   C. conclude
   D. veto   E. prorogue

10. *Administrator* is to *policy* as *clerk* is to   10.__
    A. subornation   B. organization   C. coordination
    D. direction   E. application

KEY (CORRECT ANSWERS)

1. E	6. B
2. D	7. C
3. C	8. A
4. A	9. B
5. C	10. E

VERBAL ANALOGIES
EXAMINATION SECTION

Questions 1-10.

DIRECTIONS: In each of Questions 1 through 10, a pair of related words written in capital letters is followed by four other pairs of words. For each question, select the pair of words which MOST closely expresses a relationship similar to that of the pair in capital letters.

SAMPLE QUESTION:

BOAT - DOCK
    A. airplane - hangar   B. rain - snow
    C. cloth - cotton   D. hunger - food

Choice A is the answer to this sample question since of the choices given, the relationship between airplane and hangar is most similar to the relationship between boat and dock.

1. AUTOMOBILE - FACTORY   1._____
    A. tea - lemon   B. wheel - engine
    C. pot - flower   D. paper - mill

2. GIRDER - BRIDGE   2._____
    A. petal - flower   B. street - sidewalk
    C. meat - vegetable   D. sun - storm

3. RADIUS - CIRCLE   3._____
    A. brick - building   B. tie - tracks
    C. spoke - wheel   D. axle - tire

4. DISEASE - RESEARCH   4._____
    A. death - poverty   B. speech - audience
    C. problem - conference   D. invalid - justice

5. CONCLUSION - INTRODUCTION   5._____
    A. commencement - beginning B. housing - motor
    C. caboose - engine   D. train - cabin

6. SOCIETY - LAW   6._____
    A. baseball - rules   B. jury - law
    C. cell - prisoner   D. sentence - jury

7. PLAN - ACCOMPLISHMENT
   A. deed - fact   B. method - success
   C. graph - chart   D. rules - manual

7.

8. ORDER - GOVERNMENT
   A. chaos - administration   B. confusion - pandemonium
   C. rule - stability   D. despair - hope

8.

9. TYRANNY - FREEDOM
   A. despot - mob   B. wealth - poverty
   C. nobility - commoners   D. dictatorship - democracy

9.

10. TELEGRAM - LETTER
    A. hare - tortoise   B. lie - truth
    C. number - word   D. report - research

10.

Questions 11-30.

DIRECTIONS: In Questions 11 through 30, the first two capitalized words have a relationship to each other. Determine the relationship, and then match the third capitalized word with the one of the lettered choice with which it has the same relationship as the words of the first pair have to each other.

11. CONGRESS is to SENATOR as CONVENTION is to
    A. election   B. chairman   C. delegate   D. nominee

11.

12. DIVIDEND is to INVESTOR as WAGE is to
    A. employee   B. salary   C. consumer   D. price

12.

13. TERMINATE is to COMMENCE as ADJOURN is to
    A. enact   B. convene   C. conclude   D. veto

13.

14. SANITATION is to HEALTH as EDUCATION is to
    A. school   B. hygiene   C. knowledge   D. teacher

14.

15. ADMINISTRATOR is to POLICY as CLERK is to
    A. subordinate   B. organization
    C. coordination   D. procedure

15.

16. ALLEGIANCE is to LOYALTY as TREASON is to
    A. felony   B. faithful   C. obedience   D. rebellion

16.

17. DIAMOND is to GLASS as PLATINUM is to
    A. jewelry   B. metal   C. aluminum   D. mine

17.

18. WATER is to AQUEDUCT as ELECTRICITY is to
    A. meter   B. battery   C. fuse   D. wire

18.

19. ORATORY is to FILIBUSTER as REIGN is to
    A. tyranny   B. terror   C. government   D. empire

19.

20. GRAVITY is to GAIETY as TAUNT is to
    A. ridicule   B. console   C. avoid   D. amuse

20.

21. ELECTRON is to ATOM as EARTH is to   21.___
    A. sun   B. solar system   C. moon   D. planet

22. FLATTERY is to PRAISE as CRUELTY is to   22.___
    A. pain   B. punishment   C. pleasantry   D. favoritism

23. ROWBOAT is to OAR as AUTOMOBILE is to   23.___
    A. land   B. engine   C. driver   D. passenger

24. FRICTION is to OIL as WAR is to   24.___
    A. conference   B. peace   C. munitions   D. satellite

25. DISEASE is to INFECTION as REACTION is to   25.___
    A. control   B. injury   C. relapse   D. stimulus

26. PERSECUTION is to MARTYR as SWINDLE is to   26.___
    A. embezzler   B. refugee   C. victim   D. bank

27. PHYSICIAN is to PATIENT as ATTORNEY is to   27.___
    A. court   B. client   C. counsel   D. judge

28. JUDGE is to SENTENCE as JURY is to   28.___
    A. court   B. foreman   C. defendant   D. verdict

29. REVERSAL is to AFFIRMANCE as CONVICTION is to   29.___
    A. appeal   B. acquittal   C. error   D. mistrial

30. GENUINE is to TRUE as SPURIOUS is to   30.___
    A. correct   B. conceived   C. false   D. speculative

KEY (CORRECT ANSWERS)

1. D	11. C	21. B
2. A	12. A	22. B
3. C	13. B	23. B
4. C	14. C	24. A
5. C	15. D	25. D
6. A	16. D	26. C
7. B	17. C	27. B
8. C	18. D	28. D
9. D	19. A	29. B
10. A	20. B	30. C

ABSTRACT REASONING

COMMENTARY

The mathematical or quantitative ability of the candidate is generally measured through the form of questions and/or problems involving arithmetical reasoning, algebraic problem solving, and the interpretation of visual materials -- graphs, charts, tables, diagrams, maps, cartoons, and pictures.

A more recent development, which attempts to assay facets of quantitative ability not ordinarily discernible or measurable, is the nonverbal test of reasoning of the type commonly designated as the figure analogy. Figure analogies are novel and differentiated measures of non-numerical mathematics reasoning.

Since intelligence exists in many forms or phases and the theory of differential aptitudes is now firmly established in testing, other manifestations and measurements of intelligence than verbal or purely arithmetical must be identified and measured.

Classification inventory, or figure classification, involves the aptitude of form perception, i.e., the ability to perceive pertinent detail in objects or in pictorial or graphic material. It involves making visual comparisons and discriminations and discerning slight differences in shapes and shading figures and widths and lengths of lines.

___

One aspect of this type of nonverbal question takes the form of a *positive* requirement to find the *COMPATIBLE PATTERN* (i.e., the one that *does* belong) from among two (2) sets of figure groups. The prescription for this question-type is as follows:

A group of three drawings lettered A, B, and C, respectively, is presented, followed on the same line by five (5) numbered alternative drawings labeled 1, 2, 3, 4, and 5, respectively.

The first two (2) drawings (A, B) in each question are related in some way.

The candidate is then to decide what characteristic *each* of the figures labeled A and B has that causes them to be related, and is then to select the one alternative from the five (5) numbered figures that is related to figure C in the same way that drawing B is related to drawing A.

Leading examples of presentation are the figure analogy and the figure classification. The Section that follows presents progressive and varied samplings of this type of question.

___

FIGURE ANALOGIES

Figure analogies are a novel and differentiated measure of non-numerical mathematics reasoning.

This question takes the form of, and, indeed, is similar to, the one-blank verbal analogy. However, pictures or drawings are used instead of words.

SAMPLE QUESTIONS AND EXPLANATIONS

DIRECTIONS: Each question in this part consists of 3 drawings lettered A,B,C, followed by 5 alternative drawings, numbered 1 to 5. The first 2 drawings in each question are related in some way. Choose the number of the alternative that is related to the third drawing in the same way that the second drawing is related to the first, and mark the appropriate space on your answer sheet.

1.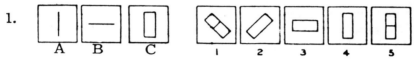

The CORRECT answer is 3. A vertical line has the same relationship to a horizontal line that a rectangle standing on its end has to a rectangle lying on its side.

2.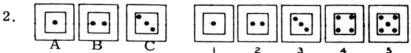

The second square has one more dot than the first square. Therefore the CORRECT answer is alternative 4, which has one more dot than the third square.

3.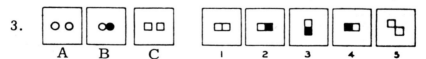

In the second drawing the circles are moved together and the circle on the right darkened. Therefore the CORRECT answer is 2, in which the squares are moved together and the right-hand square darkened.

4.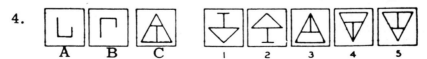

The CORRECT answer is 5. The second drawing is the inverted version of the first; alternative 5 is the inverted version of the third drawing.

2

5.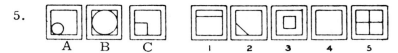

The CORRECT answer is 4. Drawing A has a small circle within a square; drawing B contains a circle completely filling the square. Drawing C has a small square within a square; in alternative 4, this small square has been magnified to its complete size within the square so that this magnified square coincides with the enclosing square, leaving the outline of only one square.

6.

The CORRECT answer is 5. Drawing A appears in a horizontal position, with a diagonal line drawn through the center dot; drawing B appears in a vertical position, with a straight line drawn through the center dot. Drawing C is similar to drawing A, except that it appears in a vertical position; drawing 5 is similar to drawing B, except that it appears in a horizontal position. Our analogy may, therefore, be verbally expressed as

A:B:C:5.

———

SUGGESTIONS FOR ANSWERING THE FIGURE ANALOGY QUESTION

1. In doing the actual questions, there can be little practical gain in rationalizing each answer that you attempt. What is needed is a quick and ready perceptive sense in this matter.

2. The BEST way to prepare for this type of question is to do the "Tests" in figure analogies that follow. By this method, you will gain enough functional skill to enable you to cope successfully with this type of question on the Examination.

———

PLEASE NOTE -- In the tests which begin on page 5, after the sample questions, the three (3) drawings are unlabeled and the answers have four (4) choices instead of five (5) labeled A,B,C and D. They are to be answered in the same way.

———

SAMPLE TEST

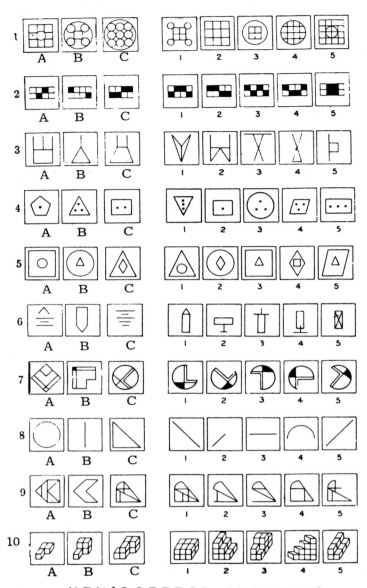

KEY(CORRECT ANSWERS)

1. 2	3. 4	5. 4	7. 3
2. 2	4. 1	6. 3	8. 2

EXPLANATION OF ANSWERS

1. In the second figure, the squares are changed to circles and the circles to squares.
2. In the second figure, the upper darkened area has moved two squares to left; the lower, two squares to right.
3. The second figure has a flat base, like the first.
4. The sum of sides and dots in the second figure equals that of the first.
5. The outside part of the second figure is the inside part of the first.
6. The second figure is constructed from the lines given in the first.
7. The second figure is obtained from the first by rotating it 135° clockwise, darkening the smaller area and deleting the larger.
8. The second figure is the bisector of the area of the first.
9. The second figure is obtained from the first by deleting all the vertical lines.
10. The second figure contains two blocks more than the first.

4

EXAMINATION SECTION

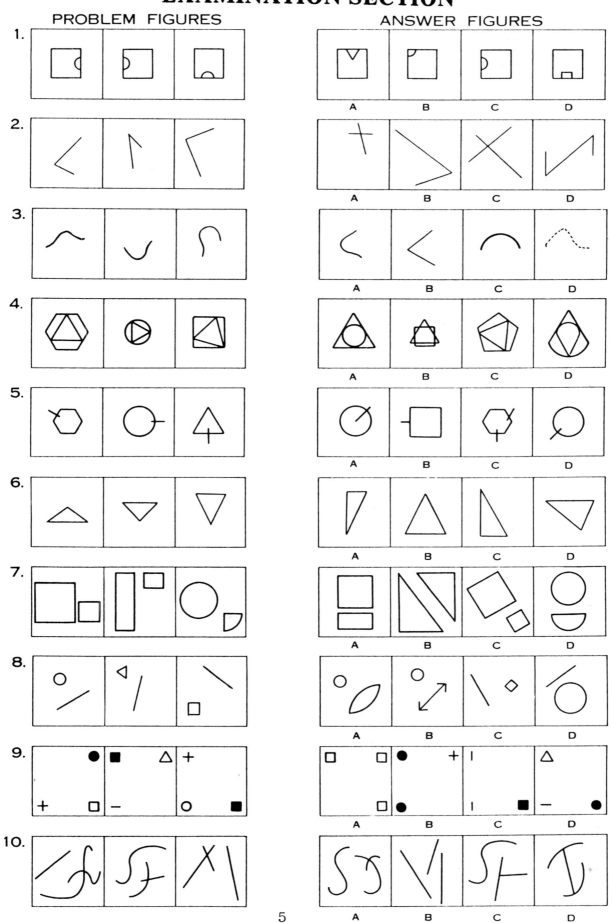

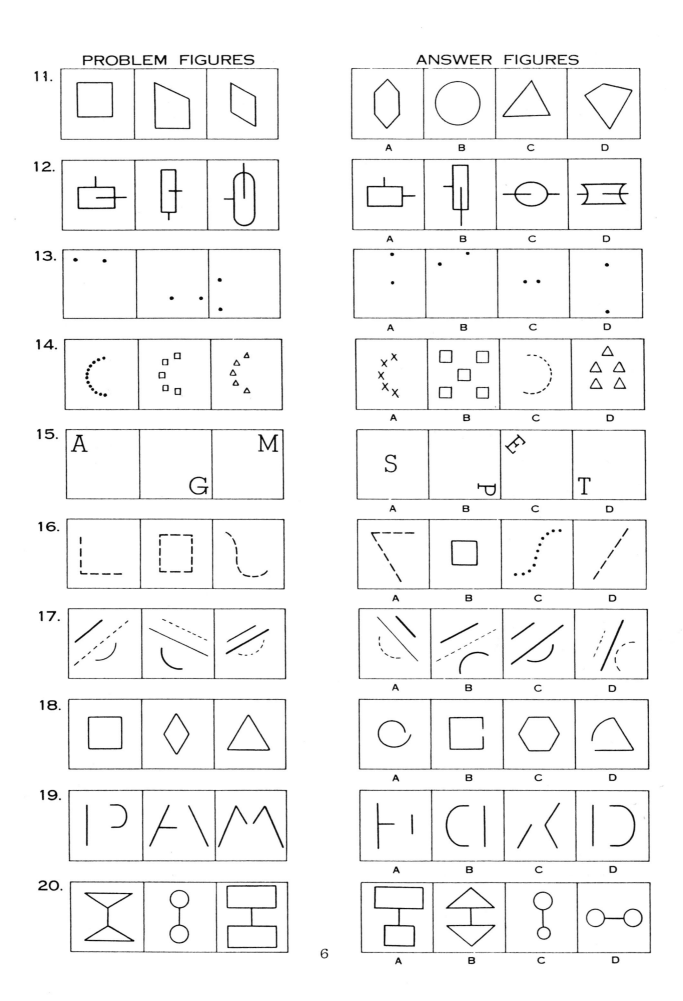

PROBLEM FIGURES

ANSWER FIGURES

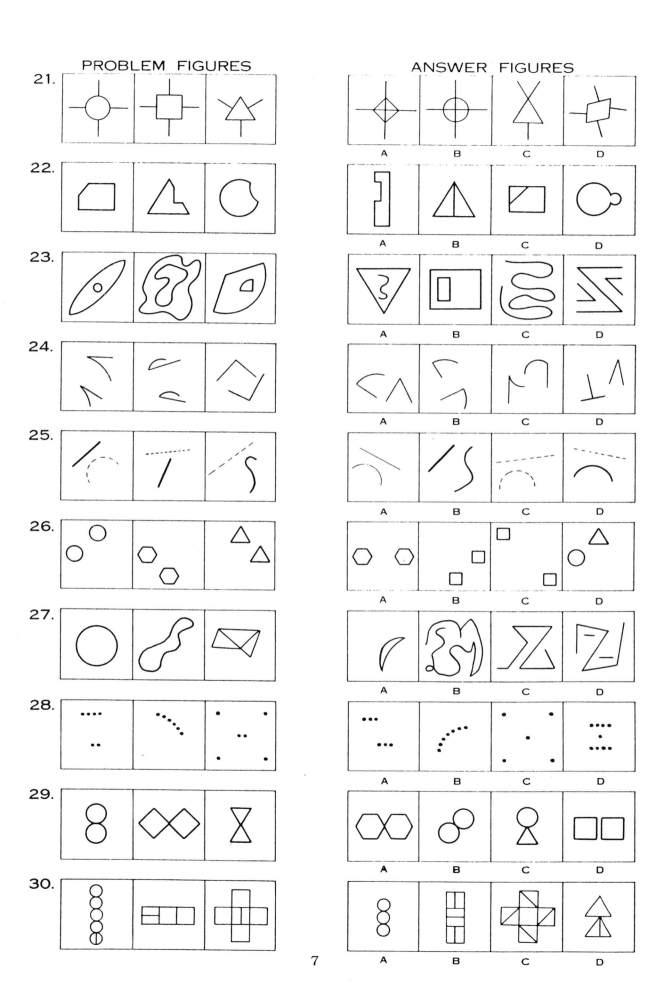

PROBLEM FIGURES

ANSWER FIGURES

21.

22.

23.

24.

25.

26.

27.

28.

29.

30.

7

PROBLEM FIGURES

ANSWER FIGURES

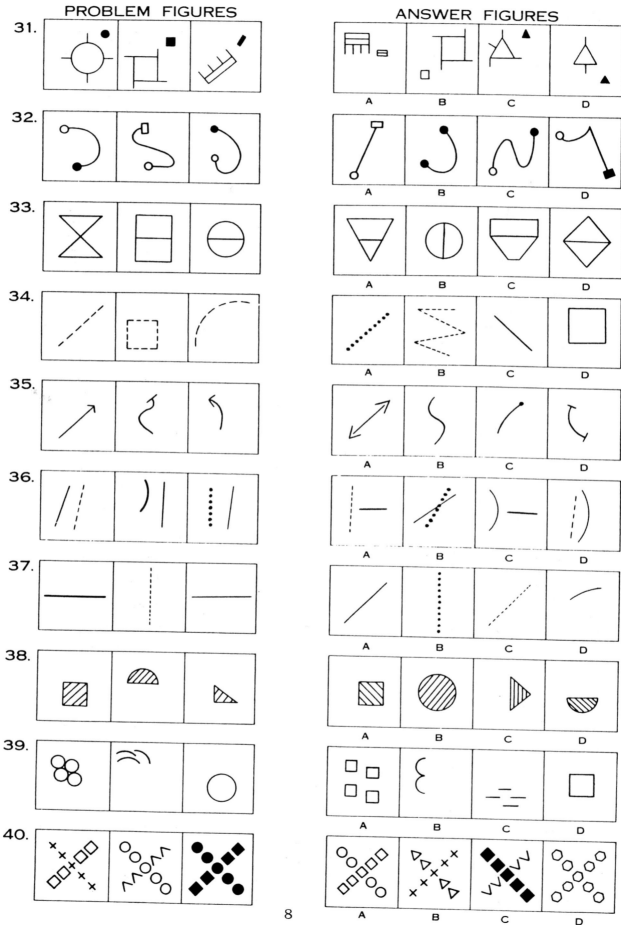

31.

32.

33.

34.

35.

36.

37.

38.

39.

40.

A   B   C   D

8

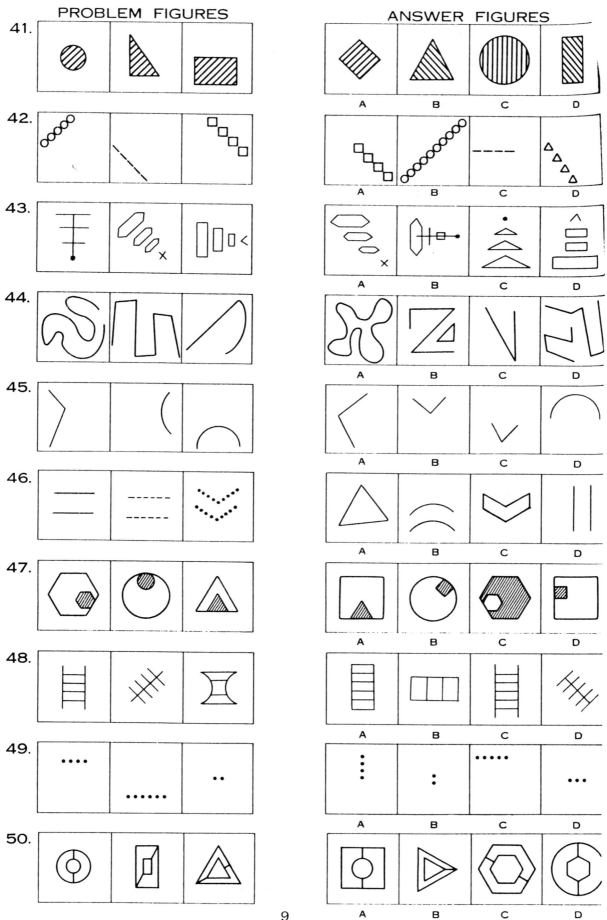

PROBLEM FIGURES

ANSWER FIGURES

41.

42.

43.

44.

45.

46.

47.

48.

49.

50.

9

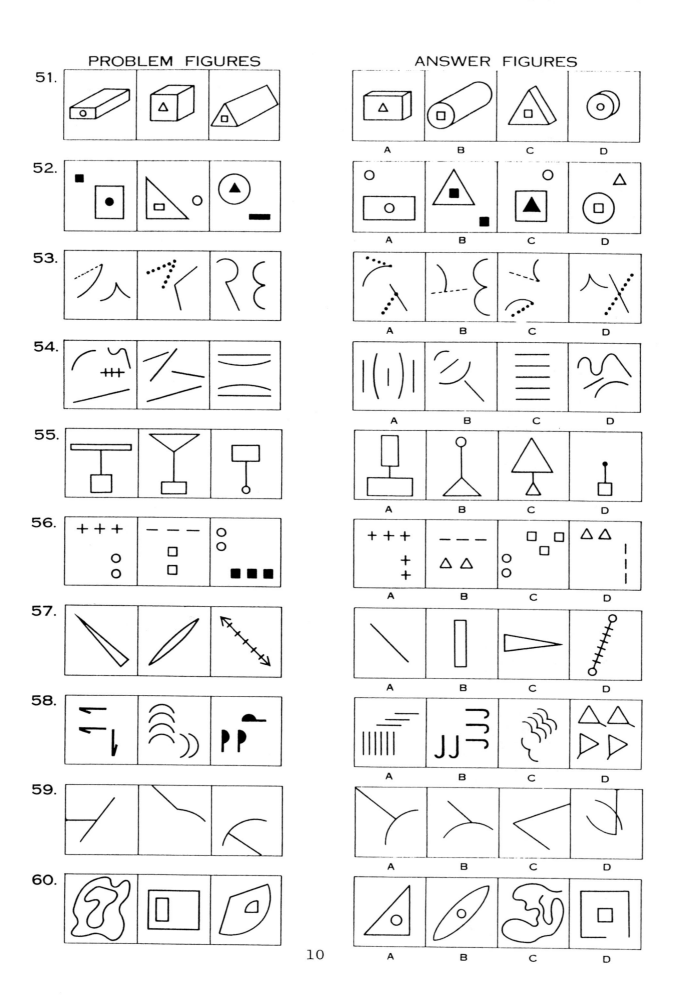

KEY (CORRECT ANSWERS)

1.	C	21.	D	41.	A		
2.	B	22.	A	42.	D		
3.	A	23.	B	43.	C		
4.	C	24.	B	44.	C		
5.	D	25.	D	45.	B		
6.	B	26.	B	46.	B		
7.	C	27.	A	47.	D		
8.	C	28.	A	48.	B		
9.	D	29.	A	49.	D		
10.	A	30.	D	50.	C		
11.	D	31.	C	51.	B		
12.	B	32.	C	52.	D		
13.	A	33.	D	53.	C		
14.	A	34.	B	54.	B		
15.	D	35.	C	55.	C		
16.	A	36.	D	56.	D		
17.	A	37.	B	57.	A		
18.	C	38.	B	58.	A		
19.	D	39.	B	59.	C		
20.	B	40.	C	60.	B		

———

ARITHMETIC

EXAMINATION SECTION

DIRECTIONS FOR THIS SECTION:
Each question or incomplete statement is followed by several suggested answers or completions. Select the one that *BEST* answers the question or completes the statement. *PRINT THE LETTER OF THE CORRECT ANSWER IN THE SPACE AT THE RIGHT.*

TEST 1

1. Add $4.34, $34.50, $6.00, $101.76, $90.67. From the result, subtract $60.54 and $10.56.   1. ...
   A. $76.17   B. $156.37   C. $166.17   D. $300.37
2. Add 2,200, 2,600, 252 and 47.96. From the result, subtract 202.70, 1,200, 2,150 and 434.43.   2. ...
   A. 1,112.83   B. 1,213.46   C. 1,341.51   D. 1,348.91
3. Multiply 1850 by .05 and multiply 3300 by .08 and, then, add both results.   3. ...
   A. 242.50   B. 264.00   C. 333.25   D. 356.50
4. Multiply 312.77 by .04. Round off the result to the nearest hundredth.   4. ...
   A. 12.52   B. 12.511   C. 12.518   D. 12.51
5. Add 362.05, 91.13, 347.81 and 17.46 and then divide the result by 6. The answer, rounded off to the nearest hundredth, is: 5. ...
   A. 138.409   B. 137.409   C. 136.41   D. 136.40
6. Add 66.25 and 15.06 and, then, multiply the result by 2 1/6. The answer is, most nearly,   6. ...
   A. 176.18   B. 176.17   C. 162.66   D. 162.62
7. Each of the following items contains three decimals. In which case do *all* three decimals have the *SAME* value?   7. ...
   A. .3; .30; .03   B. .25; .250; .2500
   C. 1.9; 1.90; 1.09   D. .35; .350; .035
8. Add 1/2 the sum of (539.84 and 479.26) to 1/3 the sum of (1461.93 and 927.27). Round off the result to the nearest whole number.   8. ...
   A. 3408   B. 2899   C. 1816   D. 1306
9. Multiply $5,906.09 by 15% and, then, divide the result by 3 and round off to the nearest cent.   9. ...
   A. $295.30   B. $885.91   C. $2,657.74   D. $29,530.45
10. Multiply 630 by 517.   10. ...
    A. 325,710   B. 345,720   C. 362,425   D. 385,660
11. Multiply 35 by 846.   11. ...
    A. 4050   B. 9450   C. 18740   D. 29610
12. Multiply 823 by 0.05.   12. ...
    A. 0.4115   B. 4.115   C. 41.15   D. 411.50
13. Multiply 1690 by 0.10.   13. ...
    A. 0.169   B. 1.69   C. 16.90   D. 169.0
14. Divide 2765 by 35.   14. ...
    A. 71   B. 79   C. 87   D. 93
15. From $18.55 subtract $6.80.   15. ...
    A. $9.75   B. $10.95   C. $11.75   D. $25.35
16. The sum of 2.75 + 4.50 + 3.60 is: 16. ...
    A. 9.75   B. 10.85   C. 11.15   D. 11.95
17. The sum of 9.63 + 11.21 + 17.25 is: 17. ...
    A. 36.09   B. 38.09   C. 39.92   D. 41.22
18. The sum of 112.0 + 16.9 + 3.84 is: 18. ...
    A. 129.3   B. 132.74   C. 136.48   D. 167.3

19. When 65 is added to the result of 14 multiplied by 13, the   19. ...
    answer is:
       A. 92   B. 182   C. 247   D. 16055
20. From $391.55 subtract $273.45.   20. ...
       A. $118.10   B. $128.20   C. $178.10   D. $218.20

TEST 2

 1. The sum of $29.61 + $101.53 + $943.64 is: 1. ...
       A. $983.88   B. $1074.78   C. $1174.98   D. $1341.42
 2. The sum of $132.25 + $85.63 + $7056.44 is: 2. ...
       A. $1694.19   B. $7274.32   C. $8464.57   D. $9346.22
 3. The sum of 4010 + 1271 + 838 + 23 is: 3. ...
       A. 6142   B. 6162   C. 6242   D. 6362
 4. The sum of 53632 + 27403 + 98765 + 75424 is: 4. ...
       A. 19214   B. 215214   C. 235224   D. 255224
 5. The sum of 76342 + 49050 + 21206 + 59989 is: 5. ...
       A. 196586   B. 206087   C. 206587   D. 234487
 6. The sum of $452.13 + $963.45 + $621.25 is: 6. ...
       A. $1936.83   B. $2036.83   C. $2095.73   D. $2135.73
 7. The sum of 36392 + 42156 + 98765 is: 7. ...
       A. 167214   B. 177203   C. 177313   D. 178213
 8. The sum of 40125 + 87123 + 24689 is: 8. ...
       A. 141827   B. 151827   C. 151937   D. 161947
 9. The sum of 2379 + 4015 + 6521 + 9986 is: 9. ...
       A. 22901   B. 22819   C. 21801   D. 21791
10. From 50962 subtract 36197.   10. ...
       A. 14675   B. 14765   C. 14865   D. 24765
11. From 90000 subtract 31928.   11. ...
       A. 58072   B. 59062   C. 68172   D. 69182
12. From 63764 subtract 21548.   12. ...
       A. 42216   B. 43122   C. 45126   D. 85312
13. From $9605.13 subtract $2715.96.   13. ...
       A. $12,321.09 B. $8,690.16 C. $6,990.07 D. $6,889.17
14. From 76421 subtract 73101.   14. ...
       A. 3642   B. 3540   C. 3320   D. 3242
15. From $8.25 subtract $6.50.   15. ...
       A. $1.25   B. $1.50   C. $1.75   D. $2.25
16. Multiply 583 by 0.50.   16. ...
       A. $291.50   B. 28.15   C. 2.815   D. 0.2815
17. Multiply 0.35 by 1045.   17. ...
       A. 0.36575   B. 3.6575   C. 36.575   D. 365.75
18. Multiply 25 by 2513.   18. ...
       A. 62825   B. 62725   C. 60825   D. 52825
19. Multiply 423 by 0.01.   19. ...
       A. 0.0423   B. 0.423   C. 4.23   D. 42.3
20. Multiply 6.70 by 3.2.   20. ...
       A. 2.1440   B. 21.440   C. 214.40   D. 2144.0

TEST 3

Questions 1-4.
DIRECTIONS: For each of Questions 1-4, perform the indicated arithmetic and choose the correct answer from among the four choices given.

2

1. 12,485
    +   347

    A. 12,038   B. 12,128   C. 12,782   D. 12,832

2. 74,137
    +   711

    A. 74,326   B. 74,848   C. 78,028   D. 78,926

3. 3,749
    - 671

    A. 3,078   B. 3,168   C. 4,028   D. 4,420

4. 19,805
    -18,904

    A. 109   B. 901   C. 1,109   D. 1,901

5. When 119 is subtracted from the sum of 2016 + 1634, the remainder is:

    A. 2460   B. 3531   C. 3650   D. 3769

6. Multiply 35 X 65 X 15.

    A. 2275   B. 24265   C. 31145   D. 34125

7. 90% expressed as a decimal is:

    A. .009   B. .09   C. .9   D. 9.0

8. Seven-tenths of a foot expressed in inches is:

    A. 5.5   B. 6.5   C. 7   D. 8.4

9. If 95 men were divided into crews of five men each, the *number* of crews that will be formed is:

    A. 16   B. 17   C. 18   D. 19

10. If a man earns $19.50 an hour, the *number* of working hours it will take him to earn $4,875 is, most nearly,

    A. 225   B. 250   C. 275   D. 300

11. If 5½ loads of gravel cost $55.00, then 6½ loads will cost:

    A. $60.   B. $62.50   C. $65.   D. $66.00

12. At $2.50 a yard, 27 yards of concrete will cost:

    A. $36.   B. $41.80   C. $54.   D. $67.50

13. A distance is measured and found to be 52.23 feet. In feet and inches, this distance is, most nearly, 52 feet *and*

    A. 2 3/4"   B. 3 1/4"   C. 3 3/4"   D. 4 1/4"

14. If a maintainer gets $5.20 per hour and time and one-half for working over 40 hours, his *gross* salary for a week in which he worked 43 hours would be

    A. $208.00   B. $223.60   C. $231.40   D. $335.40

15. The circumference of a circle is given by the formula C = ΠD, where C is the circumference, D is the diameter, and Π is about 3 1/7.
    If a coil is 15 turns of steel cable has an average diameter of 20 inches, the *total* length of cable on the coil is *nearest to*

    A. 5 feet   B. 78 feet   C. 550 feet   D. 943 feet

16. The measurements of a poured concrete foundation show that 54 cubic feet of concrete have been placed.
    If payment for this concrete is to be on the basis of cubic yards, the 54 cubic feet must be

    A. multiplied by 27   B. multiplied by 3
    C. divided by 27   D. divided by 3

17. If the cost of 4 1/2 tons of structural steel is $1,800,   17. ...
    then the cost of 12 tons is, most nearly,
    A. $4,800   B. $5,400   C. $7,200   D. $216,000

18. An hourly-paid employee working 12:00 midnight to 8:00   18. ...
a.m. is directed to report to the medical staff for a
physical examination at 11:00 a.m. of the same day.
The pay allowed him for reporting will be an extra
    A. 1 hour   B. 2 hours   C. 3 hours   D. 4 hours

19. The *total* length of four pieces of 2" pipe, whose lengths   19. ...
are 7' 3½", 4' 2 3/16", 5' 7 5/16", and 8' 5 7/8", respectively, is:
    A. 24' 6 3/4"   B. 24' 7 15/16"
    C. 25' 5 13/16"   D. 25' 6 7/8"

20. As a senior mortuary caretaker, you are preparing a month- 20. ...
ly report, using the following figures:
    No. of bodies received   983
    No. of bodies claimed   720
    No. of bodies sent to city cemetery   14
    No. of bodies sent to medical schools   9
How many bodies remained at the end of the monthly reporting period?
    A. 230   B. 240   C. 250   D. 260

KEYS (CORRECT ANSWERS)

TEST 1		TEST 2		TEST 3	
1. C	11. D	1. B	11. A	1. D	11. C
2. A	12. C	2. B	12. A	2. B	12. D
3. D	13. D	3. A	13. D	3. A	13. A
4. D	14. B	4. D	14. C	4. B	14. C
5. C	15. C	5. C	15. C	5. B	15. B
6. B	16. B	6. B	16. A	6. D	16. C
7. B	17. B	7. C	17. D	7. C	17. A
8. D	18. B	8. C	18. A	8. D	18. C
9. A	19. C	9. A	19. C	9. D	19. D
10. A	20. A	10. B	20. B	10. B	20. B

SOLUTIONS TO PROBLEMS
TEST 1

1. ($4.34 + $34.50 + $6.00 + $101.76 + $90.67) − ($60.54 + $10.56)
    = $237.27 − $71.10 = $166.17.

2. (2200 + 2600 + 252 + 47.96) − (202.70 + 1200 + 2150 + 434.43)
    = 5099.96 − 3987.13 = 1112.83

3. (1850)(.05) + (3300)(.08) = 92.5 + 264 = 356.50

4. (312.77)(.04) = 12.5108 = 12.51 to nearest hundredth

5. (362.05 + 91.13 + 347.81 + 17.46) ÷ 6 = 136.408$\overline{3}$ = 136.41
    to nearest hundredth

6. $(66.25 + 15.06)(2\frac{1}{6})$ = 176.171$\overline{6}$ ≈ 176.17

7. .25 = .250 = .2500

8. $(\frac{1}{2})$(539.84 + 479.26) + $\frac{1}{3}$(1461.93 + 927.27) = 509.55 + 796.4
    = 1305.95 = 1306 nearest whole number

9. ($5906.09)(.15) ÷ 3 = ($885.9135)/3 = 295.3045 = $295.30
    to nearest cent

10. (630)(517) = 325,710

11. (35)(846) = 29,610

12. (823)(.05) = 41.15

13. (1690)(.10) = 169.0

14. 2765 ÷ 35 = 79

15. $18.55 − $6.80 = $11.75

16. 2.75 + 4.50 + 3.60 = 10.85

17. 9.63 + 11.21 + 17.25 = 38.09

18. 112.0 + 16.9 + 3.84 = 132.74

19. 65 + (14)(13) = 65 + 182 = 247

20. $391.55 − $273.45 = $118.10

────

5

SOLUTIONS TO PROBLEMS
TEST 2

1. $29.61 + $101.53 + $943.64 = $1074.78

2. $132.25 + $85.63 + $7056.44 = $7274.32

3. 4010 + 1271 + 838 + 23 = 6142

4. 53,632 + 27,403 + 98,765 + 75,424 = 255,224

5. 76,342 + 49,050 + 21,206 + 59,989 = 206,587

6. $452.13 + $963.45 + $621.25 = $2036.83

7. 36,392 + 42,156 + 98,765 = 177,313

8. 40,125 + 87,123 + 24,689 = 151,937

9. 2379 + 4015 + 6521 + 9986 = 22,901

10. 50962 - 36197 = 14,765

11. 90,000 - 31,928 = 58,072

12. 63,764 - 21,548 = 42,216

13. $9605.13 - $2715.96 = $6889.17

14. 76,421 - 73,101 = 3320

15. $8.25 - $6.50 = $1.75

16. (583)(.50) = 291.50

17. (.35)(1045) = 365.75

18. (25)(2513) = 62,825

19. (423)(.01) = 4.23

20. (6.70)(3.2) = 21.44

SOLUTIONS TO PROBLEMS
TEST 3

1. $12,485 + 347 = 12,832$

2. $74,137 + 711 = 74,848$

3. $3749 - 671 = 3078$

4. $19,805 - 18,904 = 901$

5. $(2016 + 1634) - 119 = 3650 - 119 = 3531$

6. $(35)(65)(15) = 34,125$

7. $90\% = .90$ or $.9$

8. $(\frac{7}{10})(12) = 8.4$ inches

9. $95 \div 5 = 19$ crews

10. $\$4875 \div \$19.50 = 250$ days

11. Let x = cost. Then, $\frac{5\frac{1}{2}}{6\frac{1}{2}} = \frac{\$55.00}{x}$. $5\frac{1}{2}x = 357.50$. Solving, $x = \$65$

12. $(\$2.50)(27) = \$67.50$

13. $.23$ ft. $= 2.76$ in., so 52.23 ft ≈ 52 ft. $2\frac{3}{4}$ in. $(.76 \approx \frac{3}{4})$

14. Salary $= (\$5.20)(40) + (\$7.80)(3) = \$231.40$

15. Length $\approx (15)(3\frac{1}{7})(20) \approx 943$ in. ≈ 78 ft.

16. There are 27 cu.ft. in 1 cu.yd. To change from 54 cu.ft. to cu.yds., divide by 27.

17. $\$1800 \div 4\frac{1}{2} = \$400$ per ton. Then, 12 tons cost $(\$400)(12) = \$4800$

18. Instead of working 12 to 8, he will be staying until 11 AM, an extra 3 hours.

19. $7'3\frac{1}{2}" + 4'2\frac{3}{16}" + 5'7\frac{5}{16}" + 8'5\frac{7}{8}" = 24'17\frac{30}{16}" = 24'18\frac{7}{8}"$

20. $983 - 720 - 14 - 9 = 240$ bodies left.

ARITHMETICAL COMPUTATION AND REASONING
EXAMINATION SECTION

TEST 1

DIRECTIONS: Each question or incomplete statement is followed by several suggested answers or completions. Select the one that BEST answers the question or completes the statement. *PRINT THE LETTER OF THE CORRECT ANSWER IN THE SPACE AT THE RIGHT.*

1. 3/8 less than $40 is
   A. $25   B. $65   C. $15   D. $55   1.____

2. 27/64 expressed as a percent is
   A. 40.625%   B. 42.188%   C. 43.750%   D. 45.313%   2.____

3. 1/6 more than 36 gross is ____ gross.
   A. 6   B. 48   C. 30   D. 42   3.____

4. 15 is 20% of
   A. 18   B. 3   C. 75   D. 35   4.____

5. The number which when increased by 1/3 of itself equals 96 is
   A. 128   B. 72   C. 64   D. 32   5.____

6. 0.16 3/4 written as percent is
   A. 16 3/4%   B. 16.3/4%   C. .016 3/4%   D. .0016 3/4%   6.____

7. 55% of 15 is
   A. 82.5   B. 0.825   C. 0.0825   D. 8.25   7.____

8. The number which when decreased by 1/3 of itself equals 96 is
   A. 64   B. 32   C. 128   D. 144   8.____

9. A carpenter used a board 15 3/4 ft. long from which 3 foot-   9.____
   stools were made with sufficient lumber left over for half
   of another footstool.
   If the lumber cost 24½¢ per foot, the cost of EACH footstool was
   A. $1.54   B. $3.86   C. $1.10   D. $1.08

10. In one year, a luncheonette purchased 1231 gallons of   10.____
    milk for $907.99.
    The AVERAGE cost per half pint was
    A. $0.046   B. $0.045   C. $0.047   D. $0.044

11. The product of 23 and 9 3/4 is   11.____
    A. 191 2/3   B. 224 1/4   C. 213 3/4   D. 32 3/4

12. An order for 345 machine bolts at $4.15 per hundred will   12.____
    cost
    A. $0.1432   B. $1.1432   C. $14.32   D. $143.20

13. The fractional equivalent of .0625 is
    A. 1/16   B. 1/15   C. 1/14   D. 1/13   13.___

14. The number 0.03125 equals
    A. 3/64   B. 1/16   C. 1/64   D. 1/32   14.___

15. 21.70 divided by 1.75 equals
    A. 124   B. 12.4   C. 1.24   D. .124   15.___

16. The average cost of school lunches for 100 children varied   16.___
    as follows: Monday, $0.285; Tuesday, $0.237; Wednesday,
    $0.264; Thursday, $0.276; Friday, $0.292.
    The AVERAGE lunch cost
    A. $0.136   B. $0.270   C. $0.135   D. $0.271

17. The cost of 5 dozen eggs at $8.52 per gross is   17.___
    A. $3.50   B. $42.60   C. $3.55   D. $3.74

18. 410.07 less 38.49 equals   18.___
    A. 372.58   B. 371.58   C. 381.58   D. 382.68

19. The cost of 7 3/4 tons of coal at $20.16 per ton is   19.___
    A. $15.12   B. $151.20   C. $141.12   D. $156.24

20. The sum of 90.79, 79.09, 97.90, and 9.97 is   20.___
    A. 277.75   B. 278.56   C. 276.94   D. 277.93

KEY (CORRECT ANSWERS)

1. A			11. B	
2. B			12. C	
3. D			13. A	
4. C			14. D	
5. B			15. B	
6. A			16. D	
7. D			17. C	
8. D			18. B	
9. C			19. D	
10. A			20. A	

SOLUTIONS TO PROBLEMS

1. $(\$40)(\frac{5}{8}) = \$25$

2. $27/64 = .421875 \approx 42.188\%$

3. $(36)(1\frac{1}{6}) = 42$

4. Let x = missing number. Then, $15 = .20x$. Solving, x = 75

5. Let x = missing number. Then, $x + \frac{1}{3}x = 96$.
   Simplifying, $\frac{4}{3}x = 96$. Solving, $x = 96 \div \frac{4}{3} = 72$

6. $.16\frac{3}{4} = 16\frac{3}{4}\%$ by simply moving the decimal point two places to the right.

7. $(.55)(15) = 8.25$

8. Let x = missing number. Then, $x - \frac{1}{3}x = 96$. Simplifying,
   $\frac{2}{3}x = 96$. Solving, $x = 96 \div \frac{2}{3} = 144$

9. $15\frac{3}{4} \div 3\frac{1}{2} = 4.5$ feet per footstool. The cost of one footstool is $(\$.245)(4.5) = \$1.1025 \approx \$1.10$

10. $\$907.99 \div 1231 \approx \$.7376$ per gallon. Since there are 16 half-pints in a gallon, the average cost per half-pint is $\$.7376 \div 16 \approx \$.046$

11. $(23)(9\frac{3}{4}) = (23)(9.75) = 224.25$ or $224\frac{1}{4}$

12. $(\$4.15)(3.45) = \$14.3175 \approx \$14.32$

13. $.0625 = 625/10,000 = \frac{1}{16}$

14. $.03125 = 3125/100,000 = \frac{1}{32}$

15. $21.70 \div 1.75 = 12.4$

16. The sum of these lunches is $\$1.354$. Then, $\$1.354 \div 5$
    $= \$.2708 \approx \$.271$

17. $8.52 ÷ 12 = $.71 per dozen. Then, the cost of 5 dozen is
     ($.71)(5) = $3.55

18. 410.07 − 38.49 = 371.58

19. ($20.16)(7.75) = $156.24

20. 90.79 + 79.09 + 97.90 + 9.97 = 277.75

TEST 2

1. 1600 is 40% of what number?   1.____
    A. 6400   B. 3200   C. 4000   D. 5600

2. An executive's time card reads: Arrived 9:15 A.M., Left   2.____
    2:05 P.M.
    How many hours was he in the office? ____ hours ____ minutes.
    A. 5; 10   B. 4; 50   C. 4; 10   D. 5; 50

3. .4266 times .3333 will have the following number of   3.____
    decimals in the product:
    A. 8   B. 4   C. 1   D. None of these

4. An office floor is 25 ft. wide by 36 ft. long.   4.____
    To cover this floor with carpet will require ____ square yards.
    A. 100   B. 300   C. 900   D. 25

5. 1/8 of 1% expressed as a decimal is   5.____
    A. .125   B. .0125   C. 1.25   D. .00125

6. $\dfrac{6 \div 4}{6 \times 4}$ equals   6.____

    A. 1/16   B. 1   C. 1/6   D. 1/4

7. 1/25 of 230 equals   7.____
    A. 92.0   B. 9.20   C. .920   D. 920

8. 4 times 3/8 equals   8.____
    A. 1 3/8   B. 3/32   C. 12.125   D. 1.5

9. 3/4 divided by 4 equals   9.____
    A. 3   B. 3/16   C. 16/3   D. 16

10. 6/7 divided by 2/7 equals   10.____
    A. 6   B. 12/49   C. 3   D. 21

11. The interest on $240 for 90 days @ 6% is   11.____
    A. $4.80   B. $3.40   C. $4.20   D. $3.60

12. 16 2/3% of 1728 is   12.____
    A. 91   B. 288   C. 282   D. 280

13. 6¼% of 6400 is   13.____
    A. 2500   B. 410   C. 108   D. 400

14. $12\frac{1}{2}\%$ of 560 is   14.___
    A. 65   B. 40   C. 50   D. 70

15. 2 yards divided by 3 equals   15.___
    A. 2 feet   B. $\frac{1}{2}$ yard   C. 3 yards   D. 3 feet

16. A school has 540 pupils. 45% are boys.   16.___
    How many girls are there in this school?
    A. 243   B. 297   C. 493   D. 394

17. .1875 is equivalent to   17.___
    A. 18 3/4   B. 75/18   C. 18/75   D. 3/16

18. A kitchen cabinet listed at $42 is sold for $33.60.   18.___
    The discount allowed is
    A. 10%   B. 15%   C. 20%   D. 30%

19. 3 6/8 divided by 8 1/4 equals   19.___
    A. 9 1/8   B. 12   C. 5/11   D. 243.16

20. An agent sold goods to the amount of $1480.   20.___
    His commission at $5\frac{1}{2}\%$ was
    A. $37.50   B. $81.40   C. 76.70   D. $81.10

KEY (CORRECT ANSWERS)

1. C		11. D
2. B		12. B
3. A		13. D
4. A		14. D
5. D		15. A
6. A		16. B
7. B		17. D
8. D		18. C
9. B		19. C
10. C		20. B

SOLUTIONS TO PROBLEMS

1. Let x = missing number. Then, 1600 = .40x.
   Solving, x = 4000

2. 2:05 PM – 9:15 AM = 4 hours 50 minutes

3. The product of two 4-decimal numbers is an 8-decimal number.

4. (25 ft)(36 ft) = 900 sq.ft. = 100 sq.yds.

5. $(\frac{1}{8})(1\%) = (.125)(.01) = .00125$

6. $(6 \div 4) \div (6 \times 4) = \frac{3}{2} \div 24 = (\frac{3}{2})(\frac{1}{24}) = \frac{1}{16}$

7. $(\frac{1}{25})(230) = 9.20$

8. $(4)(\frac{3}{8}) = \frac{12}{8} = 1.5$

9. $\frac{3}{4} \div 4 = (\frac{3}{4})(\frac{1}{4}) = \frac{3}{16}$

10. $\frac{6}{7} \div \frac{2}{7} = (\frac{6}{7})(\frac{7}{2}) = 3$

11. ($240)(.06)(90/360) = $3.60

12. $(16\frac{2}{3}\%)(1728) = (\frac{1}{6})(1728) = 288$

13. $(6\frac{1}{4}\%)(6400) = (\frac{1}{16})(6400) = 400$

14. $(12\frac{1}{2}\%)(560) = (\frac{1}{8})(560) = 70$

15. 2 yds $\div$ 3 = $\frac{2}{3}$ yds = $(\frac{2}{3})(3)$ = 2 ft.

16. If 45% are boys, then 55% are girls. Thus,
    (540)(.55) = 297

17. $.1875 = 1875/10,000 = \frac{3}{16}$

18. $42 - $33.60 = $8.40.
     The discount is $8.40 ÷ $42 = .20 = 20%

19. $3\frac{6}{8} \div 8\frac{1}{4} = (\frac{30}{8})(\frac{4}{33}) = \frac{5}{11}$

20. ($1480)(.055) = $81.40

TEST 3

DIRECTIONS: Each question or incomplete statement is followed by several suggested answers or completions. Select the one that BEST answers the question or completes the statement. *PRINT THE LETTER OF THE CORRECT ANSWER IN THE SPACE AT THE RIGHT.*

1. 93.648 divided by 0.4 is
   A. 23.412   B. 234.12   C. 2.3412   D. 2341.2

   1.___

2. Add 4.3682, .0028, 34., 9.92, and from the sum subtract 1.992.
   The remainder is
   A. .46299   B. 4.6299   C. 462.99   D. 46.299

   2.___

3. At $2.88 per gross, three dozen will cost
   A. $8.64   B. $0.96   C. $0.72   D. $11.52

   3.___

4. 13 times 2.39 times 0.024 equals
   A. 745.68   B. 74.568   C. 7.4568   D. .74568

   4.___

5. A living room suite is marked $64 less 25 percent. A cash discount of 10 percent is allowed.
   The cash price is
   A. $53.20   B. $47.80   C. $36.00   D. $43.20

   5.___

6. 1/8 of 1 percent expressed as a decimal is
   A. .125   B. .0125   C. 1.25   D. .00125

   6.___

7. 16 percent of 482.11 equals
   A. 77.1376   B. 771.4240   C. 7714.2400   D. 7.71424

   7.___

8. A merchant sold a chair for $60. This was at a profit of 25 percent of what it cost him.
   The chair cost him
   A. $48   B. $45   C. $15   D. $75

   8.___

9. Add 5 hours 13 minutes, 3 hours 49 minutes, and 14 minutes.
   The sum is ____ hours ____ minutes.
   A. 9; 16   B. 9; 76   C. 8; 16   D. 8; 6

   9.___

10. 89 percent of $482 is
    A. $428.98   B. $472.36   C. $42.90   D. $47.24

    10.___

11. 200 percent of 800 is
    A. 16   B. 1600   C. 2500   D. 4

    11.___

12. Add 2 feet 3 inches, 4 feet 11 inches, 8 inches, 6 feet 6 inches.
    The sum is ____ feet ____ inches.
    A. 12; 4   B. 12; 14   C. 14; 4   D. 14; 28

    12.___

13. A merchant bought dresses at $15 each and sold them at $20 each. His overhead expenses are 20 percent of cost. His net profit on each dress is
    A. $1   B. $2   C. $3   D. $4

14. 0.0325 expressed as a percent is
    A. 325%   B. $3\frac{1}{4}$%   C. $32\frac{1}{2}$%   D. 32.5%

15. Add 3/4, 1/8, 1/32, 1/2; and from the sum subtract 4/8. The remainder is
    A. 2/32   B. 7/8   C. 29/32   D. 3/4

16. A salesman gets a commission of 4 percent on his sales. If he wants his commission to amount to $40, he will have to sell merchandise totaling
    A. $160   B. $10   C. $1,000   D. $100

17. Jones borrowed $225,000 for five years at $3\frac{1}{2}$ percent. The annual interest charge was
    A. $1,575   B. $1,555   C. $7,875   D. $39,375

18. A kitchen cabinet listed at $42 is sold for $33.60. The discount allowed is ____ percent.
    A. 10   B. 15   C. 20   D. 30

19. The exact number of days from May 5, 1987 to July 1, 1987 is ____ days.
    A. 59   B. 58   C. 56   D. 57

20. A dealer sells an article at a loss of 50% of the cost. Based on the selling price, the loss is
    A. 25%   B. 50%   C. 100%   D. none of these

KEY (CORRECT ANSWERS)

1. B	11. B
2. D	12. C
3. C	13. B
4. D	14. B
5. D	15. C
6. D	16. C
7. A	17. C
8. A	18. C
9. A	19. D
10. A	20. C

SOLUTIONS TO PROBLEMS

1. $93.648 \div .4 = 234.12$

2. $4.368 + .0028 + 34 + 9.92 - 1.992 = 48.291 - 1.992 = 46.299$

3. $2.88 for 12 dozen means $.24 per dozen. Three dozen will cost $(3)($.24) = $.72$

4. $(13)(2.39)(.024) = .74568$

5. $($64)(.75)(.90) = 43.20

6. $(\frac{1}{8})(1\%) = (.125)(.01) = .00125$

7. $(.16)(482.11) = 77.1376$

8. Let x = cost. Then, $1.25x = 60. Solving, $x = 48

9. 5 hrs. 13 min. + 3 hrs. 49 min. + 14 min = 8 hrs. 76 min. = 9 hrs. 16 min.

10. $(.89)($482) = 428.98

11. $200\% = 2$. So, $(200\%)(800) = (2)(800) = 1600$

12. 2 ft. 3 in. + 4 ft. 11 in. + 8 in. + 6 ft. 6 in. + 12 ft. 28 in. = 14 ft. 4 in.

13. Overhead is $(.20)($15) = 3. The net profit is $20 - $15 - $3 = 2

14. $.0325 = 3.25\% = 3\frac{1}{4}\%$

15. $\frac{3}{4} + \frac{1}{8} + \frac{1}{32} + \frac{1}{2} - \frac{4}{8} = \frac{45}{32} - \frac{4}{8} = \frac{29}{32}$

16. Let x = sales. Then, $40 = .04x$. Solving, $x = 1000

17. Annual interest is $($225,000)(.035) \times 1 = 7875$

18. $42 - $33.60 = 8.40. Then, $8.40 \div $42 = .20 = 20\%$

19. The number of days left for May, June, July is 26, 30, and 1. Thus, $26 + 30 + 1 = 57$

20. Let x = cost, so that $.50x$ = selling price. The loss is represented by $.50x \div .50x = 1 = 100\%$ on the selling price. (Note: The loss in dollars is $x - .50x = .50x$)

———

ARITHMETICAL REASONING
EXAMINATION SECTION
TEST 1

DIRECTIONS: Each question or incomplete statement is followed by
several suggested answers or completions. Select the
one that BEST answers the question or completes the
statement. *PRINT THE LETTER OF THE CORRECT ANSWER IN
THE SPACE AT THE RIGHT.*

Questions 1-4.

DIRECTIONS: In answering questions 1-4, assume that
you are working in a medical facility
and are responsible for maintaining inventory and stock.

1. The following quantities of disposable syringes were used   1.____
    during the first six weeks of the year: 840, 756, 772,
    794, 723, and 789.
    If the cost of a disposable syringe is seventy cents, the
    average weekly cost for disposable syringes is MOST NEARLY
        A. $550   B. $780   C. $850   D. $3,270

2. Four pieces of glass tubing measuring 4 feet 3 inches,   2.____
    6 feet 8 inches, 7 feet 2 inches, and 7 feet 6 inches
    are to be cut into 5-inch pieces.
    The TOTAL number of 5-inch pieces that can be cut from
    the four pieces is
        A. 60   B. 61   C. 62   D. 63

3. Assume that a 55-gallon drum of disinfectant is to be   3.____
    distributed equally among eight work stations.
    The amount of disinfectant that each work station should
    receive is
        A. 7.5 gallons   B. 27.5 pints
        C. 55 pints   D. 55 quarts

4. On June 30, an inventory indicated that there were 13   4.____
    dozen petri dishes in the stockroom. During the next
    four weeks in July, the following quantities of petri
    dishes were given out by the stockroom: 23, 56, 37, and
    31. On August 1, no petri dishes were given out, but
    9 dozen were delivered to the stockroom.
    The number of petri dishes in the stockroom AFTER delivery
    on August 1 is
        A. 18   B. 108   C. 110   D. 117

5. A table of composition of foods lists the protein value   5.____
    of a 100 gram portion of hamburger at 22 grams.
    The protein value of a 45 gram portion of hamburger is,
    therefore, _____ grams.
        A. 5   B. 9.9   C. 11.3   D. 12.4

6. To cover a room 15' x 18' with wall-to-wall carpeting 6.___
    requires _____ square yards.
        A. 25   B. 30   C. 35   D. 90

7. Assume that you are in a hospital whose x-ray department 7.___
    is open from 8 A.M. to 12 Noon and from 1 P.M. to 6 P.M.
    You have assigned one of your technicians to schedule all
    the x-ray appointments for the clinic cases. Your
    instructions to him are not to make more than 12 appoint-
    ments per half hour in the morning session and not more
    15 per hour for the afternoon session.
    The GREATEST number of patients he can schedule in the
    entire day will be
        A. 75   B. 96   C. 123   D. 171

8. 1,000,000 may be represented as   8.___
        A. 10^3 B. 10^5 C. 10^6 D. 10^{10}

9. 35° Centigrade equals   9.___
        A. 70°F   B. 95°F   C. 100°F   D. 120°F

10. $10^3 \times 10^4$ equals   10.___
        A. 10^7 B. 10^{12} C. 100^7 D. 100^{12}

11. If a mixture is made up of one part Substance A, 3 parts 11.___
    Substance B, and 12 parts Substance C, the proportion of
    Substance A in the mixture is
        A. 4%   B. $6\frac{1}{4}$%   C. 16%   D. $62\frac{1}{2}$%

12. If 5 grams of a chemical are enough to perform a certain 12.___
    laboratory test 9 times, the quantity of the chemical
    needed to perform this test 1,350 times would be _____
    grams.
        A. 30   B. 150   C. 270   D. 750

13. If it takes 7 grams of a certain substance to make 5   13.___
    liters of a solution, the quantity of the substance
    needed to make 4 liters of the solution is _____ grams.
        A. 2.85   B. 4.70   C. 5.60   D. 8.75

14. If it takes 3 grams of Substance A and 7 grams of Sub-   14.___
    stance B to make 4 liters of a solution, how many grams
    of Substances A and B does it take to make 5 liters of
    the solution?
    _____ of Substance A and _____ of Substance B.
        A. 3.35; 6.65   B. 3.50; 7.50
        C. 3.75; 8.75   D. 4; 7

15. A certain type of laboratory test can be performed by a   15.___
    laboratory technician in 20 minutes.
    Three laboratory technicians can perform 243 such tests
    in _____ hours.
        A. 16   B. 20   C. 27   D. 81

16. Pairs of shatterproof plastic safety glasses cost $38.00   16.____
    each, but an 8% discount is given on orders of six pairs
    or more. Pairs of straight blade dissecting scissors
    cost $144 a dozen with a 12% discount on orders of two
    dozen or more.
    The TOTAL cost of eight pairs of safety glasses and 30
    pairs of dissecting scissors is MOST NEARLY
       A. $596.50   B. $621.00   C. $664.00   D. $731.50

17. On July 1, your laboratory has 280 usable 20-gauge   17.____
    needles on hand. On August 1, 15% of these needles have
    been lost or damaged beyond repair. On August 15, a new
    shipment of 50 needles is received by the laboratory,
    but 10% of these arrive damaged and are returned to the
    seller.
    At this point, the number of usable 20-gauge needles on
    hand would be
       A. 238   B. 283   C. 288   D. 325

18. A certain laboratory procedure can be completed by a   18.____
    laboratory technician in 15 minutes.
    If your lab is assigned 30 such tests, and they must be
    completed within 3 hours, the MINIMUM number of techni-
    cians that would have to be assigned to this task is
       A. 2   B. 3   C. 4   D. 5

19. A patient's hospital bill is $24,600. The patient has   19.____
    three different medical insurance plans, each of which
    will make partial payment toward his bill. One plan
    will pay $6,500 of the patient's bill, another will pay
    $7,300 of the bill, and the third will pay $8,832 of
    the bill.
    The percentage of the bill that the patient's three
    insurance plans combined do NOT pay for is
       A. 5%   B. 8%   C. 10%   D. 20%

20. A patient has stayed at a hospital for which the all-   20.____
    inclusive daily rate is $205.00. The patient was hos-
    pitalized for 27 days. The patient is covered by a
    private insurance plan that will pay the hospital 2/3
    of the patient's total hospital bill.
    The one of the following that MOST NEARLY indicates how
    much of the patient's hospital bill would NOT be covered
    by this insurance plan is
       A. $1,845   B. $2,078   C. $3,690   D. $3,156

21. A hospital charges a flat daily rate for all hospital   21.____
    services. In February 2000, the hospital charged a patient
    $2,772 for 14 days of hospitalization. In April 2002,
    the same patient was charged for 16 days of hospitaliza-
    tion at the same hospital.
    If the daily rate charged by the hospital increased by $7
    between the patient's 2000 hospitalization and his 2002
    hospitalization, the total amount that the patient must pay
    for the 2002 hospitalization is
       A. $3,296   B. $3,280   C. $3,264   D. $3,248

22. A hospital insurance plan that previously covered 3/5 of the total hospital charges for its subscribers has recently been improved, and coverage for total hospital charges has been increased by 25% of the previous rate. A subscriber to this plan has just completed a hospital stay and has received a bill for total hospital charges of $6,200.
Assuming that the hospital stay is covered by the recently improved plan, the one of the following that MOST NEARLY indicates how much the plan now provides the patient toward the payment of the hospital bill is

    A. $1,550   B. $3,720   C. $4,650   D. $5,270

22.___

Questions 23-25.

DIRECTIONS: Questions 23 through 25 are to be answered on the basis of the following situation.

You have been asked to keep records of the time spent with each patient by the doctors in the clinic where you are assigned. Your notes show that Dr. Jones spent the following amount of time with each patient he examined on a certain day: Patient A - 14 minutes, Patient B - 13 minutes, Patient C - 34 minutes, Patient D - 48 minutes, Patient E - 26 minutes, Patient F - 20 minutes, Patient G - 25 minutes.

23. The average number of minutes spent by Dr. Jones with each patient is MOST NEARLY

    A. 20   B. 25   C. 30   D. 35

23.___

24. If Dr. Jones is to take care of the seven patients mentioned above at one session, the number of hours he will have to remain at the clinic is MOST NEARLY _____ hour(s).

    A. 1   B. 2   C. 3   D. 4

24.___

25. The one of the following groups of patients that required the LEAST time to examine is Patients _____ and _____.

    A. A, C; E   B. B, D; F   C. C, E; G   D. A,D; G

25.___

KEY (CORRECT ANSWERS)

1. A	6. B	11. B	16. A	21. B
2. B	7. D	12. D	17. B	22. C
3. C	8. C	13. C	18. B	23. B
4. D	9. B	14. C	19. B	24. C
5. B	10. A	15. C	20. A	25. A

SOLUTIONS TO PROBLEMS

1. $(840+756+772+794+723+789) \div 6 = 779$. Then, $(779)(.70) = \$545.30 \approx \$550$

2. $4'3'' + 6'8'' + 7'2'' + 7'6'' = 25'7'' = 307''$. Then, $307 \div 5 = 61.4$, so 61 5-inch pieces exist.

3. $55 \div 8 = 6.875$ gallons = 55 pints

4. $(13)(12) - 23 - 56 - 37 - 31 + (9)(12) = 117$ dishes

5. Let x = protein value. Then, $\frac{22}{100} = \frac{x}{45}$. Solving, x = 9.9 grams

6. $(15')(18') = 270$ sq.ft. = 30 sq.yds.

7. Maximum number of appointments = $(12)(8) + (15)(5) = 171$

8. $1,000,000 = 10^6$

9. $F = \frac{9}{5}C + 32$. If C = 35, $F = (\frac{9}{5})(35) + 32 = 95$

10. $10^3 \times 10^4 = 10^7$. When multiplying with like bases, add the exponents.

11. $\frac{1}{1+3+12} = \frac{1}{16} = 6\frac{1}{4}\%$

12. Let x = grams needed. Then, $\frac{5}{9} = \frac{x}{1350}$. Solving, x = 750

13. Let x = grams needed. Then, $\frac{7}{5} = \frac{x}{4}$. Solving, x = 5.6

14. Let x = grams of A needed and y = grams of B needed. Then, $\frac{3}{4} = \frac{x}{5}$ and $\frac{7}{4} = \frac{y}{5}$. Solving, x = 3.75, y = 8.75

15. The test requires $\frac{1}{3}$ technician-hrs. Now, $(243)(\frac{1}{3}) = 81$ technician-hrs., and $81 \div 3 = 27$ hours

16. $(8)(\$38.00)(.92) + (2\frac{1}{2})(\$144)(.88) = \$596.48 \approx \$596.50$

17. $280 - (.15)(280) + 50 - (.10)(50) = 283$ needles on hand

18. The test requires $\frac{1}{4}$ technician-hrs., so 30 tests require $7\frac{1}{2}$ technician-hrs. Since 3 hrs. is the time limit for these 30 tests, $7\frac{1}{2} \div 3 = 2.5$ or 3 technicians at a minimum are needed.

19. $24,600 − ($6500+$7300+$8832) = $1968, and $\dfrac{1968}{24,600}$ = 8%

20. Amount not covered = $(\frac{1}{3})$($205)(27) = $1845

21. Daily rate for 2000 = $2772 ÷ 14 = $198, so for 2002 the daily rate = $205. Finally, ($205)(16) = $3280

22. The new plan covers (.60)(1.25) = .75 or 75% of the bill. Then, (.75)($6200) = $4650

23. (14+13+34+48+26+20+25) ÷ 7 ≈ 26 min., closest to 25 min.

24. 180 min. = 3 hours

25. Patients A, C, E: 74 min.; patients B, D, F: 81 min.; patients C, E, G: 85 min.; patients A, D, G: 87 min. So, the 1st group requires the least time.

TEST 2

DIRECTIONS: Each question or incomplete statement is followed by several suggested answers or completions. Select the one that BEST answers the question or completes the statement. *PRINT THE LETTER OF THE CORRECT ANSWER IN THE SPACE AT THE RIGHT.*

1. A stack of cartons containing pesticides is 10 cartons long, 9 cartons wide, and 5 cartons high.
   The number of cartons in the stack is
      A. 24   B. 55   C. 95   D. 450   1.____

2. Assume that you have bags of corn meal, each of the same weight. The total weight of 25 bags is 125 pounds.
   How many of these bags would it take to make a TOTAL weight of 50 pounds?
      A. 2   B. 5   C. 6   D. 10   2.____

3. You are working in the sub-basement of a project building, and the foreman tells you to get two boards from the maintenance shop to stand on. One of the boards is 5 yards long, and the other $3\frac{1}{2}$ feet long.
   The TOTAL length, in feet, of the two boards is
      A. $8\frac{1}{2}$ B. $9\frac{1}{2}$ C. $17\frac{1}{2}$ D. $18\frac{1}{2}$ 3.____

4. Three hundred plastic bags of rat-mix, each bag weighing four ounces, are packed in a carton. The carton weighed one pound before the rat-mix was packed in it.
   The TOTAL weight of the filled carton is _____ pounds.
      A. $37\frac{1}{2}$ B. $38\frac{1}{2}$ C. 75   D. 76   4.____

5. Of 180 families that relocated in a given month, 1/5 moved into Finder's Fee apartments, 1/4 moved into tenant-found apartments, 1/3 moved into public housing, and the rest moved out of the city.
   How many moved out of the city?
      A. 36   B. 39   C. 45   D. 60   5.____

6. If a space treatment device covers 1,000 cubic feet in six seconds, how long should it run in order to treat a room that is 30 feet long, 20 feet wide, and 15 feet high?
      A. 18 seconds   B. 54 seconds
      C. 1 minute 24 seconds   D. 1 minute 48 seconds   6.____

7. If you have to prepare five gallons of 0.5 Diazinon emulsion using water and 20% Diazinon emulsifiable concentrate, what is the amount of concentrate that is necessary? _____ ounces.
      A. 1.6   B. 3.2   C. 16.0   D. 64.0   7.____

8. Suppose you have 15 5/6 ounces of a certain chemical on hand.
   If you later receive shipments of $6\frac{1}{2}$ ounces and 8 3/4 ounces of this chemical, the TOTAL number of ounces you should then have on hand is

      A. 29 7/8   B. 30 5/6   C. 31 1/12   D. 31 3/4

   8.__

9. You are told to prepare 60 pounds of 2% pyrethrum dust using talc and 5% pyrethrum dust concentrate.
   What is the amount of concentrate that is required in the mixture?
   _____ pounds.

      A. 24   B. 28   C. $30\frac{1}{2}$ D. 36

   9.__

10. In the pest control shop of a certain housing development, there is a supply of 4 one-gallon containers of insecticide. This week, the exterminator will use up five quarts of this insecticide in his work, and for each week thereafter he will use up five quarts. Deliveries are made on the first day of the week.
    Next week, and each week thereafter, the shop will get a delivery of one gallon of insecticide.
    The exterminator will need an additional supply of insecticide by the end of the _____ week.

       A. 4th   B. 12th   C. 24th   D. 29th

    10.__

11. There are 22 boxes of rat mix in a certain pest control shop.
    If each box contains $7\frac{1}{2}$ pounds of rat mix, the TOTAL amount of rat mix in the shop is _____ pounds.

       A. 165   B. $172\frac{1}{2}$ C. 180   D. $182\frac{1}{2}$

    11.__

12. A pest control shop has a supply of 26 one-gallon cans of insecticide.
    If the exterminator works 5 days a week and uses 32 ounces of the liquid a day, the number of work weeks this supply of insecticide will last is MOST NEARLY

       A. 10   B. 20   C. 28   D. 32

    12.__

13. A certain supplier packs two dozen mousetraps to a box.
    If the exterminator gets a delivery of 20 boxes and finds that two of these boxes are half-full, the TOTAL number of traps the exterminator received from this supplier is

       A. 408   B. 432   C. 456   D. 480

    13.__

14. Assume that a truck which contains a shipment of pesticides is parked outside your exterminating shop. You are able to unload the truck in one hour.
    How long would it take four exterminators, starting at the same time and working at the same rate as you, to unload four trucks similar to the one you unloaded?

       A. 15 minutes   B. 1 hour
       C. 2 hours   D. 4 hours

    14.__

15. A certain building in a housing development has 142 apartments. It takes one exterminator an average of six minutes to treat one apartment.
At that rate, approximately how long should it take him to treat all 142 apartments?
_____ hours.
   A. 2   B. 14   C. 24   D. 85

15.____

16. A crate contains 3 pieces of pesticide equipment weighing 73, 84, and 47 pounds, respectively.
If the crate is lifted by 4 exterminators, each lifting one corner of the crate, the average number of pounds, in addition to the weight of the crate, lifted by each of the exterminators is
   A. 51   B. 65   C. 71   D. 78

16.____

17. Of the following, the pair that is NOT a set of equivalents is
   A. .014%   .00014   B. 1/5%   .002
   C. 1.5%   3/200   D. 115%   .115

17.____

18. 10^{-2} is equal to
   A. 0.001   B. 0.01   C. 0.1   D. 100.0

18.____

19. $10^2 \times 10^3$ is equal to
   A. 10^5 B. 10^6 C. 100^5 D. 100^6

19.____

20. The length of two objects are in the ratio of 2:1.
If each were 3 inches shorter, the ratio would be 3:1.
The longer object is _____ inches.
   A. 8   B. 10   C. 12   D. 14

20.____

21. If the weight of water is 62.4 pounds per cubic foot, the weight of the water that fills a rectangular container 6 inches by 6 inches by 1 foot is _____ pounds.
   A. 7.8   B. 15.6   C. 31.2   D. 46.8

21.____

22. The formula for converting degrees Centigrade to degrees Fahrenheit is as follows:
   Fahrenheit = 9/5 of Centigrade + 32°, or
   multiply the number of degrees Centigrade by 9, divide by 5 and add 32).
If the Centigrade thermometer reads 25°, the temperature in degrees Fahrenheit is
   A. 13   B. 45   C. 53   D. 77

22.____

23. To make a certain preparation, you have been told to mix one ounce of Liquid A and 3 ounces of Liquid B.
If you have used 18 ounces of Liquid B in preparing a larger amount, the number of ounces of Liquid A you should use is
   A. 6   B. 15   C. 21   D. 54

23.____

24. If one inch is equal to approximately 2.5 centimeters,   24.__
    the number of inches in fifteen centimeters is MOST NEARLY
        A. 1.6   B. 6   C. 12.5   D. 37.5

25. You are in charge of a small lawn area of 1,850 sq. ft.   25.__
    You are asked to apply lime on this lawn at the rate of
    40 pounds per 1,000 sq. ft.
    The number of pounds of lime you will need to cover the
    entire area of the lawn is MOST NEARLY _____ pounds.
        A. 74   B. 86   C. 87   D. 89

KEY (CORRECT ANSWERS)

1. D		11. A
2. D		12. B
3. D		13. C
4. D		14. B
5. B		15. B
6. B		16. A
7. C		17. D
8. C		18. B
9. A		19. A
10. B		20. C

21. B
22. D
23. A
24. B
25. A

SOLUTIONS TO PROBLEMS

1. $(10)(9)(5) = 450$ cartons

2. Let x = number of bags. Then, $\frac{25}{125} = \frac{x}{50}$. Solving, x = 10

3. 5 yds. + $3\frac{1}{2}$ ft. = 15 ft. + $3\frac{1}{2}$ ft. = $18\frac{1}{2}$ ft.

4. Total weight = $1 + (300)(\frac{4}{16}) = 76$ pounds

5. $1 - \frac{1}{5} - \frac{1}{4} - \frac{1}{3} = \frac{13}{60}$. Then, $(180)(\frac{13}{60}) = 39$ families

6. $(30')(20')(15') = 9000$ cu.ft. Let x = number of seconds
   Then, $\frac{1000}{6} = \frac{9000}{x}$. Solving, x = 54

7. 1 qt. of concentrate = 16 oz.

8. $15\frac{5}{6} + 6\frac{1}{2} + 8\frac{3}{4} = 29\frac{25}{12} = 31\frac{1}{12}$ ounces

9. $.05x = .02(60)$
   $x = 24$

10. For the 1st week (end), there will be 16 - 5 = 11 qts. left. For each additional week, since 4 qts. are delivered but 5 qts. are used, there will be a net loss of 1 qt. Thus, at the end of 12 weeks, the supply of insecticide will be gone.

11. $(22)(7\frac{1}{2}) = 165$ pounds

12. $(26)(128) = 3328$ oz., and $(32)(5) = 160$ oz. used each week. Finally, $3328 \div 160 = 20.8$, closest to 20 oz.

13. $(24)(18) + (12)(2) = 456$ mousetraps

14. 4 trucks require 4 man-hours. Then, $4 \div 4 = 1$ hour

15. $(142)(6) = 852$ min. = 14.2 hrs. $\approx$ 14 hrs.

16. Total weight = 204 lbs. Then, $204 \div 4 = 51$ lbs.

17. 115% = 1.15, not .115

18. $10^{-2} = \frac{1}{100} = .01$

19. $10^2 \times 10^3 = 10^5$. When multiplying with like bases, add the exponents.

20. Let x, $\frac{1}{2}$x = lengths of the longer and shorter objects. Then, x - 3 = 3($\frac{1}{2}$x-3). Simplifying, x - 3 = $\frac{3}{2}$x - 9. Solving, x = 12 i

21. $(\frac{1}{2}')(\frac{1}{2}')(1') = \frac{1}{4}$ cu.ft. Then, $(62.4)(\frac{1}{4}) = 15.6$ pounds

22. F = $(\frac{9}{5})(25°) + 32° = 77°$

23. Let x = number of ounces of liquid A. Then, $\frac{1}{3} = \frac{x}{18}$. Solving, x = 6

24. 15 cm. = $\frac{15}{\approx 2.5}$ or approx. 6 in.

25. $(40)(\frac{1850}{1000}) = 74$ pounds

READING COMPREHENSION
UNDERSTANDING AND INTERPRETING WRITTEN MATERIAL
TEST 1

DIRECTIONS: Each question or incomplete statement is followed by several suggested answers or completions. Select the one that BEST answers the question or completes the statement. *PRINT THE LETTER OF THE CORRECT ANSWER IN THE SPACE AT THE RIGHT.*

Questions 1-4.

DIRECTIONS: Questions 1 through 4 are to be answered ONLY according to the information given in the following passage.

HANDLING HOSPITAL LAUNDRY

In a hospital, care must be taken when handling laundry in order to reduce the chance of germs spreading. There is always the possibility that dirty laundry will be carrying dangerous germs. To avoid catching germs when they are working with dirty laundry, laundry workers should be sure that any cuts or wounds they have are bandaged before they touch the dirty laundry. They should also be careful when handling this laundry not to rub their eyes, nose, or mouth. Just like all other hospital workers, laundry workers should also protect themselves against germs by washing and rinsing their hands thoroughly before eating meals and before leaving work at the end of the day.

To be sure that germs from dirty laundry do not pass onto clean laundry and thereby increase the danger to patients, clean and dirty laundry should not be handled near each other or by the same person. Special care also has to be taken with laundry that comes from a patient who has a dangerous, highly contagious disease so that as few people as possible come in direct contact with this laundry. Laundry from this patient, therefore, should be kept separate from other dirty laundry at all times.

1. According to the above passage, when working with dirty laundry, laundry workers should
   A. destroy laundry carrying dangerous germs
   B. have any cuts bandaged before touching the dirty laundry
   C. never touch the dirty laundry directly
   D. rub their eyes, nose, and mouth to protect them from germs

1.____

2. According to the above passage, all hospital workers should wash their hands thoroughly
   A. after eating meals to remove any trace of food from their hands
   B. at every opportunity to show good example to the patients
   C. before eating meals to protect themselves against germs
   D. before starting work in the morning to feel fresh and ready to do a good day's work

2.____

3. According to the above passage, the danger to patients   3.___
   will increase
   A. unless a worker handles dirty and clean laundry at
      the same time
   B. unless clean and dirty laundry are handled near each
      other
   C. when clean laundry is ironed frequently
   D. when germs pass from dirty laundry to clean laundry

4. According to the above passage, laundry from a patient   4.___
   with a dangerous, highly contagious disease should be
   A. given special care so that as few people as possible
      come in direct contact with it
   B. handled in the same way as any other dirty laundry
   C. washed by hand
   D. separated from the other dirty laundry just before
      it is washed

Questions 5-8.

DIRECTIONS: Questions 5 through 8 are to be answered ONLY according
              to the information given in the following passage.

MARKING PROCEDURES FOR PERSONAL WASH

As soon as a bundle of personal wash is brought into the laundry,
it is taken to a marking section. Here an employee marks the individual pieces so that pieces following different courses through the
laundry may be brought together when work upon them has been completed. The wash is identified either by visible markings, invisible
markings, or by labels. Serial numbers and letters, often coded
identifying the wash, are marked upon each article.

Visible markings should be placed on the concealed parts of the
wash, such as trouser waistbands, either with a marking pencil or by
a machine with a keyboard which looks like a typewriter. A similar
machine is also used in laundries to mark pieces with invisible ink.
These marks need not be concealed since they can be seen only under
ultraviolet light. Labels with the markings on them, may be stapled
or sewed onto each piece of wash. In addition to identifying, the
marker has the task of listing, counting, and marking on a printed
laundry list each piece in the bundle. After the wash has been
marked, the marker then classifies the wash into groups that can be
laundered together.

This is the only work done in the marking section.

5. According to the above passage, an IMPORTANT reason for   5.___
   placing identifying marks on personal wash is to
   A. keep a correct record of how many pounds of laundry
      are washed
   B. make sure that all the pieces in the bundle of laundry
      are washed together
   C. classify the pieces in the bundle according to the
      way they are washed
   D. make it possible to bring together later pieces that
      are washed separately

6. According to the above passage, in order to see a laundry 6.___
   mark made with invisible ink, it is necessary to
   A. use an ultraviolet light
   B. wet it
   C. use a special machine
   D. treat it with a mild acid

7. According to the above passage, an advantage of using 7.___
   invisible ink to mark laundry is that
   A. it is cheaper
   B. the mark can be made with an ordinary pencil
   C. the mark can be put any place on the wash and doesn't
      have to be hidden
   D. it takes less time to do the marking

8. According to the above passage, the marker does NOT 8.___
   A. put identifying marks on the wash
   B. sew small rips in torn wash
   C. check the number of pieces in each bundle of wash
   D. group the pieces of wash that can be laundered together

Questions 9-12.

DIRECTIONS: Questions 9 through 12 are to be answered ONLY according
             to the information given in the following passage.

THE HANDLING OF RAYON IN THE LAUNDRY

Rayon is an artificial fabric manufactured from wood pulp and
short cotton fibres. It is extensively used in such items as
shirtings, dress goods, and curtains, and may compose the entire
fabric or simply be a part of the weave. While quite strong and
substantial in its dry state, rayon is weak when wet and must,
therefore, be handled with great care in the washing process. It
should not be rubbed or stretched and should always be placed in
nets to relieve as much strain as possible while in the washwheel.
Rayon should preferably be washed in cold water with the proper
materials for cold water washing. If there is any doubt as to
whether a fabric is silk or rayon, a small thread or particle may
be burnt. If it is silk, the threads will burn slowly and leave a
small ball of ash at the end of the thread. Rayon, however, burns
quickly and leaves no ash or tell-tale ball.

9. According to the above passage, rayon is made from a 9.___
    combination of _____ and _____.
    A. wood; silk   B. wool; linen
    C. cotton; wood   D. silk; linen

10. According to the above passage, a manufacturer would 10.___
    probably NOT use rayon to make
    A. kitchen window curtains   B. dish towels
    C. nurses' uniforms   D. men's shirts

11. According to the above passage, the MAIN reason for   11.___
    putting rayon fabrics in a net when they are to be washed
    is that rayon is
    A. washable only in cold water
    B. a manufactured fabric
    C. easily stained by the materials from the washwheel
    D. not a strong material when wet

12. According to the above passage, threads of rayon burn   12.___
    ____ and leave ____ ash.
    A. slowly; no   B. fast; no
    C. slowly; a ball of   D. fast; a ball of

Questions 13-17.

DIRECTIONS: Questions 13 through 17 are to be answered ONLY according
              to the information given in the following paragraph.

REPORT FOR THE YEAR 2005 - LAUNDRY DIVISION

    The Area A Central Laundry, which cost about 4½ million dollars
with the equipment, was opened in December 2005, enabling the Department of Hospitals to close a number of out-of-date laundries in some
Area A hospitals. The new Area A Central Laundry can now process
8,000 pounds of linen in an hour, or about 17½ million pounds a year.
It has sufficient space for additional equipment to increase the
capacity to 10,000 pounds per hour. The cost of processing laundry
in 2004 at the old laundries was about twelve cents per pound. However, in 2005, the cost at the new laundry was about six cents per
pound. Area A now does all the laundry for the municipal hospitals
in that city and for the Area B Hospital Center.

    During 2005, the laundries in Area C, D, E, and F Hospitals were
also shut down and their work assigned to Area G laundry. About
one-quarter of the original laundry staff was retained at each
hospital to sort soiled linen and distribute clean linen -- the other
employees were reassigned to other laundries.

13. According to the above passage, can the new Area A Central   13.___
    Laundry do more than 8,000 pounds of linen an hour?
    A. Yes, if it gets more equipment
    B. Yes, only if it gets more space
    C. No, 8,000 pounds is the maximum capacity
    D. It is not possible to find this out from the passage

14. According to the above passage, the cost of processing   14.___
    laundry at the new Area A Laundry in 2005, as compared
    with the cost at the old laundries in 2004, was
    A. twice as much   B. about the same
    C. about half   D. only slightly less

15. According to the above passage, the cost of processing   15.___
    laundry in the new laundry was
    A. greater than at the old laundries
    B. equal to the cost at the laundries in Area C, D, E,
       and F Hospitals

C. greater by 10,000 pounds per hour
D. less by more than five cents per pound

16. According to the above passage, dirty linen from Area E   16.___
Hospital is now laundred at the Area
    A. G laundry   B. A Central Laundry
    C. B Center Laundry   D. E Hospital

17. According to the above passage, what happened to the   17.___
laundry workers at Area F Hospital when the laundry there
was shut down?
    A. One-quarter of them went to Area A Central Laundry
       and the rest to the Area G laundry.
    B. Half of them were given jobs in other municipal depart-
       ments and the rest were sent to other laundries.
    C. About three-quarters of them went to work at other
       laundries in the department.
    D. All of them were assigned to other hospital laundries
       to work on sorting and giving out laundry.

Questions 18-22.

DIRECTIONS: Questions 18 through 22 are to be answered ONLY according
             to the information given in the following paragraph.

    The fact that your hospital has been ordered to make certain
budgetary cutbacks has angered and frightened the community. A
peaceful demonstration has been taking place for the last three
days on hospital grounds. The group's leader has met with the
hospital administrator; and although the meeting was amicable,
nothing was resolved and the community still feels abused by the
hospital, the health and hospitals corporation, and the city.
Because you fear that the demonstration may become violent, you
arrange to discuss first with the hospital administration and then
with your staff what actions may become necessary.

18. Which of the following actions SHOULD be included in your   18.___
preliminary plans?
    A. Notifying the media of a possible altercation at the
       hospital.
    B. Determining the location of the command post.
    C. Blocking all entrances and exits to the facility with
       furniture.
    D. Calling the administration and ordering them to leave
       the premises immediately.

19. Of the following, which is the MOST important topic you   19.___
should discuss with your subordinates prior to the possible
increased activity by the community?
    A. The nature of the group's complaints against the
       hospital and the city
    B. Your view on the hospital's position in this matter
    C. The need for self-control by all security personnel
    D. Hand-to-hand fighting techniques which may be
       necessary if the community group becomes violent

20. Assume that your concerns prove correct and the demonstra-   20.
    tion becomes less organized, less controlled, and poten-
    tially violent.
    As the supervisor of security personnel, your CHIEF
    responsibility is to
        A. join your men in quelling any disturbance
        B. maintain a clearly defined chain of command so that
           orders remain clear and concise
        C. prevent the demonstration's leaders from entering
           the hospital administration building so that hospital
           routines may continue without interruption
        D. meet with demonstration leaders as soon as possible

21. The one of the following choices that contains only the   21. __
    MOST important items of information a security officer
    should transmit to his hospital administrator in the
    situation described above is the
        A. approximate size of the group of demonstrators, the
           security measures already taken, and the number of
           officers on duty
        B. number of available parking spaces, the demands of
           the demonstrators, and the names of community leaders
           seen
        C. number of officers on leave, the number of patients
           in the hospital, and the approximate size of the group
           of demonstrators
        D. number of officers on leave, the demands of the
           demonstrators, and the number of plant maintenance
           staff on duty

22. Of the following, the area whose security is LEAST   22. __
    important to protect during the demonstrations is the
        A. pharmacy   B. patients' accounts office
        C. pathology laboratory   D. linen storage rooms

Questions 23-25.

DIRECTIONS: Questions 23 through 25 are to be answered ONLY according
             to the information given in the following statement.

      When a Voluntary hospital admits a Blue Cross subscriber who
has been referred from a city hospital, a concurrent submission of
the case shall be made by it to both Blue Cross and the city
Investigator who routinely visits the Voluntary hospital. This
procedure will be advantageous to both the Voluntary hospital and
the city since the hospital would be notified immediately of the
ability of the city to reimburse should Blue Cross coverage be
inapplicable or insufficient. Furthermore, the city will be able
to assure itself of potential State Aid for those cases for whom it
may have to assume some responsibility. Necessary time limits to
process applications for State Aid can also be made if this referral
is concurrent, such as for state charges and relief clients, who
are frequently Blue Cross members. This investigation can best be
conducted by the city staff assigned to the Voluntary hospital,
rather than by the staff in the referring Municipal hospital.

23. According to the above statement, one responsibility of a   23.____
    Voluntary hospital with respect to an admission who is a
    Blue Cross subscriber is to
    A. get the city to reimburse its fair share if Blue Cross
       coverage is inapplicable or insufficient
    B. refer the case to the city hospital for possible
       collection of State Aid
    C. submit the case concurrently to both Blue Cross and
       the city Investigator
    D. submit the case to the city investigator if the
       patient has been referred by a city hospital

24. According to the above statement, it is NOT an advantage   24.____
    of the procedure described that the
    A. city can make sure of getting possible State Aid for
       those cases for whom it may be partly responsible
    B. cost of caring for the cases referred to will be shared
       by Blue Cross, the Voluntary hospital, the city, and
       the State
    C. needed time limits to handle State Aid applications
       can be made
    D. Voluntary hospitals will know immediately if the city
       will pay for its referrals who do not have enough Blue
       Cross coverage

25. According to the above statement, the investigation   25.____
    referred to can be carried out MOST advantageously by the
    A. city investigator who routinely visits the Voluntary
       hospital
    B. city staff assigned to the hospital that admitted the
       patient
    C. staff of the hospital that referred the patient
    D. staff of the Voluntary hospital that accepted the
       referral

_____

KEY (CORRECT ANSWERS)

_____

TEST 2

DIRECTIONS: Each question consists of a statement. You are to indicate whether the statement is TRUE (T) or FALSE (F). *PRINT THE LETTER OF THE CORRECT ANSWER IN THE SPACE AT THE RIGHT.*

Questions 1-9.

DIRECTIONS: Questions 1 through 9 are to be answered SOLELY on the basis of the information contained in the following passage.

All deaths must be reported to the Department of Health by the licensed physician in attendance at the time of death if death is from natural causes and does not occur in a hospital, or by the person in charge of a hospital if the death occurs there from natural causes, or by the office of the chief medical examiner if the death is apparently from other than natural causes such as violence or suicide. The physician in attendance or the person in charge of a hospital must file a death certificate accompanied by a confidential medical report. The office of the medical examiner files only a death certificate. These papers should be filed within twenty-four hours after death or finding of the remains, with the office of the Department of Health in the borough in which the death occurs or in which the remains are found. However, this requirement is also considered fulfilled if such papers are delivered immediately upon demand and within the twenty-four hours either to a funeral director or undertaker authorized to take charge of the remains or to the city superintendent of mortuaries for those cases in which the remains are to be buried in the city cemetery. These persons receiving the papers must then file the certificates and confidential report with the Department of Health within 48 hours following death or the finding of the remains.

1. A death from heart disease at home must be reported to the Department of Health by the licensed physician in attendance at the time of death.   1.__

2. All deaths outside a hospital must be reported to the Department of Health by the physician in attendance.   2.__

3. The Police Department reports all violent deaths to the Department of Health.   3.__

4. When the death is a suicide, a confidential medical report is filed by the medical examiner.   4.__

5. If a person dies in a hospital from other than natural causes, the death certificate must be filed by the office of the medical examiner.   5.__

6. If a person who lives in Brooklyn dies in Manhattan, the death certificate must be filed in Manhattan.   6.____

7. The physician in attendance who is required to file a death certificate must do so within 24 hours after the death.   7.____

8. The death certificate may also be delivered to an authorized undertaker instead of filing it directly with the Department of Health.   8.____

9. The authorized funeral director who has the death certificate must file it with the Department of Health within twenty-four hours after he has received it.   9.____

Questions 10-22.

DIRECTIONS: Questions 10 through 22 are to be answered SOLELY on the basis of the information contained in the following paragraph.

THE HUMAN BODY

The vertebrae of the spinal column all have the same general shape in that each has a thick body of bone in front, from the sides of which two lighter extensions of bone pass backwards and around to join each other, thus forming an opening in the center. These openings, placed in line with each other as in an intact spinal column, help form the spinal canal which encloses and protects the spinal cord. Cartilage plates between the bodies of the upper twenty-four vertebrae permit considerable movement of the vertebrae and cushion the shock of falling. The sternum is a long, flat bone forming the middle part of the chest's front wall. The upper end of the sternum is a long, flat bone forming the middle part of the chest's front wall. The upper end of the sternum supports the collarbones, and most of the ribs on each side of the chest are attached to the sternum by means of cartilage. Each of the twelve ribs on each side of the chest's bony framework is joined to the spinal column by a movable joint. The first seven ribs, on each side, called true ribs, are joined in front to the sternum by cartilage, and the next three, called false ribs, are each joined similarly to the rib immediately above. The lowest two, called floating ribs, are not fastened at all by their front ends. The pelvis, a basin-shaped ring of bones, is located between the movable vertebrae of the spinal column, which it supports, and the lower limbs, on which it rests. The pelvis, forming the floor of the abdominal cavity and providing deep pockets into which the heads of the thighbones fit, consists of four bones: the sacrum and coccyx behind, and the two hip bones at the sides and front.

10. The vertebrae have a bony part only in the front.   10.____

11. The spinal cord passes through the openings in the center   11.___
     of the vertebrae.

12. The total number of ribs in the body is 24.   12.___

13. The spinal cord is made up of the openings in the verte-   13.___
     brae.

14. The shock of falling is eased by cartilage plates between   14.___
     the vertebrae.

15. The sternum is at the rear of the chest cavity.   15.___

16. The collarbones are supported by the top part of the   16.___
     sternum.

17. All the ribs are joined in the front to the sternum by   17.___
     cartilage.

18. The floating ribs are not fastened to the spinal column   18.___
     at all.

19. The pelvis is a bony structure.   19.___

20. The hip bones are a part of the pelvis.   20.___

21. The pelvis is at the bottom of the abdominal cavity.   21.___

Questions 22-26.

DIRECTIONS: Questions 22 through 26 are to be answered SOLELY on the
              basis of the information contained in the following
              paragraph.

RELEASE OF HUMAN REMAINS FROM CITY MORTUARY

When human remains which have been removed to the city mortuary
are subsequently claimed, the superintendent of city mortuaries shall
deliver the remains, on demand, only to a funeral director or undertaker. The latter must submit a written statement that he or the
funeral establishment with which he is associated has been employed
by the next of kin, legal representative, or, in the absence of
arrangements by such next of kin or legal representative, by a friend
of the deceased. Together with the remains, the superintendent shall
deliver the certificate of death or fetal death and confidential
medical report, if any, or, any permit issued by the Department
authorizing burial in the city cemetery. No burial permit may be
issued unless the certificate of death has been filed with the
Department of Health.

22. To secure the release of human remains from the city   22.___
     mortuary, the next of kin must advise the mortuaries
     superintendent by telephone of the name of the undertaker.

23. The superintendent of city mortuaries cannot release a   23.___
    body directly to the next of kin.

24. If there is a confidential medical report, the superin-   24.___
    tendent of city mortuaries is supposed to deliver this
    with the body to the person authorized to receive the
    body.

25. The permit for burial in the city cemetery is shown to   25.___
    the duly employed undertaker, but is kept by the super-
    intendent of city mortuaries.

26. If a certificate of death has not been filed with the   26.___
    Department of Health, no burial permit may be issued.

Questions 27-30.

DIRECTIONS: Questions 27 through 30 are to be answered SOLELY on
             the basis of the information given in this paragraph.

CARBON MONOXIDE GAS

Carbon monoxide is a deadly gas from the effects of which no one
is immune. Any person's strength will be cut down considerably by
breathing this gas, even though he does not take in enough to overcome him. Wearing a handkerchief tied around the nose and mouth
offers some protection against the irritating fumes of ordinary smoke,
but many people have died convinced that a handkerchief will stop
carbon monoxide. Any person entering a room filled with this deadly
gas should wear a mask equipped with an air hose, or even better, an
oxygen breathing apparatus.

27. Some people get no ill effects from carbon monoxide gas   27.___
    until they are overcome.

28. A person can die from breathing carbon monoxide gas.   28.___

29. A handkerchief around the mouth and nose gives some   29.___
    protection against the effects of ordinary smoke.

30. It is better for a person entering a room filled with   30.___
    carbon monoxide to wear a mask equipped with an air hose
    than an oxygen breathing apparatus.

KEY (CORRECT ANSWERS)

1.	T	11.	T	21.	T
2.	F	12.	T	22.	F
3.	F	13.	T	23.	T
4.	F	14.	T	24.	T
5.	T	15.	F	25.	F
6.	T	16.	T	26.	T
7.	T	17.	F	27.	F
8.	T	18.	F	28.	T
9.	F	19.	T	29.	T
10.	F	20.	T	30.	F

———

SCIENCE READING COMPREHENSION
EXAMINATION SECTION

DIRECTIONS FOR THIS SECTION:

Each question or incomplete statement is followed by several suggested answers or completions. Select the one that BEST answers the question or completes the statement. *PRINT THE LETTER OF THE CORRECT ANSWER IN THE SPACE AT THE RIGHT.*

TEST 1

PASSAGE

Photosynthesis is a complex process with many intermediate steps. Ideas differ greatly as to the details of these steps, but the general nature of the process and its outcome are well established. Water, usually from the soil, is conducted through the xylem of root, stem and leaf to the chlorophyl-containing cells of a leaf. In consequence of the abundance of water within the latter cells, their walls are saturated with water. Carbon dioxide, diffusing from the air through the stomata and into the intercellular spaces of the leaf, comes into contact with the water in the walls of the cells which adjoin the intercellular spaces. The carbon dioxide becomes dissolved in the water of these walls, and in solution diffuses through the walls and the plasma membranes into the cells. By the agency of chlorophyl in the chloroplasts of the cells, the energy of light is transformed into chemical energy. This chemical energy is used to decompose the carbon dioxide and water, and the products of their decomposition are recombined into a new compound. The compound first formed is successively built up into more and more complex substances until finally a sugar is produced.

Questions 1-8.

1. The union of carbon dioxide and water to form starch results in an excess of   1. ...
   A. hydrogen   B. carbon   C. oxygen
   D. carbon monoxide E. hydrogen peroxide

2. Synthesis of carbohydrates takes place   2. ...
   A. in the stomata
   B. in the intercellular spaces of leaves
   C. in the walls of plant cells
   D. within the plasma membranes of plant cells
   E. within plant cells that contain chloroplasts

3. In the process of photosynthesis, chlorophyl acts as a   3. ...
   A. carbohydrate   B. source of carbon dioxide
   C. catalyst   D. source of chemical energy
   E. plasma membrane

4. In which of the following places are there the GREATEST   4. ...
   number of hours in which photosynthesis can take place
   during the month of December?
   A. Buenos Aires, Argentina B. Caracas, Venezuela
   C. Fairbanks, Alaska   D. Quito, Ecuador
   E. Calcutta, India

5. During photosynthesis, molecules of carbon dioxide enter   5. ...
   the stomata of leaves because
   A. the molecules are already in motion
   B. they are forced through the stomata by the son's rays
   C. chlorophyl attracts them
   D. a chemical change takes place in the stomata
   E. oxygen passes out through the stomata

1

6. Besides food manufacture, another USEFUL result of photo- 6. ...
synthesis is that it
    A. aids in removing poisonous gases from the air
    B. helps to maintain the existing proportion of gases in
       the air
    C. changes complex compounds into simpler compounds
    D. changes certain waste products into hydrocarbons
    E. changes chlorophyl into useful substances
7. A process that is almost the exact reverse of photosynthesis 7. ...
is the
    A. rusting of iron   B. burning of wood
    C. digestion of starch   D. ripening of fruit
    E. storage of food in seeds
8. The leaf of the tomato plant will be unable to carry on   8. ...
photosynthesis if the
    A. upper surface of the leaf is coated with vaseline
    B. upper surface of the leaf is coated with lampblack
    C. lower surface of the leaf is coated with lard
    D. leaf is placed in an atmosphere of pure carbon dioxide
    E. entire leaf is coated with lime

TEST 2

PASSAGE

The only carbohydrate which the human body can absorb and oxidize
is the simple sugar glucose. Therefore, all carbohydrates which are
consumed must be changed to glucose by the body before they can be
used. There are specific enzymes in the mouth, the stomach, and the
small intestine which break down complex carbohydrates. All the
monosaccharides are changed to glucose by enzymes secreted by the
intestinal glands, and the glucose is absorbed by the capillaries
of the villi.

The following simple test is used to determine the presence of a
reducing sugar. If Benedict's solution is added to a solution containing glucose or one of the other reducing sugars and the resulting mixture is heated, a brick-red precipitate will be formed. This
test was carried out on several substances and the information in the
following table was obtained. "P" indicates that the precipitate was
formed and "N" indicates that no reaction was observed.

Material Tested	Observation
Crushed grapes in water	P
Cane sugar in water	N
Fructose	P
Molasses	N

Questions 1-2.
1. From the results of the test made upon crushed grapes in   1. ...
water, one may say that grapes contain
    A. glucose   B. sucrose   C. a reducing sugar
    D. no sucrose   E. no glucose
2. Which one of the following foods probably undergoes the   2. ...
LEAST change during the process of carbohydrate digestion
in the human body?
    A. Cane sugar   B. Fructose   C. Molasses
    D. Bread   E. Potato

2

TEST 3

PASSAGE

The British pressure suit was made in two pieces and joined around the middle in contrast to the other suits, which were one-piece suits with a removable helmet. Oxygen was supplied through a tube, and a container of soda lime absorbed carbon dioxide and water vapor. The pressure was adjusted to a maximum of 2 1/2 pounds per square inch (130 millimeters) higher than the surrounding air. Since pure oxygen was used, this produced a partial pressure of 130 millimeters, which is sufficient to sustain the flier at any altitude.

Using this pressure suit, the British established a world's altitude record of 49,944 feet in 1936 and succeeded in raising it to 53,937 feet the following year. The pressure suit is a compromise solution to the altitude problem. Full sea-level pressure can not be maintained, as the suit would be so rigid that the flier could not move arms or legs. Hence a pressure one third to one fifth that of sea level has been used. Because of these lower pressures, oxygen has been used to raise the partial pressure of alveolar oxygen to normal.

Questions 1-9.

1. The MAIN constituent of air not admitted to the pressure suit described was   1. ...
    A. oxygen   B. nitrogen   C. water vapor
    D. carbon dioxide   E. hydrogen

2. The pressure within the suit exceeded that of the surrounding air by an amount equal to 130 millimeters of   2. ...
    A. mercury   B. water   C. air
    D. oxygen   E. carbon dioxide

3. The normal atmospheric pressure at sea level is   3. ...
    A. 130 mm   B. 250 mm   C. 760 mm
    D. 1000 mm   E. 1300 mm

4. The water vapor that was absorbed by the soda lime came from   4. ...
    A. condensation
    B. the union of oxygen with carbon dioxide
    C. body metabolism
    D. the air within the pressure suit
    E. water particles in the upper air

5. The HIGHEST altitude that has been reached with the British pressure suit is about   5. ...
    A. 130 miles   B. 2 1/2 miles   C. 6 miles
    D. 10 miles   E. 5 miles

6. If the pressure suit should develop a leak, the   6. ...
    A. oxygen supply would be cut off
    B. suit would fill up with air instead of oxygen
    C. pressure within the suit would drop to zero
    D. pressure within the suit would drop to that of the surrounding air
    E. suit would become so rigid that the flier would be unable to move arms or legs

7. The reason why oxygen helmets are unsatisfactory for use in efforts to set higher altitude records is that   7. ...
    A. it is impossible to maintain a tight enough fit at the neck

3

B. oxygen helmets are too heavy
C. they do not conserve the heat of the body as pressure suits do
D. if a parachute jump becomes necessary, it can not be made while such a helmet is being worn
E. oxygen helmets are too rigid

8. The pressure suit is termed a compromise solution because   8. ...
    A. it is not adequate for stratosphere flying
    B. aviators can not stand sea-level pressure at high altitudes
    C. some suits are made in two pieces, others in one
    D. other factors than maintenance of pressure have to be accommodated
    E. full atmospheric pressure can not be maintained at high altitudes

9. The passage implies that   9. ...
    A. the air pressure at 49,944 feet is approximately the same as it is at 53,937 feet
    B. pressure cabin planes are not practical at extremely high altitudes
    C. a flier's oxygen requirement is approximately the same at high altitudes as it is at sea level
    D. one-piece pressure suits with removable helmets are unsafe
    E. a normal alveolar oxygen supply is maintained if the air pressure is between one third and one fifth that of sea level

---

TEST 4

PASSAGE

Chemical investigations show that during muscle contraction the store of organic phosphates in the muscle fibers is altered as energy is released. In doing so, the organic phosphates (chiefly adenoisine triphosphate and phospho-creatine) are transformed an-aerobically to organic compounds plus phosphates. As soon as the organic phosphates begin to break down in muscle contraction, the glycogen in the muscle fibers also transforms into lactic acid plus free energy; this energy the muscle fiber uses to return the organic compounds plus phosphates into high-energy organic phosphates ready for another contraction. In the presence of oxygen, the lactic acid from the glycogen decomposition is changed also. About one-fifth of it is oxidized to form water and carbon dioxide and to yield another supply of energy. This time the energy is used to transform the re-maining four-fifths of the lactic acid into glycogen again.

Questions 1-5.

1. The energy for muscle contraction comes directly from the   1. ...
    A. breakdown of lactic acid into glycogen
    B. resynthesis of adenosine triphosphate
    C. breakdown of glycogen into lactic acid
    D. oxidation of lactic acid
    E. breakdown of the organic phosphates

2. Lactic acid does NOT accumulate in a muscle that   2. ...
   A. is in a state of lacking oxygen
   B. has an ample supply of oxygen
   C. is in a state of fatigue
   D. is repeatedly being stimulated
   E. has an ample supply of glycogen

3. The energy for the resynthesis of adenosine triphosphate   3. ...
  and phospho-creatine comes from the
   A. oxidation of lactic acid
   B. synthesis of organic phosphates
   C. change from glycogen to lactic acid
   D. resynthesis of glycogen
   E. change from lactic acid to glycogen

4. The energy for the resynthesis of glycogen comes from the   4. ...
   A. breakdown of organic phosphates
   B. resynthesis of organic phosphates
   C. change occurring in one-fifth of the lactic acid
   D. change occurring in four-fifths of the lactic acid
   E. change occurring in four-fifths of glycogen

5. The breakdown of the organic phosphates into organic com-   5. ...
  pounds plus phosphates is an
   A. anobolic reaction   B. aerobic reaction
   C. endothermic reaction   D. exothermic reaction
   E. anaerobic reaction

TEST 5

PASSAGE

And with respect to that theory of the origin of the forms of life peopling our globe, with which Darwin's name is bound up as closely as that of Newton with the theory of gravitation, nothing seems to be further from the mind of the present generation than any attempt to smother it with ridicule or to crush it by vehemence of denunciation. "The struggle for existence," and "natural selection," have become household words and every-day conceptions. The reality and the importance of the natural processes on which Darwin founds his deductions are no more doubted than those of growth and multiplication; and, whether the full potency attributed to them is admitted or not, no one is unmindful of or at all doubts their vast and far-reaching significance. Wherever the biological sciences are studied, the "Origin of Species" lights the path of the investigator; wherever they are taught it permeates the course of instruction. Nor has the influence of Darwinian ideas been less profound beyond the realms of biology. The oldest of all philosophies, that of evolution, was bound hand and foot and cast into utter darkness during the millennium of theological scholasticism. But Darwin poured new life-blood into the ancient frame; the bonds burst, and the revivified thought of ancient Greece has proved itself to be a more adequate expression of the universal order of things than any of the schemes which have been accepted by the credulity and welcomed by the super-stition of seventy later generations of men.

5

Questions 1-7.
1. Darwin's theory of the origin of the species is based on   1. ...
   A. theological deductions   B. the theory of gravitation
   C. Greek mythology
   D. natural processes evident in the universe
   E. extensive reading in the biological sciences
2. The passage implies that   2. ...
   A. thought in ancient Greece was dead
   B. the theory of evolution is now universally accepted
   C. the "Origin of Species" was seized by the Church
   D. Darwin was influenced by Newton
   E. the theories of "the struggle for existence" and
      "natural selection" are too evident to be scientific
3. The idea of evolution   3. ...
   A. was suppressed for 1,000 years
   B. is falsely claimed by Darwin
   C. has swept aside all superstition
   D. was outworn even in ancient Greece
   E. has revolutionized the universe
4. The processes of growth and multiplication   4. ...
   A. have been replaced by others discovered by Darwin
   B. were the basis for the theory of gravitation
   C. are "the struggle for existence" and "natural selection"
   D. are scientific theories not yet proved
   E. are accepted as fundamental processes of nature
5. Darwin's treatise on evolution   5. ...
   A. traces life on the planets from the beginning of time
      to the present day
   B. was translated from the Greek
   C. contains an ancient philosophy in modern, scientific
      guise
   D. has had a profound effect on evolution
   E. has had little notice outside scientific circles
6. The theory of evolution   6. ...
   A. was first advanced in the "Origin of Species"
   B. was suppressed by the ancient Greeks
   C. did not get beyond the monasteries during the millennium
   D. is philosophical, not scientific
   E. was elaborated and revived by Darwin
7. Darwin has contributed GREATLY toward   7. ...
   A. a universal acceptance of the processes of nature
   B. reviving the Greek intellect
   C. ending the millennium of theological scholasticism
   D. a satisfactory explanation of scientific theory
   E. easing the struggle for existence

TEST 6

PASSAGE

The higher forms of plants and animals, such as seed plants and vertebrates, are similar or alike in many respects but decidedly different in others. For example, both of these groups of organisms carry on digestion, respiration, reproduction, conduction, growth, and exhibit sensitivity to various stimuli. On the other hand, a

number of basic differences are evident. Plants have no excretory
systems comparable to those of animals. Plants have no heart or
similar pumping organ. Plants are very limited in their movements.
Plants have nothing similar to the animal nervous system. In addition, animals can not synthesize carbohydrates from inorganic substances. Animals do not have special regions of growth, comparable
to terminal and lateral meristems in plants, which persist throughout the life span of the organism. And, finally, the animal cell "wall"
is only a membrane, while plant cell walls are more rigid, usually
thicker, and may be composed of such substances as cellulose, lignin,
pectin, cutin, and suberin. These characteristics are important to
an understanding of living organisms and their functions and should,
consequently, be carefully considered in plant and animal studies.
Questions 1-7.

1. Which of the following do animals lack?   1. ...
   A. Ability to react to stimuli
   B. Ability to conduct substances from one place to another
   C. Reproduction by gametes
   D. A cell membrane
   E. A terminal growth region
2. Which of the following statements is false?   2. ...
   A. Animal cell "walls" are composed of cellulose.
   B. Plants grow as long as they live.
   C. Plants produce sperms and eggs.
   D. All vertebrates have hearts.
   E. Wood is dead at maturity.
3. Respiration in plants takes place   3. ...
   A. only during the day
   B. only in the presence of carbon dioxide
   C. both day and night
   D. only at night
   E. only in the presence of certain stimuli
4. An example of a vertebrate is the   4. ...
   A. earthworm   B. starfish   C. amoeba
   D. cow   E. insect
5. Which of the following statements is true?   5. ...
   A. All animals eat plants as a source of food.
   B. Respiration, in many ways, is the reverse of photo-
      synthesis.
   C. Man is an invertebrate animal.
   D. Since plants have no hearts, they can not develop
      high pressures in their cells.
   E. Plants can not move.
6. Which of the following do plants lack?   6. ...
   A. A means of movement   B. Pumping structures
   C. Special regions of growth
   D. Reproduction by gametes
   E. A digestive process
7. A substance that can be synthesized by green plants but NOT 7. ...
   by animals is
   A. protein   B. cellulose   C. carbon dioxide
   D. uric acid   E. water

7

TEST 7

PASSAGE

Sodium chloride, being by far the largest constituent of the mineral matter of the blood, assumes special significance in the regulation of water exchanges in the organism. And, as Cannon has emphasized repeatedly, these latter are more extensive and more important than may at first thought appear. He points out "there are a number of circulations of the fluid out of the body and back again, without loss." Thus, by example, it is estimated that from a quart and one-half of water daily "leaves the body" when it enters the mouth as saliva; another one or two quarts are passed out as gastric juice; and perhaps the same amount is contained in the bile and the secretions of the pancreas and the intestinal wall. This large volume of water enters the digestive processes; and practically all of it is reabsorbed through the intestinal wall, where it performs the equally important function of carrying in the digested foodstuffs. These and other instances of what Cannon calls "the conservative use of water in our bodies" involve essentially osmotic pressure relationships in which the concentration of sodium chloride plays an important part.

Questions 1-11.

1. This passage implies that   1. ...
    A. the contents of the alimentary canal are not to be considered within the body
    B. sodium chloride does not actually enter the body
    C. every particle of water ingested is used over and over again
    D. water can not be absorbed by the body unless it contains sodium chloride
    E. substances can pass through the intestinal wall in only one direction

2. According to this passage, which of the following processes   2. ... requires MOST water? The
    A. absorption of digested foods
    B. secretion of gastric juice
    C. secretion of saliva
    D. production of bile
    E. concentration of sodium chloride solution

3. A body fluid that is NOT saline is   3. ...
    A. blood   B. urine   C. bile
    D. gastric juice   E. saliva

4. An organ that functions as a storage reservoir from which   4. ... large quantities of water are reabsorbed into the body is the
    A. kidney   B. liver   C. large intestine
    D. mouth   E. pancreas

5. Water is reabsorbed into the body by the process of   5. ...
    A. secretion   B. excretion   C. digestion
    D. osmosis   E. oxidation

6. Digested food enters the body PRINCIPALLY through the   6. ...
    A. mouth   B. liver   C. villi
    D. pancreas   E. stomach

7. The metallic element found in the blood in compound form   7. ...
   and present there in larger quantities than any other
   metallic element is
      A. iron   B. calcium   C. magnesium
      D. chlorine   E. sodium
8. An organ that removes water from the body and prevents   8. ...
   its reabsorption for use in the body processes is the
      A. pancreas   B. liver   C. small intestine
      D. lungs   E. large intestine
9. In which of the following processes is sodium chloride   9. ...
   removed MOST rapidly from the body?
      A. Digestion   B. Breathing   C. Oxidation
      D. Respiration   E. Perspiration
10. Which of the following liquids would pass from the ali-   10. ...
    mentary canal into the blood MOST rapidly?
      A. A dilute solution of sodium chloride in water
      B. Gastric juice
      C. A concentrated solution of sodium chloride in water
      D. Digested food
      E. Distilled water
11. The reason why it is unsafe to drink ocean water even   11. ...
    under conditions of extreme thirst is that it
      A. would reduce the salinity of the blood to a dangerous
         level
      B. contains dangerous disease germs
      C. contains poisonous salts
      D. would greatly increase the salinity of the blood
      E. would cause salt crystals to form in the blood stream

TEST 8

PASSAGE

The discovery of antitoxin and its specific antagonistic effect upon toxin furnished an opportunity for the accurate investigation of the relationship of a bacterial antigen and its antibody. Toxin-antitoxin reactions were the first immunological processes to which experimental precision could be applied, and the discovery of principles of great importance resulted from such studies. A great deal of the work was done with diphtheria toxin and antitoxin and the facts elucidated with these materials are in principle applicable to similar substances.

The simplest assumption to account for the manner in which an antitoxin renders a toxin innocuous would be that the antitoxin destroys the toxin. Roux and Buchner, however, advanced the opinion that the antitoxin did not act directly upon the toxin, but affected it indirectly through the mediation of tissue cells. Ehrlich, on the other hand, conceived the reaction of toxin and antitoxin as a direct union, analogous to the chemical neutralization of an acid by a base.

The conception of toxin destruction was conclusively refuted by the experiments of Calmette. This observer, working with snake poison, found that the poison itself (unlike most other toxins) possessed the property of resisting heat to 100 degrees C, while its specific antitoxin, like other antitoxins, was destroyed at or about

9

70 degrees C. Nontoxic mixtures of the two substanues, when sub-
jected to heat, regained their toxic properties.   The natural
inference from these observations was that the toxin in the original
mixture had not been destroyed, but had been merely inactiviated by
the presence of the antitoxin and again set free after destruction
of the antitoxin by heat.

Questions 1-10.

1. Both toxins and antitoxins ORDINARILY   1. ...
    A. are completely destroyed at body temperatures
    B. are extremely resistant to heat
    C. can exist only in combination
    D. are destroyed at 180°F
    E. are products of nonliving processes
2. MOST toxins can be destroyed by   2. ...
    A. bacterial action   B. salt solutions
    C. boiling   D. diphtheria antitoxin
    E. other toxins
3. Very few disease organisms release a true toxin into the   3. ...
   blood stream. It would follow, then, that
    A. studies of snake venom reactions have no value
    B. studies of toxin-antitoxin reactions are of little
       importance
    C. the treatment of most diseases must depend upon in-
       formation obtained from study of a few
    D. antitoxin plays an important part in the body defense
       against the great majority of germs
    E. only toxin producers are dangerous
4. A person becomes susceptible to infection again immediate-   4. ...
   ly after recovering from
    A. mumps   B. tetanus   C. diphtheria
    D. smallpox   E. tuberculosis
5. City people are more frequently immune to communicable   5. ...
   diseases than country people are because
    A. country people eat better food
    B. city doctors are better than country doctors
    C. the air is more healthful in the country
    D. country people have fewer contacts with disease car-
       riers
    E. there are more doctors in the city than in the country
6. The substances that provide us with immunity to disease   6. ...
   are found in the body in the
    A. blood serum   B. gastric juice   C. urine
    D. white blood cells   E. red blood cells
7. A person ill with diphtheria would MOST likely be treated   7. ...
   with
    A. diphtheria toxin   B. diphtheria toxoid
    C. dead diphtheria germs   D. diphtheria antitoxin
    E. live diphtheria germs
8. To determine susceptibility to diphtheria, an individual   8. ...
   may be given the
    A. Wassermann test   B. Schick test
    C. Widal test   D. Dick test
    E. Kahn test
9. Since few babies under six months of age contract diph-   9. ...
   theria, young babies PROBABLY
    A. are never exposed to diphtheria germs

B. have high body temperatures that destroy the toxin
   if acquired
C. acquire immunity from their mothers
D. acquire immunity from their fathers
E. are too young to become infected

10. Calmette's findings   10. ...
   A. contradicted both Roux and Buchner's opinion and
      Ehrlich's conception
   B. contradicted Roux and Buchner, but supported Ehrlich
   C. contradicted Ehrlich, but supported Roux and Buchner
   D. were consistent with both theories
   E. had no bearing on the point at issue

TEST 9

PASSAGE

In the days of sailing ships, when voyages were long and uncertain, provisions for many months were stored without refrigeration
in the holds of the ships. Naturally no fresh or perishable foods
could be included. Toward the end of particularly long voyages the
crews of such ships became ill and often many died from scurvy. Many
men, both scientific and otherwise, tried to devise a cure for scurvy.
Among the latter was John Hall, a son-in-law of William Shakespeare,
who cured some cases of scurvy by administering a sour brew made from
scurvy grass and water cress.

The next step was the suggestion of William Harvey that scurvy
could be prevented by giving the men lemon juice. He thought that
the beneficial substance was the acid contained in the fruit.

The third step was taken by Dr. James Lind, an English naval surgeon, who performed the following experiment with 12 sailors, all of
whom were sick with scurvy: Each was given the same diet, except
that four of the men received small amounts of dilute sulfuric acid,
four others were given vinegar and the remaining four were given
lemons. Only those who received the fruit recovered.

Questions 1-7.

1. Credit for solving the problem described above belongs to   1. ...
   A. Hall, because he first devised a cure for scurvy
   B. Harvey, because he first proposed a solution of the
      problem
   C. Lind, because he proved the solution by means of an
      experiment
   D. both Harvey and Lind, because they found that lemons
      are more effective than scurvy grass or water cress
   E. all three men, because each made some contribution

2. A good substitute for lemons in the treatment of scurvy is   2. ...
   A. fresh eggs   B. tomato juice   C. cod-liver oil
   D. liver   E. whole-wheat bread

3. The number of control groups that Dr. Lind used in his ex-   3. ...
   periment was
   A. one   B. two   C. three   D. four   E. none

4. A substance that will turn blue litmus red is   4. ...
   A. aniline   B. lye   C. ice
   D. vinegar   E. table salt

5. The hypothesis tested by Lind was: 5. ...
   A. Lemons contain some substance not present in vinegar.
   B. Citric acid is the most effective treatment for scurvy.
   C. Lemons contain some unknown acid that will cure scurvy.
   D. Some specific substance, rather than acids in general, is needed to cure scurvy.
   E. The substance needed to cure scurvy is found only in lemons.

6. A problem that Lind's experiment did NOT solve was: 6. ...
   A. Will citric acid alone cure scurvy?
   B. Will lemons cure scurvy?
   C. Will either sulfuric acid or vinegar cure scurvy?
   D. Are all substances that contain acids equally effective as a treatment for scurvy?
   E. Are lemons more effective than either vinegar or sulfuric acid in the treatment of scurvy?

7. The PRIMARY purpose of a controlled scientific experiment 7. ...
is to
   A. get rid of superstitions
   B. prove a hypothesis is correct
   C. disprove a theory that is false
   D. determine whether a hypothesis is true or false
   E. discover new facts

TEST 10

PASSAGE

The formed elements of the blood are the red corpuscles or erythrocytes, the white corpuscles or leucocytes, the blood platelets, and the so-called blood dust or hemoconiae. Together, these constitute 30-40 per cent by volume of the whole blood, the remainder being taken up by the plasma. In man, there are normally 5,000,000 red cells per cubic millimeter of blood; the count is somewhat lower in women. Variations occur frequently, especially after exercise or a heavy meal, or at high altitudes. Except in camels, which have elliptical corpuscles, the shape of the mammalian corpuscle is that of a circular, nonnucleated, bi-concave disk. The average diameter usually given is 7.7 microns, a value obtained by examining dried preparations of blood and considered by Ponder to be too low. Ponder's own observations, made on red cells in the fresh state, show the human corpuscle to have an average diameter of 8.8 microns. When circulating in the blood vessels, the red cell does not maintain a fixed shape but changes its form constantly, especially in the small capillaries. The red blood corpuscles are continually undergoing destruction, new corpuscles being formed to replace them. The average life of red corpuscles has been estimated by various investigators to be between three and six weeks. Preceding destruction, changes in the composition of the cells are believed to occur which render them less resistant. In the process of destruction, the lipids of the membrane are dissolved and the hemoglobin which is liberated is the most important, though probably not the only, source of bilirubin. The belief that the liver is the only site of red cell destruction is no longer generally held. The leucocytes, of which

there are several forms, usually number between 7000 and 9000 per cubic millimeter of blood. These increase in number in disease, particularly when there is bacterial infection.
Questions 1-10.
1. Leukemia is a disease involving the   1. ...
   A. red cells   B. white cells   C. plasma
   D. blood platelets E. blood dust
2. Are the erythrocytes in the blood increased in number after 2. ...
   a heavy meal? The paragraph implies that this
    A. is true   B. holds only for camels
    C. is not true   D. may be true
    E. depends on the number of white cells
3. When blood is dried, the red cells   3. ...
    A. contract   B. remain the same size
    C. disintegrate   D. expand
    E. become elliptical
4. Ponder is probably classified as a professional 4. ...
    A. pharmacist   B. physicist   C. psychologist
    D. physiologist   E. psychiatrist
5. The term "erythema" when applied to skin conditions sig- 5. ...
   nifies
    A. redness   B. swelling   C. irritation
    D. pain   E. roughness
6. Lipids are insoluble in water and soluble in such solvents 6. ...
   as ether, chloroform and benzene. It may be inferred that
   the membranes of red cells MOST closely resemble
    A. egg white   B. sugar   C. bone
    D. butter   E. cotton fiber
7. Analysis of a sample of blood yields cell counts of 7. ...
   4,800,000 erythrocytes and 16,000 leucocytes per cubic
   millimeter. These data suggest that the patient from whom
   the blood was taken
    A. is anemic
    B. has been injuriously invaded by germs
    C. has been exposed to high-pressure air
    D. has a normal cell count
    E. has lost a great deal of blood
8. Bilirubin, a bile pigment, is   8. ...
    A. an end product of several different reactions
    B. formed only in the liver
    C. formed from the remnants of the cell membranes of
      erythrocytes
    D. derived from hemoglobin exclusively
    E. a precursor of hemoglobin
9. Bancroft found that the blood count of the natives in the 9. ...
   Peruvian Andes differed from that usually accepted as normal. The blood PROBABLY differed in respect to
    A. leucocytes   B. blood platelets C. cell shapes
    D. erythrocytes E. hemoconiae
10. Hemoglobin is probably NEVER found   10. ...
    A. free in the blood stream
    B. in the red cells
    C. in women's blood
    D. in the blood after exercise
    E. in the leucocytes

TEST 11

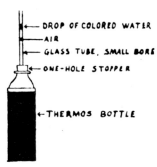

Questions 1-7.
1. The device shown in the diagram above indicates changes   1. ...
   that are measured more accurately by a(n)
      A. thermometer   B. hygrometer   C. anemometer
      D. hydrometer   E. barometer
2. If the device is placed in a cold refrigerator for 72   2. ...
   hours, which of the following is MOST likely to happen?
      A. The stopper will be forced out of the bottle.
      B. The drop of water will evaporate.
      C. The drop will move downward.
      D. The drop will move upward.
      E. No change will take place.
3. When the device was carried in an elevator from the first   3. ...
   floor to the sixth floor of a building, the drop of colored
   water moved about 1/4 inch in the tube. Which of the following is MOST probably true? The drop moved
      A. *downward* because there was a decrease in the air pressure
      B. *upward* because there was a decrease in the air pressure
      C. *downward* because there was an increase in the air tem-
         perature
      D. *upward* because there was an increase in the air temper-
         ature
      E. *downward* because there was an increase in the tempera-
         ture and a decrease in the pressure
4. The part of a thermos bottle into which liquids are poured 4. ...
   consists of
      A. a single-walled, metal flask coated with silver
      B. two flasks, one of glass and one of silvered metal
      C. two silvered-glass flasks separated by a vacuum
      D. two silver flasks separated by a vacuum
      E. a single-walled, glass flask with a silver-colored
         coating
5. The thermos bottle is MOST similar in principle to   5. ...
      A. the freezing unit in an electric refrigerator
      B. radiant heaters
      C. solar heating systems
      D. storm windows
      E. a thermostatically controlled heating system
6. In a plane flying at an altitude where the air pressure is 6. ...
   only half the normal pressure at sea level, the plane's
   altimeter should read, *approximately*,
      A. 3000 feet   B. 9000 feet   C. 18000 feet
      D. 27000 feet   E. 60000 feet

7. Which of the following is the POOREST conductor of heat?   7. ...
   A. Air under a pressure of 1.5 pounds per square inch
   B. Air under a pressure of 15 pounds per square inch
   C. Unsilvered glass
   D. Silvered glass
   E. Silver

TEST 12

PASSAGE

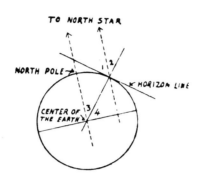

The latitude of any point on the earth's surface is the angle between a plumb line dropped to the center of the earth from that point and the plane of the earth's equator. Since it is impossible to go to the center of the earth to measure latitude, the latitude of any point may be determined indirectly as shown in the accompanying diagram.

It will be recalled that the axis of the earth, if extended outward, passes very near the North Star. Since the North Star is, for all practical purposes, infinitely distant, the line of sight to the North Star of an observer on the surface of the earth is virtually parallel with the earth's axis. Angle 1, then, in the diagram represents the angular distance of the North Star above the horizon. Angle 2 is equal to angle 3, because when two parallel lines are intersected by a straight line, the corresponding angles are equal. Angle 1 plus angle 2 is a right angle and so is angle 3 plus angle 4. Therefore, angle 1 equals angle 4 because when equals are subtracted from equals the results are equal.

Questions 1-10.
1. If an observer finds that the angular distance of the North 1. ...
   Star above the horizon is 30°, his latitude is
     A. 15°N   B. 30°N   C. 60°N   D. 90°N   E. 120°N
2. To an observer on the equator, the North Star would be   2. ...
   A. 30° above the horizon   B. 60° above the horizon
   C. 90° above the horizon   D. on the horizon
   E. below the horizon
3. To an observer on the Arctic Circle, the North Star would   3. ...
   be
   A. directly overhead   B. 23 1/2° above the horizon
   C. 66 1/2° above the horizon
   D. on the horizon
   E. below the horizon

4. The distance around the earth along a certain parallel of   4. ...
   latitude is 3600 miles. At that latitude, how many miles
   are there in one degree of longitude?
       A. 1 mile   B. 10 miles   C. 30 miles
       D. 69 miles   E. 100 miles
5. At which of the following latitudes would the sun be   5. ...
   DIRECTLY overhead at noon on June 21?
       A. 0°   B. 23 1/2°S   C. 23 1/2°N
       D. 66 1/2°N   E. 66 1/2°S
6. On March 21 the number of hours of daylight at places on   6. ...
   the Arctic Circle is
       A. none   B. 8   C. 12   D. 16   E. 24
7. The distance from the equator to the 45th parallel, meas-   7. ...
   ured along a meridian, is, *approximately,*
       A. 450 miles   B. 900 miles   C. 1250 miles
       D. 3125 miles   E. 6250 miles
8. The difference in time between the meridians that pass   8. ...
   through longitude 45°E and longitude 105°W is
       A. 6 hours   B. 2 hours   C. 8 hours
       D. 4 hours   E. 10 hours
9. Which of the following is NOT a great circle or part of a   9. ...
   great circle?
       A. Arctic Circle   B. 100th meridian   C. Equator
       D. Shortest distance between New York and London
       E. Greenwich meridian
10. At which of the following places does the sun set EARLIEST 10. ...
    on June 21?
        A. Montreal, Canada   B. Santiago, Chile
        C. Mexico City, Mexico   D. Lima, Peru
        E. Manila, P.I.

KEY (CORRECT ANSWERS)

TEST 1	TEST 4	TEST 7	TEST 9	TEST 11
1. C	1. A	1. A	1. E	1. A
2. E	2. B	2. A	2. B	2. C
3. C	3. C	3. D	3. B	3. B
4. A	4. C	4. C	4. D	4. C
5. A	5. D	5. D	5. D	5. D
6. B		6. C	6. A	6. C
7. B	TEST 5	7. E	7. D	7. A
8. C	1. D	8. D		
	2. B	9. E	TEST 10	TEST 12
TEST 2	3. A	10. E	1. B	1. B
1. C	4. E		2. D	2. D
2. B	5. D	TEST 8	3. A	3. C
	6. E	1. D	4. D	4. B
TEST 3	7. A	2. C	5. A	5. C
1. B		3. C	6. D	6. C
2. A	TEST 6	4. E	7. B	7. D
3. C	1. E	5. D	8. A	8. E
4. C	2. A	6. A	9. D	9. A
5. D	3. C	7. D	10. E	10. B
6. D	4. D	8. B		
7. D	5. B	9. C		
8. E	6. B	10. D		
9. C	7. B			

EXAMINATION SECTION
TEST 1

DIRECTIONS: Each question or incomplete statement is followed by
several suggested answers or completions. Select the
one that BEST answers the question or completes the
statement. *PRINT THE LETTER OF THE CORRECT ANSWER
IN THE SPACE AT THE RIGHT.*

Questions 1-8.
DIRECTIONS: Questions 1-8 refer to the passage that follows.
Base your choice on the information given in the selection
and on your own understanding of science.

Whenever micro-organisms have successfully invaded the body and are
growing at the expense of the tissues, the process is called an infection. The term *infection* should always imply the existence of an ab-
normal state or unnatural condition resulting from the harmful action
of micro-organisms. In other words, the simple presence of an organism
is not sufficient to cause disease.

Infection may arise from the admission of microorganisms to the tissues through the gastrointestinal tract, through the upper air passages,
through wounds made by contaminated teeth or claws of animals or by
contaminated weapons, and by the bite of suctorial insects. Another
type of infection sometimes occurs when for some reason the body has
become vulnerable to the pathogenic action of bacteria whose normal
habitat is the body.

The reaction of the body to the attack of an invading organism results in the formation of substances of a specific nature. Those reaction bodies which circulate mainly in the blood serum are known as
antibodies and are classified according to their activity. Some known
as antitoxins, neutralize poisonous substances produced by the infecting organism. Others, called bacteriolysins, destroy bacteria by
dissolving them. Opsonins or bacteriotropins prepare the bacteria for
destruction by phagocytes, while precipitins and agglutinins have the
property of grouping the invading agents into small clumps or precipi-
tates. The formation of defensive substances is specific for each
organism.

1. The passage states "the formation of defensive substances   1. ___
   is specific for each organism." This implies that
   A. organisms inherit the ability to produce antibodies
   B. only specific organisms can produce antibodies
   C. the same organism cannot cause the production of two
      kinds of antibodies
   D. diphtheria antitoxin will not neutralize tetanus toxin
   E. only specific microorganisms can cause the production
      of antibodies in the human body

2. The passage you have read defines the term *infection*. In   2. ___
   the light of what it says, which of the following conditions

would illustrate an infection?
   A. A guinea pig is injected with diphtheria toxin. It be-
      comes very ill and dies.
   B. A nurse taking care of a tubercular patient inhales
      some tuberculosis bacilli.
   C. A man cuts his finger with a dirty knife. He uses no
      antiseptic.
   D. A student examines his saliva with a microscope. Under
      high power he observes some streptococci.
   E. An anopheles mosquito bites a healthy soldier. Some
      time thereafter, the soldier experiences alternate
      periods of chill and fever.

3. Phagocytes are mentioned in the last paragraph of the pas-   3. ___
   sage. Of the following, the statement that is TRUE of
   phagocytes is:
   A. All white corpuscles are phagocytes.
   B. Some white corpuscles are phagocytes.
   C. Phagocytes are always red corpuscles.
   D. Phagocytes are usually platelets.
   E. Parasitic amebas are phagocytes.

4. In their control of infection the phagocytes are aided by   4. ___
   A. enzymes   B. insulin   C. fibrinogen   D. lipids
   E. lymph glands

5. The passage mentions several ways in which germs may enter   5. ___
   the body. One of those mentioned is by way of the gastrointestinal tract. A disease that enters in this way is
   A. beriberi   B. typhoid   C. typhus
   D. yellow fever   E. cancer of the stomach

6. With which of the following statements would the author   6. ___
   of the passage agree?
   A. The white blood corpuscles help ward off infection by
      distributing antibodies to all parts of the body.
   B. A disease organism may live in the body of a person with-
      out having any bad effect on the person.
   C. Antibodies are classified according to the type of or-
      ganism they attack.
   D. Infection is usually accompanied by swelling and the for-
      mation of pus.
   E. Antitoxins are formed against every organism which enters
      the body.

7. A child comes down with diphtheria. His brother, who has   7. ___
   never had diphtheria and has never been immunized against
   it, should receive
   A. the Shick test
   B. injections of diphtheria toxin
   C. injections of diphtheria antitoxin
   D. injections of diphtheria toxoid
   E. nothing, as any treatment would be ineffective

2

8. Not long ago a child in a large city died of diphtheria.   8. ___
   The following opinions were expressed by different people
   when they read about this. Which opinion is in best keep-
   ing with modern medical knowledge and practice?
   A. In the struggle for existence the weak die off. There-
      fore, the death of this child is of advantage to so-
      ciety because the child was probably a weakling.
   B. Diphtheria is a disease of childhood and some children
      must die of it.
   C. In a large city some deaths from diphtheria must be
      expected despite all precautions.
   D. This death was unnecessary. The child could have been
      saved if the proper medical care had been provided while
      the child was ill.
   E. No child should sicken with diphtheria, much less die of
      it. Where children still die of diphtheria, either the
      parents are ignorant of the fact that it is preventable
      or they are negligent of the welfare of their children.

9. Accidents in the home occur MOST frequently from   9. ___
   A. burns   B. falls   C. firearms   D. poisons
   E. suffocation

10. When a motor car is going 20 miles per hour, its brakes   10. ___
    can stop it in 40 feet. When the same car is going 40
    miles per hour, its brakes ought to stop it in about
    A. 40 ft.   B. 80 ft.   C. 160 ft.   D. 200 ft.
    E. 240 ft.

11. Emotional stability is a characteristic of mental health   11. ___
    that is MOST important to
    A. clearness of complexion   B. digestion
    C. muscle tone
    D. resistance to infectious disease
    E. respiration

12. Anne and Margaret went to a restaurant for lunch. Anne   12. ___
    had a cup of consommé, four saltines, a square of butter,
    a serving of plain jello and a gingersnap. Margaret had
    a cup of tomato soup, two slices of buttered toast, a glass
    of milk and a baked apple. Comparison of their lunches in-
    dicated that
    A. Margaret's lunch was a poorer source of calcium than
       Anne's
    B. Margaret's lunch was a poorer source of vitamin C
    C. Anne's lunch was higher in caloric value than Mar-
       garet's
    D. Anne's lunch was a better source of iron than Mar-
       garet's
    E. Anne's lunch was a poorer source of vitamin A

13. A family consists of father, mother and three children
    aged fifteen, thirteen and five. The MINIMUM amount of
    milk the family should buy per week is
        A. 7 quarts   B. 14 quarts   C. 21 quarts
        D. 28 quarts   E. 35 quarts

13. ____

14. In buying citrus fruit for juice it is MOST economical
    to select the fruit
        A. with thick skins   B. heavy for their size
        C. extra large in size   D. small in size
        E. with most highly colored skins

14. ____

15. In selecting eggs for the family, it is BEST to buy
    those that
        A. are fertile   B. are whitest in color
        C. seem light in the hand   D. have smooth, shiny shells
        E. have rough, dull shells

15. ____

16. In caring for plastics (such as bakelite), it is impor-
    tant to know that
        A. an abrasive is a good cleanser for them
        B. they can be subjected to high temperatures
        C. they are resistant to water and most chemicals
        D. they are molded
        E. their colors are apt to fade

16. ____

17. Which of the following circuits could you wire from this
    diagram?

17. ____

    1. code oscillator   B. doorbell system
    C. electric chime   D. radio receiving set
    E. electric train signal

18. Which process does the illustration represent?

18. ____

    1. heading a rivet   B. flattening a bolt
    C. setting a nail   D. clinching a nail
    E. forming the head of a screw

4

19. Which drawing illustrates a wired edge in sheet metal work? 19. ___

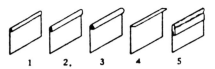

20. Which symbol represents an electrical ground connection? 20. ___

21. With what kind of saw should the type of curve illustrated below be cut? 21. ___

   1. back saw   B. coping saw   C. dovetail saw
   D. key-hole saw D. rip saw

22. In squaring up a piece of rough lumber, which of the surfaces indicated would you plane first? 22. ___

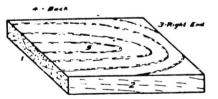

23. Which diagram illustrates the CORRECT method of determining the position of a circle? 23. ___

5

24. All of the following are drawing instruments EXCEPT   24. ____
     A. T-square   B. compass   C. triangle
     D. scale rule   E. plumb bob

25. The instrument used to regulate the temperature of a   25. ____
    refrigerator is a
     A. thermocouple   B. thermograph
     C. thermometer   D. thermoscope
     E. thermostat

26. The source from which MOST electromagnetic waves ra-   26. ____
    diate is
     A. electromagnets   B. power plants   C. the spectrum
     D. the sun   E. uranium 235

27. If the bulb of a glass thermometer is plunged into hot   27. ____
    water, the mercury first falls before rising because the
     A. air above the mercury expands
     B. mercury contracts from the shock
     C. glass expands faster than the mercury
     D. mercury has a negative coefficient of expansion
     E. expanding glass absorbs heat from the mercury

28. A Diesel engine operates without   28. ____
     A. a crankshaft   B. a cooling system
     C. an ignition coil   D. a flywheel
     E. pistons

29. Electric clocks commonly used in homes rarely need set-   29. ____
    ting because they
     A. are well regulated at the factory
     B. keep in step with carefully regulated generators
     C. are manufactured with such fine tolerances
     D. contain ingenious governors
     E. are kept wound by small motors

30. The fuse in a household wiring circuit is a metal with   30. ____
    a high
     A. capacity   B. combustion point
     C. coefficient of expansion   D. melting point
     E. resistance

31. The area of a regular-size postage stamp is about   31. ____
     A. 8 square millimeters   B. 1 square centimeter
     C. 5 square centimeters   D. 50 square centimeters
     E. 2.4 square decimeters

32. The spectroscope is used to   32. ____
     A. calibrate periscopes
     B. study the interior of the lungs
     C. magnify small objects enormously
     D. analyze the composition of hot materials
     E. discover the defects in large castings

33. The Beaufort scale is used in the measurement of   33. ___
    A. wind velocity
    B. very low temperatures
    C. earthquake intensities
    D. light intensity
    E. small changes in gravitational forces

34. Electrons are   34. ___
    A. neutral particles   B. the nuclei of atoms
    C. negative particles   D. neutralized protons
    E. positive particles

35. The differential in an **automobile** is a device that al- 35. ___
    lows
    A. a continuous change of gear ratio
    B. the rear wheels to turn independently of each other
    C. a variable battery-charging voltage
    D. traction for one rear wheel when the other is on a
       slippery surface
    E. compensation for gasolines of various octane ratings

36. A railroad locomotive stopped with a crankshaft on dead 36. ___
    center is started forward by
    A. an auxiliary engine
    B. the stored inertia from previous motion
    C. the opposite piston
    D. cranking the crankshaft off center
    E. first backing up

37. The exhaust gas of an automobile is mainly carbon, car- 37. ___
    bon dioxide, carbon monoxide, nitrogen, and
    A. hydrogen   B. oxygen   C. steam
    C. gasoline vapor   E. silicon carbide

38. A woman bought a navy blue dress with white polka dots   38. ___
    in a store illuminated with a pure yellow light. The
    colors of the dress as they appeared in the store were
    A. blue with yellow polka dots
    B. black with white polka dots
    C. black with yellow polka dots
    D. green with white polka dots
    E. green with yellow polka dots

39. Of the following, the one that weighs MOST is   39. ___
    A. 50 grams of feathers
    B. 1 pound of cotton
    C. 12 ounces of lead
    D. 1 cubic centimeter of mercury
    E. 600,000 milligrams of sulfur

40. Water is obtained from an artesian well   40. ___
    A. with a shallow lift pump B. with a shallow force pump

7

C. with a deep lift pump   D. with a deep force pump
E. without a pump

41. Which one of the following items would NOT have to be   41. ___
    seriously considered by a group of scientists exploring
    on the moon?
       A. Effects of insolation
       B. Effects of gravity
       C. Temperature changes after nightfall
       D. Changing weather conditions
       E. Communication with the earth

42. Each day between March 21 and June 21, the sun appears   42. ___
    to set a tiny bit farther north of west than it rose
    north of east because the
       A. days are getting longer
       B. earth has moved on its orbit during the day
       C. earth's axis tilts a little more each day
       D. earth rotates on its axis
       E. earth is coming closer to the sun

43. The twinkling of a star is caused by   43. ___
       A. the star itself
       B. interplanetary dust
       C. defects in the structure of the human eye
       D. objects passing between the star and our eyes
       E. turbulence within the atmosphere

44. The Aurora borealis and the Aurora australis are indi-   44. ___
    cations that
       A. the earth's atmosphere is more than 200 miles in
          depth
       B. large ice sheets reflect considerable light
       C. the earth's orbit and its axis are not mutually
          perpendicular
       D. moonlight is reflected from cirrus clouds

45. A point on the earth's surface diametrically opposite   45. ___
    latitude 40°N, longitude 70°W is
       A. 40°N 70°E   B. 40°S 70°E   C. 50°S 110°E
       D. 40°S 110°E   E. 50°S 70°E

46. The BEST estimate of the age of the earth comes from   46. ___
    studies of
       A. the total thickness of sedimentary rocks
       B. certain changes in radioactive minerals
       C. the amount of salt in the ocean
       D. the amount of erosion
       E. the mineralization of the lowest fossil-bearing
          rock

47. Which of the following elements related to the process of   47. ___
    nuclear fission does NOT occur in nature?
    A. barium   B. curium   C. radium   D. thorium
    E. uranium

48. The nucleus of an atom of uranium 235 contains   48. ___
    A. 235 protons
    B. 235 neutrons
    C. 92 protons and 143 neutrons
    D. 90 protons and 146 neutrons
    E. 146 protons and 89 neutrons

49. A mineral mined in large quantities in the East is   49. ___
    A. aluminum   B. coal   C. magnesium   D. salt
    E. sulfur

50. Certain metals are added to increase the hardness and   50. ___
    toughness of steel. A group of such metals is
    A. magnesium, cadmium, antimony
    B. manganese, chromium, nickel
    C. carbon, tin, copper
    D. zinc, lead, aluminum
    E. nickel, tin, zinc

___

KEY (CORRECT ANSWERS)

1.	D	11.	B	21.	B	31.	C	41.	D
2.	E	12.	E	22.	E	32.	D	42.	B
3.	B	13.	D	23.	A	33.	A	43.	E
4.	E	14.	B	24.	E	34.	C	44.	A
5.	B	15.	E	25.	E	35.	B	45.	D
6.	B	16.	C	26.	D	36.	C	46.	B
7.	C	17.	D	27.	C	37.	C	47.	B
8.	E	18.	A	28.	C	38.	C	48.	C
9.	B	19.	C	29.	B	39.	E	49.	D
10.	C	20.	C	30.	E	40.	E	50.	B

___

TEST 2

DIRECTIONS: Each question or incomplete statement is followed by several suggested answers or completions. Select the one that *BEST* answers the question or completes the statement. *PRINT THE LETTER OF THE CORRECT ANSWER IN THE SPACE AT THE RIGHT.*

1. A relatively inert gas, such as argon, is included in many incandescent electric lamps because the gas   1.___
   A. excludes oxygen, which would corrode the filament
   B. glows when electrically excited
   C. reacts with the filament to cause the glow
   D. permits rapid vaporization around the filament
   E. prevents rapid vaporization around the filament

2. Wet wood will usually burn but does *NOT* make good tinder because   2.___
   A. water does not burn
   B. so much heat is needed to evaporate the water
   C. wet wood has a higher kindling temperature than dry wood
   D. the water vapor produced smothers the fire
   E. wet wood has a lower kindling temperature than dry wood

3. When coal burns in a furnace, the weight of all the substances derived from the burning will be equal to the weight of   3.___
   A. the coal
   B. the ashes taken from the furnace
   C. all the air entering the furnace
   D. the air entering the furnace plus the weight of the ashes
   E. the oxygen entering the furnace plus the weight of the coal

4. Hard coal burns with less smoke than soft coal because hard coal   4.___
   A. is more nearly pure carbon
   B. contains more volatile materials
   C. has a lower kindling temperature
   D. undergoes chemical change more readily
   E. contains more smoke-reducing compounds

5. A metal much used in the construction of permanent magnets is   5.___
   A. brass   B. copper
   C. nickel   D. tin
   E. zinc

6. The frequency of visible light falls between that of   6.____
   A. infrared rays and radio waves
   B. X rays and cosmic rays
   C. ultraviolet rays and X rays
   D. short radio waves and long radio waves
   E. ultraviolet rays and infrared waves

7. In the visible spectrum, yellow is between   7.____
   A. red and orange   B. orange and green
   C. green and blue   D. green and blue
   E. blue and violet

8. The centripetal force that holds the earth in a   8.____
   nearly circular orbit is
   A. the momentum of the earth
   B. the inertia of the earth
   C. the gravitational attraction of the earth and sun
      for each other
   D. the atomic energy of the sun
   E. the electromagnetic attraction of the sun for the
      iron core of the earth

9. A light year is a measure of   9.____
   A. acceleration   B. distance
   C. intensity   D. time
   E. velocity

10. The atmosphere contains about 1%   10.____
    A. argon   B. carbon dioxide
    C. helium   D. hydrogen
    E. krypton

11. Air that has a relative humidity of 50%   11.____
    A. has half as much water vapor as it can hold
    B. is half water vapor and half air
    C. has half its water vapor condensed
    D. has its water vapor half way condensed
    E. has half its water content condensed and half
       evaporated

12. As a mass of air rises   12.____
    A. its temperature increases and its pressure
       increases
    B. its temperature decreases and its pressure
       increases
    C. its temperature decreases and its pressure
       decreases
    D. its temperature increases and its pressure
       decreases
    E. its temperature stays the same and its pressure
       increases

13. The meridian at which the time is 5 hours earlier   13.____
    than the time at Greenwich is
        A. 105° E   B. 105° W
        C. 75° E   D. 75° W
        E. none of these answers

14. Which of the following will absorb *MOST* water per   14.____
    given volume?
        A. gravel   B. humus
        C. quartz   D. sand
        E. sandy loam

15. Coal consists of organic matter which, during   15.____
    geologic ages, was
        A. thoroughly decayed   B. unable to oxidize
        C. thoroughly oxidized   D. preserved unchanged
        E. incompletely calcified

16. The plants of which of the following groups act as   16.____
    hosts to nitrogen-fixing bacteria?
        A. Wheat, oats, rye
        B. Corn, rye, barley
        C. Pumpkins, squash, cucumbers
        D. Beets, carrots, turnips
        E. Clover, alfalfa, soybeans

17. Of the following deciduous trees, the one that loses   17.____
    its leaves *LAST* after a summer's growing season is the
        A. box elder   B. elm
        C. oak   D. poplar
        E. sumac

18. Seedless orange trees are produced by   18.____
        A. planting oranges that contain no seeds
        B. cross-pollination
        C. careful breeding
        D. budding or grafting
        E. planting an orange segment that has no seeds

19. The oxygen absorbed from water by aquatic animals is   19.____
        A. dissolved in the water
        B. produced by the respiration of plants
        C. produced by the respiration of animals
        D. derived by breaking down water into hydrogen
           and oxygen
        E. produced by oxidation of decaying materials

20. Which of the following is the *BEST* definition of   20.____
    photosynthesis? The
      A. action of sunlight on chlorophyl
      B. process by which plants give off oxygen
      C. building of protoplasm by a plant
      D. manufacture of carbohydrate by a green plant
      E. process by which plants use carbon dioxide

21. Muskrats share with beavers the habit of   21. ___
      A. cutting down trees
      B. building dams
      C. building lodges
      D. slapping the water with their tails when alarmed
      E. digging canals

22. The primary source of fish food in a pond is   22.____
      A. one-celled animals   B. one-celled plants
      C. crayfish and snails   D. large water plants
      E. insects falling in or washed in from the land

23. The principal food of our larger hawks is   23.____
      A. calves   B. chickens
      C. game birds   D. small rodents
      E. songbirds

24. The young of houseflies are   24.____
      A. caterpillars   B. cocoons
      C. small flies   D. gnats
      E. maggots

25. Of the following, the animal that is *MOST* dangerous   25.____
    to man in America is the
      A. black bear   B. housefly
      C. mountain lion   D. rattlesnake
      E. black widow spider

26. All of the following diseases are spread by animals   26.____
    EXCEPT
      A. bubonic plague   B. malaria
      C. scarlet fever   D. tularemia
      E. yellow fever

27. All of the following are parasitic diseases   27.____
    EXCEPT
      A. diabetes   B. malaria
      C. tuberculosis   D. typhoid fever
      E. streptococcic sore throat

28. A sharp blow in the front of the abdomen just   28._____
    below the ribs may cause a momentary stoppage of
    breathing because
      A. so much air has been knocked from one's lungs
      B. the secretion of adrenalin has been temporarily ended

13

    C. the portion of the autonomic nervous system
       which is centered in the solar plexus is affected
    D. the aveoli of the lungs have collapsed
    E. the diaphragm muscles are no longer stimulated
       by the cerebrum

29. In the control of disease, it has been found that   29._____
    A. all diseases can be prevented by vaccines or
       serums
    B. all communicable diseases can be cured by
       specific drugs
    C. effective treatment for all diseases is not known
       at the present time
    D. an individual who follows hygienic practices will
       avoid illness.
    E. a low-caloric diet should be given to all who are
       seriously ill

30. Children are **not** being successfully immunized to   30._____
  prevent
    A. chicken pox   B. **measles**
    C. mumps   D. pneumonia
    E. whooping cough

31. A disease that is highly infectious, incurable if not   31._____
  immediately treated and transmissible to unborn children is
    A. cancer   B. measles
    C. syphilis   D. tuberculosis
    E. infantile paralysis

32. The greatest danger from malaria is that it   32._____
    A. produces chills and a high fever
    B. attacks brain cells
    C. causes dysentery
    D. destroys red blood corpuscles
    E. upsets hormone distribution

33. Binocular vision is a type of eye functioning that   33._____
    A. is acquired at birth
    B. results in double vision
    C. is the simultaneous use of both eyes
    D. causes squinting
    E. is the result of discordant movements of the eyes

34. Infantile paralysis often causes immediate damage to   34._____
    A. blood vessels   B. bones
    C. muscles   D. the spinal cord
    E. connective tissues

35. In one type of treatment of hay fever, the patient   35._____
  is given, over a period of a month, increasing doses of

the pollen that causes his allergy. This type of treatment resembles most closely
    A. the injection of antitoxin for curative purposes
    B. the Pasteur treatment for rabies
    C. vaccination against smallpox
    D. the toxoid treatment for tetanus
    E. the use of penicillin

36. When a person is confined to his bed by diphtheria,
    A. everything should be removed from the sickroom
       except the bed, table and chair
    B. a window should be kept open
    C. liquids should be given as the best nourishment
    D. anyone entering the room should wear a gown
       over the regular clothing
    E. the room should be fumigated immediately upon
       recovery

36.____

37. In many states, the health officer should be notified
    when a person has
    A. measles   B. pellagra
    C. mumps   D. scabies
    E. scurvy

37.____

38. Depilatories are used to
    A. relieve pain
    B. overcome constipation
    C. remove hair
    D. check perspiration
    E. remedy skin blemishes

38.____

39. The ultraviolet rays of the sun are especially
    beneficial in
    A. eczema   B. measles
    C. rickets   D. scabies
    E. scurvy

39.____

40. Safe drinking water in small quantities can be
    obtained quickly and economically
    A. from a spring   B. by chlorination
    C. by distillation   D. by filtration
    E. by exposure to the sun

40.____

41. The principal minerals that food should provide for
    building and preserving sound teeth are
    A. iodine and phosphorus
    B. iron and calcium
    C. calcium and phosphorus
    D. magnesium and iron
    E. phosphorus and iron

41.____

42. The enamel of one's permanent teeth is

42.____

A. formed entirely before eruption
B. formed entirely after eruption
C. partially formed before eruption and added constantly after eruption
D. entirely formed before eruption and added as needed to replace damage
E. partially formed before eruption and added at certain periods through one's life

43. The vitamin that affects the clotting of the blood is   43.____
    A. ascorbic acid   B. riboflavin
    C. thiamin   D. vitamin D
    E. vitamin K

44. One function of the liver is the   44.____
    A. secretion of adrenalin
    B. formation of red blood cells
    C. temporary storage of glycogen
    D. digestion and absorption of starches
    E. absorption of fats from the intestinal tract

45. The principal function of red blood cells is to   45.____
    A. destroy disease germs
    B. carry oxygen to cells
    C. act as toxins in the blood stream
    D. cause the blood to coagulate
    E. give the blood a red color

46. The use of iodine in the body is most closely   46.____
    related to the functioning of the
    A. gall bladder   B. kidneys
    C. lymph nodes   D. pancreas
    E. thyroid

47. One function of the projections (villi) of the small   47.____
    intestine is to
    A. produce digestive hormones
    B. aid in the grinding of foods
    C. synchronize the peristaltic action of the intestine
    D. increase the absorptive surface of the intestine
    E. reverse peristaltic action

48. One function of sweat is to   48.____
    A. cleanse the pores   B. lubricate the skin
    C. nourish the hair   D. cool the body
    E. produce perspiration

49. An example of an enzyme is   49.____
    A. adrenalin   B. ptyalin   C. thiamin   D. thyroxine
    E. trichinosis

50. The acid found in our stomachs is _____ acid.   50.____
    A. acetic B. formic C. hydrochloric   D. nitric
    E. sulfuric

_____

KEY (CORRECT ANSWERS)

1.	E	11.	A	21.	C	31.	C	41.	C
2.	C	12.	C	22.	B	32.	D	42.	A
3.	E	13.	D	23.	D	33.	C	43.	E
4.	A	14.	B	24.	E	34.	D	44.	C
5.	C	15.	B	25.	B	35.	B	45.	B
6.	E	16.	E	26.	C	36.	D	46.	E
7.	B	17.	C	27.	A	37.	A	47.	D
8.	C	18.	D	28.	C	38.	C	48.	D
9.	B	19.	A	29.	C	39.	C	49.	B
10.	A	20.	D	30.	D	40.	B	50.	C

————

TEST 3

DIRECTIONS: Each question or incomplete statement is followed by several suggested answers or completions. Select the one that BEST answers the question or completes the statement.

1. Petroleum consists MAINLY of   1. ___
   A. carbon and hydrogen   B. hydrogen and oxygen
   C. oxygen and nitrogen   D. nitrogen and carbon
   E. carbon and oxygen

2. If a strong solution of table salt is poured on the soil   2. ___
   of a potted plant,
   A. much salt will diffuse into the juices of the plant
   B. the plant will be unaffected
   C. minerals dissolved in the plant juices will diffuse
      into the salt solution
   D. the plant will lose water through its roots
   E. root pressure will be increased and the plant will
      become turgid

3. The MAIN function of humus in soil is to   3. ___
   A. keep the soil "sweet"
   B. provide carbon dioxide for photosynthesis in the
      roots
   C. conserve moisture
   D. absorb nitrogen from the air
   E. live symbiotically with the plants

4. Fungi procure their food   4. ___
   A. by photosynthesis
   B. from the air
   C. from materials produced by other organisms
   D. from soil minerals
   E. by combining inorganic materials

5. A grain of wheat is PRIMARILY   5. ___
   A. a fertilized plant egg
   B. an embryo plant plus a food supply
   C. a developed pollen grain
   D. a miniature of the adult plant
   E. a food supply for the unfertilized plant egg

6. An oak tree increases in diameter because of the growth   6. ___
   that takes place
   A. in the bark
   B. just under the bark
   C. in the center of the trunk
   D. uniformly throughout the trunk
   E. in the size of each cell in the tree

7. Grapefruit are so named because they   7. ____
    A. are closely related to a species of tropical grapes
    B. grow in clusters
    C. are mutants of a domestic grape
    D. grow on trees whose leaves are almost indistinguish-
       able from grape leaves
    E. are produced on vines

8. Of the following, the plant that requires two growing   8. ____
seasons to complete its life cycle is the
    A. bean   B. cabbage   C. corn   D. tomato
    E. watermelon

9. The flounder   9. ____
    A. swims in its unique manner from birth
    B. has a symmetrical head
    C. has one eye that migrates to the opposite side of
       its head
    D. is a surface feeder
    E. is the main enemy of the oyster

10. One can drink water from a brook with his head lower than 10. ____
his feet because of the
    A. peristaltic action of the esophagus
    B. capillary action in the throat
    C. difference in pressure between the stomach and the
       atmosphere
    D. pumping action of the diaphragm
    E. valvular action of the larynx

11. Radioactive isotopes have been used in medicine to   11. ____
    A. trace the course of certain compounds through the
       body
    B. cure anema
    C. determine the amount of phosphorus in the body
    D. supplement the bactericidal action of streptomycin
    E. make vaccines for the treatment of cancer

12. The effect of a specific antibody in the blood is to   12. ____
cause
    A. disintegration of white blood corpuscles
    B. destruction of all disease-producing bacteria
    C. disintegration of most bacteria
    D. destruction of specific bacteria
    E. rapid blood-clotting in wounds

13. Expressed in the centigrade scale, the average normal   13. ____
temperature of the human body is
    A. 37°C   B. 55°C   C. 68°C   D. 98°C   E. 212°C

14. The incubation period of a disease is the   14. ____
    A. time required for the bacterium to hatch

19

B. time from infection until the appearance of
   symptoms
C. length of the life cycle of the infecting organism
D. period during which the patient should be confined
   to bed
E. length of exposure necessary to acquire a disease

15. As individual may do much to protect himself against hook-   15. ____
    worm in an infected area by
    A. being vaccinated against hookworm
    B. taking preventive medicine
    C. avoiding all pork
    D. eating only food that has been cooked under pres-
       sure
    E. wearing shoes

16. The iron lung is a device that   16. ____
    A. replaces one lobe of the lungs
    B. blows air into the lungs
    C. raises and lowers the pressure on the outside of the
       body
    D. supplies pure oxygen to invalids
    E. increases peristaltic action

17. Sir Alexander Fleming is BEST known for his work in con-   17. ____
    nection with the
    A. discovery of insulin
    B. development of the iron lung
    C. use of X-rays in the treatment of cancer
    D. prevention of yellow fever
    E. discovery of penicillin

18. Radioactive isotopes produced by atomic energy have al-   18. ____
    ready been used successfully in the
    A. removal of superfluous hair
    B. treatment of certain types of goiter
    C. prevention of tooth decay
    D. treatment of certain forms of mental disease
    E. treatment of water supplies to kill dangerous bacteria

19. When caring for an invalid in the home, one should remem-   19. ____
    ber that
    A. unless a person is ill, the body temperature is always
       98.6°F.
    B. the red arrow point on a clinical thermometer is at
       100°F.
    C. the normal body temperature may vary as much as one and
       one-half degrees during the day
    D. a rectal temperature of 98°F. is considered normal
    E. the body temperature is usually lowest at about 4 p.m.
       and highest at about 3 a.m.

20. Which of the following statements is TRUE?   20. ___
    A. Salivation is a sign that a baby is teething.
    B. After a baby has had an accidental fall, the mother
       should try to put it to sleep as soon as possible.
    C. Breast-fed babies usually have greater immunity to
       contagious diseases than bottle-fed babies have.
    D. Thumb sucking is a sign that a baby is not getting
       enough to eat.
    E. Infant mortality is higher in females than in males.

21. A disease to which a person is USUALLY permanently im-   21. ___
    mune after recovering from an attack is
    A. influenza   B. malaria   C. pneumonia
    D. poliomyelitis   E. syphilis

22. Of the following, the BEST treatment for someone who   22. ___
    looks as if he were about to faint is to
    A. have him sit down in a chair and close his eyes
       for a few minutes
    B. have him hold his arms above his head
    C. have someone take hold of him on either side and
       keep him walking
    D. have him sit down on the floor or ground with his
       head between his knees
    E. slap him vigorously on the back several times

23. Of the following, the BEST first-aid treatment for a   23. ___
    person whose eyes have been exposed to irritating fumes
    is to
    A. flush the eyes with water from a drinking fountain
    B. put powdered boracic acid in the eyes
    C. apply cold towels to the eyes
    D. rub the eyes to stimulate the flow of tears
    E. rush the patient to the nearest physician

24. The MOST serious type of fatigue is induced by   24. ___
    A. emotional strain
    B. mental work
    C. physical activity
    D. sedentary occupations
    E. inadequate sleep over several days

25. The BEST body position in going to sleep has been found   25. ___
    to be
    A. on the abdomen   B. on the left side
    C. on the right side   D. flat on one's back
    E. any way that is comfortable

26. The use of a common towel by two or more persons may re-   26. ___
    sult in the spread of
    A. eczema   B. hives   C. impetigo   D. rickets
    E. shingles

27. Legally prohibiting expectoration in public places helps   27. ___
    prevent
    A. cancer   B. pneumonia   C. scabies   D. tetanus
    E. typhoid fever

28. When in need of a stimulant, one may BEST use   28. ___
    A. brandy   B. hot milk   C. orange juice D. tea
    E. bicarbonate of soda in water

29. Toasted bread is more digestible than untoasted bread be-   29. ___
    cause the toasting process changes a part of the carbohy-
    drate into
    A. dextrin   B. heparin   C. melanin   D. opsonin
    E. palmitin

30. Insufficient calcium in the diet of a child **may** cause   30. ___
    A. bowlegs   B. impaired vision   C. infantile paralysis
    D. wryneck   E. tuberculosis of the bones

31. A generous supply of vitamin C may be included in a day's   31. ___
    diet by using a sufficient quantity of
    A. broiled mackerel   B. stewed prunes
    C. pork chops   D. tomato juice
    E. whole wheat bread or cereals

32. Of the following, the food nutrient that provides energy   32. ___
    in the diet is
    A. cellulose   B. iron   C. protein   D. riboflavin
    E. thiamin

33. Of the foods listed below, the one that will contribute   33. ___
    the GREATEST number of calories to the diet is
    A. one cup of milk
    B. two cups of cabbage
    C. one-half cup of cornstarch pudding
    D. four tablespoonfuls of mayonnaise
    E. two medium-sized white potatoes

34. In case of high price or shortage of meat, other foods   34. ___
    rich in protein may be used. The BEST substitute from
    the following list is
    A. egg plant   B. dark rice   C. spaghetti
    D. string beans E. red kidney beans

35. The BEST of the following lunches for a two-year old   35. ___
    child would be
    A. egg yolk, baked potato, whole wheat toast, chopped
       peas, milk
    B. cream soup, cabbage, graham crackers, custard, milk
    C. meat loaf, cabbage salad, toast, chocolate pudding,
       milk
    D. soft cooked egg, pineapple and raw carrot salad, toast,
       junket, milk

E. creamed corn, toast, weak cocoa, custard

36. Which of the following statements is TRUE?   36. ___
    A. One can become physically ill from ailments that
       are purely imaginary.
    B. A receding chin usually indicates a weak will.
    C. Good and bad personality traits are sometimes in-
       herited.
    D. Believing that a thing is true often makes it true.
    E. A person's intelligence can always be improved
       through education

37. Which of the following would be injured if a baking soda 37. ___
    solution were allowed to stand in it overnight?
    A. An earthenware casserole
    B. An enamel saucepan
    C. A pyrex double boiler
    D. An aluminum saucepan
    E. A stainless steel pressure saucepan

38. The illustration below represents a   38. ___

    A. brad   B. casing nail   C. common nail
    D. cut nail   E. finishing nail

39. A doorbell is USUALLY connected to the household circuit 39. ___
    (A.C.) through a
    A. base plug   B. condenser   C. rectifier
    D. resistor   E. transformer

40. An ordinary automobile storage battery consists of   40. ___
    A. one large dry cell   B. several dry cells
    C. one large wet cell   D. several wet cells
    E. a chemical rectifier

41. The tool illustrated below is used MOST often by   41. ___

    A. an electrician   B. a machinist   C. a printer
    D. a plumber   E. a garage mechanic

42. The term "kiln dried" applies to   42. ___
    A. linseed oil   B. lumber   C. plaster
    D. pottery   E. cold-rolled steel

43. A "stud" in a frame building is a part of the   43. ___
    A. ceiling   B. floor   C. foundation
    D. roof   E. side wall

23

44. The joint shown below is a   44. ___

    A. butt   B. dado   C. dovetail   D. half lap   E. rabbet

45. Which of the following prevents a saw from binding?   45. ___
    A. set   B. sharpness   C. curve of back
    D. number of teeth   E. thickness of blade

46. Two men are pulling on ropes attached to a rock. It is 46. ___
found that their resultant force is less than that used
by either man. It MUST be that the forces are
    A. acting at less than 90° to each other
    B. acting at more than 90° to each other
    C. acting at 90° to each other
    D. both large
    E. both small

47. An observer is moving away from a vibrating object with 47. ___
the speed of sound. The observer will
    A. hear a note an octave higher
    B. hear a note an octave lower
    C. hear the same note but more faintly
    D. hear the same note emphasized
    E. not hear the emitted note

48. The extraction of nitrogenous wastes from the blood is 48. ___
the CHIEF function of the
    A. bladder   B. kidneys   C. large intestine
    D. liver   E. lungs

49. The surface of the earth has been changed the MOST by 49. ___
    A. winds   B. glaciers   C. running water
    D. volcanos   E. chemical action of the atmosphere

50. Molds are to spores as green plants are to   50. ___
    A. flowers   B. leaves   C. roots   D. seeds
    E. stems

KEY (CORRECT ANSWERS)

1.	A	11.	A	21.	D	31.	D	41.	D
2.	D	12.	D	22.	D	32.	C	42.	B
3.	C	13.	A	23.	A	33.	D	43.	E
4.	C	14.	B	24.	A	34.	E	44.	B
5.	B	15.	E	25.	E	35.	A	45.	A
6.	B	16.	C	26.	C	36.	A	46.	B
7.	B	17.	E	27.	B	37.	D	47.	E
8.	B	18.	B	28.	D	38.	C	48.	B
9.	C	19.	C	29.	A	39.	E	49.	C
10.	A	20.	C	30.	A	40.	D	50.	D

TEST 4

DIRECTIONS: Each question or incomplete statement is followed by several suggested answers or completions. Select the one that BEST answers the question or completes the statement.

1. The dinosaur was a prehistoric   1. ___
   A. amphibian   B. arthropod   C. mammal
   D. primate   E. reptile

2. Evidence indicating that great climatic changes have oc-   2. ___
   curred in the past is found in
   A. the appearance of mountains
   B. the delta of the Mississippi
   C. coal deposits in Alaska
   D. lava deposits
   E. the records of the United States Department of Agri-
      culture

3. A structure that helps to keep air pressure in the middle   3. ___
   ear equal to atmospheric pressure is the
   A. eardrum   B. Eustachian tube
   C. Islands of Langerhans   D. nasal passage
   E. semicircular canal

4. One factor NOT necessary for photosynthesis is   4. ___
   A. carbon dioxide   B. chlorophyll
   C. free oxygen   D. sunlight
   E. water

5. Carbon grains are an essential part of a   5. ___
   A. doorbell   B. radio loudspeaker
   C. storage battery   D. transformer
   E. telephone transmitter

6. A container of water is placed on a scale and the scale   6. ___
   reading is 100 pounds. If a block of wood weighing 25 pounds
   is then floated half submerged in the water, the scale will
   read
   A. 75 pounds   B. 87.5 pounds   C. 100 pounds
   D. 112.5 pounds E. 125 pounds

7. Most evidence seems to indicate that the first vertebrate   7. ___
   animal to appear on the earth was the
   A. amphibian   B. bird   C. fish   D. mammal   E. reptile

8. The earth's crust contains about 50% oxygen by weight.   8. ___
   The next MOST abundant element in the earth's crust is
   A. aluminum   B. calcium   C. hydrogen   D. iron
   E. silicon

25

9. A large steel drum containing air at normal atmospheric
   pressure is found to float with 40% of its volume under
   water. When compressed air is forced into the drum until its
   pressure is doubled, the drum will
   A. float at the same level
   B. float higher in the water
   C. float lower in the water
   D. sink to a depth between the surface and the bottom
   E. sink to the bottom
   9. ___

10. When a bacterial cell is submerged in a strong salt solu-
    tion, the cell shrinks because
    A. minerals enter the cell
    B. the cytoplasm within the cell decomposes
    C. the salt dissolves the cell wall
    D. the salt enters the cell
    E. water leaves the cell
    10. ___

11. Mosaic vision is characteristic of
    A. bacteria   B. bees   C. earthworms   D. man   E. robins
    11. ___

12. Ambergris, a substance used to make perfume, comes from
    A. an inflammation in the body of the sperm whale
    B. distilled attar of roses
    C. the hardened resin from pine trees
    D. the musk-producing organs of a deer
    E. the nectar-producing organs of the honeysuckle vine
    12. ___

13. Blood plasma consists CHIEFLY of
    A. amino acids   B. fats   C. glucose   D. water
    E. urea and uric acids
    13. ___

14. Appendicitis is generally accompanied by
    A. daily fluctuation of red cell count
    B. high red cell count
    C. high white cell count
    D. low white cell count
    E. pain in the carotids
    14. ___

15. The dead red corpuscles in the blood stream are removed
    and decomposed by the
    A. heart   B. liver   C. lungs   D. small intestine
    E. white corpuscles
    15. ___

16. Auxins are
    A. growth hormones   B. insect poisons   C. new plastics
    D. new textiles   E. respiratory enzymes
    16. ___

17. On the desert the Arabs are able to keep water cool in
    earthenware jugs because
    A. particles of earthenware dissolve in the water and
       lower its temperature
    17. ___

26

B. the attraction between the molecules of the jug and
   the water is a cooling process
C. the change of some of the water to a vapor lowers
   the temperature
D. the jug is a good conductor of heat
E. the rough surface of the jug radiates heat more
   rapidly

18. An object weighs 10 pounds in air and floats in water with 18. ____
one half of its volume above the surface. The MINIMUM force
that must be added to submerge the object is
   A. 5 pounds B. 10 pounds   C. 20 pounds D. 31.25 pounds
   E. 62.5 pounds

19. A hot stove poker is held near the face. The rays of   19. ____
light chiefly responsible for the sensation felt on the
cheek are those of
   A. blue light   B. infrared light   C. red light
   D. ultraviolet light   E. white light

20. Plastic-coated screen is often used in place of glass in   20. ____
chicken coops and barns because
   A. glass filters out most of the infrared rays of sun-
      light
   B. glass filters out most of the ultraviolet rays of sun-
      light
   C. plastic filters out harmful rays of light
   D. plastic is far safer for the cattle or chickens since
      it will not shatter
   E. plastic transmits more of the rays of visible light

21. When smoke from a locomotive tends to settle to the ground, 21. ____
it may indicate that an area of rainy weather is approach-
ing because
   A. the air is less dense and will not support the smoke
      particles
   B. the air is rising in a low pressure area
   C. the air is sinking near the low pressure area
   D. the smoke is sucked into the low pressure area
   E. there is less oxygen so that the smoke particles are
      not completely burned and are heavier

22. In order to overcome losses during long-distance trans-   22. ____
mission of electrical energy, it is common practice to
   A. decrease both the voltage and the current
   B. decrease the voltage and increase the current
   C. increase both the voltage and the current
   D. increase the voltage and keep the current constant
   E. increase the voltage and decrease the current

23. Oil is poured on water to reduce the height of waves be-   23. ___
cause the
   A. added weight of the oil makes the waves break at a
      lesser height
   B. oil is a lubricant
   C. chemical action between oil and water produces a
      heavier substance
   D. oil fills up the troughs of the waves
   E. surface tension of the water will be weakened

24. The MOST penetrating of the following forms of radiation   24. ___
is
   A. heat   B. infrared light   C. the cosmic ray
   D. the X-ray   E. ultraviolet light

25. A good index of the health of a community is its death   25. ___
rate from
   A. arteriosclerosis   B. diphtheria   C. influenza
   D. meningitis   E. typhoid

26. Fehling's solution is added to a test tube containing a   26. ___
sample of breakfast cereal that has been heated in water.
If the Fehling's solution turns brick red, the breakfast
food PROBABLY contains
   A. animal fat   B. grape sugar   C. protein   D. starch
   E. vitamin C

27. The part of the eye that corresponds to the diaphragm of   27. ___
the camera is the
   A. cornea   B. iris   C. lens   D. pupil   E. retina

28. The pneumothorax treatment is used in cases of   28. ___
   A. cancer   B. heart disease   C. tuberculosis
   D. pneumonia   E. paralysis of the upper thorax

29. In outer space, where there is no atmosphere, a jet-pro-   29. ___
pelled rocket
   A. cannot be stopped
   B. cannot change its direction
   C. will not operate since there is no air against which
      the expelled gases can push
   D. will not operate since there is no air to supply oxy-
      gen for combustion of the fuel
   E. will operate more efficiently because there is no air
      resistance

30. A man has a cup of hot coffee, a teaspoonful of sugar, an   30. ___
ounce of cream. He desires to drink the combination at the
lowest temperature possible at the end of three minutes. He
should add the
   A. cream at once and the sugar in three minutes
   B. cream at once and the sugar slowly throughout the three-
      minute period

28

    C. sugar and cream at the end of three minutes
    D. sugar and cream immediately
    E. sugar at once and the cream slowly throughout the
       three-minute period

31. In one State, the average temperature on August 6 is   31. ___
    USUALLY higher than on June 21. This is BEST explained by
    A. the fact that August 6 is midway between June 21 and
       September 21
    B. the fact that the humidity is higher on August 6
    C. the reason that accounts for 2 p.m. usually being warmer
       than noon
    D. the sun's rays being more vertical on August 6

32. Ordinary photographic film is developed under a ruby-   32. ___
    colored light because the film is
    A. not sensitive to long wave lengths of visible light
    B. not sensitive to short wave lengths of visible light
    C. not sensitive to ultraviolet light
    D. not sensitive to visible light
    E. sensitive to all wave lengths of visible light

33. In a plant the semipermeable membrane which surrounds the 33. ___
    cell is the
    A. cell membrane B. cell wall C. vacuole membrane
    D. nuclear membrane   E. cytoplasmic inclusion

34. Tobacco mosaic is due to   34. ___
    A. a bacterium B. a lack of iron C. too much sun
    D. a virus   E. a lack of magnesium

35. When sheets are washed, bluing is sometimes added to the   35. ___
    water because
    A. a chemical change called bleaching will occur
    B. it destroys most water-borne bacteria
    C. it is a water softener
    D. its color is complementary to yellow
    E. the soap is made less harsh

36. The HIGHEST clouds are   36. ___
    A. alto-cumulus B. cirrus C. cumulus D. nimbus
    E. stratus

37. Acetylcholine is a substance that controls the   37. ___
    A. absorption of vitamins B. action of nerves
    C. digestion of food D. germination of seeds
    E. storage of fat

38. The PRINCIPAL function of the white blood cells is to   38. ___
    A. act as toxins in the blood stream
    B. carry away waste products
    C. carry oxygen to the cells

D. destroy disease germs
E. produce antitoxins

39. There are indications that decay is retarded by treating   39. ___
the teeth of children with a compound of
    A. bromine   B. chlorine   C. fluorine   D. iodine
    E. sulfur

40. Poisons manufactured by bacteria are called   40. ___
    A. molds   B. phagocytes C. septics   D. toxins
    E. viruses

41. Aero-embolism is a body disturbance commonly known as   41. ___
    A. appendicitis   B. bends   C. infantile paralysis
    D. pneumonia   E. sugar diabetes

42. Diabetes is caused by the improper functioning of the   42. ___
    A. adrenals   B. digestive juices C. pancreas
    D. parathyroids   E. thyroid

43. The air we exhale, compared to the air we inhale, con-   43. ___
tains
    A. less carbon dioxide   B. less nitrogen
    C. more nitrogen   D. more oxygen
    E. more water vapor

44. Studies of sleep by psychologists and health specialists   44. ___
indicate that
    A. a tired, stuporous feeling sometimes following a
       profound sleep is attributed to tossing too much
    B. adults reveal considerable individual differences in
       their need of sleep, but infants and pre-school child-
       ren reveal insignificant differences at a given age
    C. best rest is obtained from sleep when the stomach is
       empty
    D. the typically healthy sleeper usually changes from one
       gross bodily position to another between twenty and
       forty-five times during eight hours of sleep
    E. young children show more movements in sleep than older
       children and adults

45. Edward Jenner perfected a method of making people immune   45. ___
to
    A. anthrax   B. bubonic plague   C. diphtheria
    D. smallpox   E. yellow fever

46. A file clerk who has the habit of moistening her finger   46. ___
to facilitate the turning of pages can MOST easily break
the habit by
    A. applying a bitter but harmless substance to her finger
    B. asking a co-worker to remind her when she puts her
       finger to her tongue

C. making a practice of using the eraser of a pencil to turn pages
D. placing a large sign in a conspicuous place on her desk
E. putting a piece of adhesive plaster on her finger as a reminder

47. Ascorbic acid is the scientific name for   47. ___
    A. a narcotic obtained from poppies
    B. a poisonous substance in tobacco
    C. acid in the stomach
    D. digitalis
    E. vitamin C

48. The HIGHEST concentration of oxygen is found in the   48. ___
    A. hepatic vein   B. jugular vein   C. pulmonary artery
    D. pulmonary vein   E. right auricle

49. A workman was injured by a blunt piece of flying steel.   49. ___
    The wound, close to his eye, was dirty and lacerated but
    there was only slight bleeding. In giving first aid, his
    co-worker should
    A. apply a mild tincture of iodine and cover the wound
       with sterile gauze
    B. clean the wound carefully with alcohol and cover with
       sterile gauze
    C. cover the wound with sterile gauze and leave the clean-
       ing to a physician
    D. remove the specks of dirt with a sterile swab before
       covering the wound with sterile gauze
    E. wash the wound carefully with soap and water and cover
       it with sterile gauze

50. Which one of the following statements concerning first   50. ___
    aid is TRUE?
    A. A tourniquet should be loosened every 30 or 40 minutes
       to prevent stoppage of circulation and possible gangrene.
    B. It is essential to wash the hands before applying digital
       pressure to an open wound.
    C. It is useless to continue artificial respiration for more
       than one hour of there is no sign of returning conscious-
       ness.
    D. The pulse of a person suffering from shock is rapid and
       weak.
    E. Whiskey is a good stimulant to give a person bitten by
       a poisonous snake.

KEY (CORRECT ANSWERS)

1.	E	11.	B	21.	A	31.	C	41.	B
2.	C	12.	A	22.	E	32.	A	42.	C
3.	B	13.	D	23.	E	33.	A	43.	E
4.	C	14.	C	24.	C	34.	D	44.	D
5.	E	15.	B	25.	E	35.	D	45.	D
6.	E	16.	A	26.	B	36.	B	46.	C
7.	C	17.	C	27.	B	37.	B	47.	E
8.	E	18.	B	28.	C	38.	D	48.	D
9.	C	19.	B	29.	E	39.	C	49.	C
10.	E	20.	B	30.	C	40.	D	50.	D

TEST 5

DIRECTIONS: Each question or incomplete statement is followed by several suggested answers or completions. Select the one that BEST answers the question or completes the statement. *PRINT THE LETTER OF THE CORRECT ANSWER IN THE SPACE AT THE RIGHT.*

1. Of the following, the BEST source of vitamin E is   1. ___
   A. citrus fruits   B. cod liver oil
   C. halibut liver oil   D. wheat germ oil
   E. milk and milk products

2. Which one of the following may be caused by a plant?   2. ___
   A. amoebic dysentery   B. influenza   C. malaria
   D. ringworm   E. yellow fever

3. Which one of the following parts of the circulatory sys-   3. ___
   tem carries digested fats away from the intestines?
   A. arterial capillaries   B. lacteals
   C. pancreatic duct   D. pulmonary artery
   E. venal capillaries

4. At which one of the following points should digital pres- 4. ___
   sure be applied to stop arterial bleeding in the hand or
   forearm?
   A. brachial   B. carotid   C. femoral   D. subclavian
   E. temporal

5. The hormone that regulates the general metabolism of the   5. ___
   body is
   A. adrenalin   B. gastrin   C. insulin   D. pituitrin
   E. thyroxin

6. The small dipper seems to turn about the North Star once   6. ___
   each day because
   A. all stars move in great circles on the celestial sphere
   B. the earth turns on its axis
   C. the North Star is the last star in the handle of the
      dipper
   D. the planets revolve around the sun
   E. the solar system rotates about a fixed star

7. The component of the atmosphere that shows the GREATEST   7. ___
   percentage of variation is
   A. argon   B. carbon dioxide   C. nitrogen   D. oxygen
   E. water vapor

8. Slate is to shale as marble is to
   A. feldspar   B. gneiss   C. limestone   D. mica schist
   E. sandstone

9. A disease caused by the malfunction of the pancreas is   9. ___
    A. coronary thrombosis   B. diabetes   C. gallstones
    D. rickets   E. tuberculosis

10. Respiration is to carbon dioxide as photosynthesis is to   10. ___
    A. carbon dioxide   B. chlorophyll   C. oxygen
    D. starch   E. sunlight

11. When a machine that is 80% efficient does 1000 foot-   11. ___
    pounds of work, the work input MUST be
    A. 80 foot-pounds   B. 800 foot-pounds
    C. 1000 foot-pounds   D. 1250 foot-pounds
    E. 1800 foot-pounds

12. A siphon is NOT used to empty the water out of the hold   12. ___
    of a ship into the ocean because
    A. a siphon does not create a sufficient vacuum
    B. a siphon will not operate at sea level
    C. salt water is heavier than fresh water
    D. the air pressure is less on the ocean's surface
       than it is in the hold
    E. the hold is beneath the ocean's surface

13. A full moon might be seen   13. ___
    A. faintly at noon
    B. high in the sky at sunset
    C. low in the east in the evening
    D. low in the east in the morning
    E. low in the west at midnight

14. A kerosene lamp burns with a yellow flame due to the   14. ___
    A. burning of hydrogen
    B. complete burning of the hydrocarbons
    C. heating of the wick
    D. incandescence of unburned carbon particles
    E. natural color of any burning kerosene

15. On which one of the following days will a person's sha-   15. ___
    dow be LONGEST at noon in the East?
    A. Christmas   B. Easter Sunday   C. Fourth of July
    D. Labor Day   E. Thanksgiving

16. Perfume is made by dissolving oils containing the essence   16. ___
    of the desired odor in
    A. alcohol   B. banana oil   C. distilled water
    D. glycerin   E. volatile mineral oil

17. Which one of the following is produced naturally by   17. ___
    living things?
    A. aspirin   B. atabrine   C. lysol   D. quinine
    E. sulfanilamide

18. Which one of the following terms is NOT associated with   18. ___
    the others?
    A. beriberi   B. leukemia   C. rickets   D. scurvy
    E. xerophthalmia

19. Like most great caverns, the Howe Caverns of New York State 19. ___
    A. are made of sandstone   B. are the result of glaciation
    C. occur in limestone rock D. were formed by earthquakes
    E. were formed by wind erosion

20. The unrelated member of the following group is   20. ___
    A. cyclotron   B. deuteron   C. electron   D. neutron
    E. positron

21. Fossils are MOST likely to be found in   21. ___
    A. igneous rocks   B. marble quarries
    C. metamorphic rocks   D. ocean deeps
    E. sedimentary rocks

22. The watershed of a river has reference to   22. ___
    A. its delta
    B. its flood plain
    C. the body of water into which the river drains
    D. the land from which water drains into the river
    E. the river and its tributaries

23. An increase of temperature from 10°C. to 30°C. is equi-   23. ___
    valent to an increase of
    A. 11 1/2°F.   B. 36°F.   C. 43 1/2°F.   D. 68°F.
    E. 86°F.

24. The body proper of all insects consists of three parts,   24. ___
    namely, the head, the abdomen and the
    A. antennae   B. legs   C. shell   D. thorax
    E. wings

25. The rate of sugar storage in the liver may be studied by   25. ___
    using radioactive
    A. calcium   B. carbon   C. carbon dioxide   D. iron
    E. nitrogen

26. A water table is   26. ___
    A. a flat rock mass eroded by waves   B. a rain gauge
    C. a river flood stage   D. the sea level
    E. an underground water level

27. We can see only one side of the moon because the period   27. ___
    of the moon's
    A. revolution about the earth equals that of the earth's
       revolution about the sun
    B. rotation is equal to its period of revolution about the
       earth

35

C. rotation is equal to that of the earth's rotation
D. rotation is half that of the earth's rotation
E. rotation is twice that of the earth's rotation

28. The term that includes all others in the following group 2 . ___
is
   A. absorption   B. assimilation   C. circulation
   D. digestion   E. nutrition

29. The unrelated member of the following group is   29. ___
   A. adrenin   B. amylopsin   C. insulin
   D. parathormone   E. thyroxin

30. An object that weighs 500 pounds in air appears to lose   30. ___
   200 pounds when submerged in water to a depth of 10 feet.
   If the object is then lowered to a depth of 20 feet, its
   apparent weight will be
   A. 100 lb.   B. 200 lb.   C. 300 lb.   D. 400 lb.
   E. 500 lb.

31. The color of the sky is blue because   31. ___
   A. blue light is reflected from the Heaviside layer
   B. cosmic rays transmit blue light
   C. dust particles are blue in color
   D. the short wave lengths of visible light are scattered
      most
   E. there is an excess of ultraviolet rays in the strato-
      sphere

32. If you were placed in the middle of a room where the   32. ___
   floor was perfectly frictionless, the BEST method to use in
   betting to a side wall would be to
   A. crawl over
   B. roll over
   C. throw an object horizontally
   D. walk over
   E. wave your arms violently up and down

33. A disease caused by a protozoan is   33. ___
   A. arteriosclerosis   B. endocarditis   C. malaria
   D. poliomyelitis   E. tuberculosis

34. A one-cubic meter, closed, rigid tank contains air and   34. ___
   11 grams of water vapor at a temperature of 20°C. If the
   temperature of the confined air is raised to 35°C., which
   one of the following will result?
   A. The absolute himidity will rise.
   B. The absolute humidity will fall.
   C. The relative humidity will rise.
   D. The relative humidity will fall.
   E. No change will occur in either absolute or relative
      humidity

35. The use of a soda-acid type fire extinguisher is re-   35. ___
commended for putting out fires involving burning
   A. dry chemicals   B. fats or vegetable oils
   C. gasoline   D. painted woodwork
   E. insulation on wires carrying 110-220 volts

36. The alloy, alnico, is widely used in making   36. ___
   A. aluminum utensils   B. cutting tools
   C. permanent magnets   D. springs
   E. thermostats

37. A container is filled to the brim with ice water in   37. ___
which is floating an ice cube with 10 cc. of its volume
above the surface. The specific gravity of ice is about
0.9. After the ice has completely melted,
   A. about one cc. of water will have overflowed
   B. about nine cc. of water will have overflowed
   C. about ten cc. of water will have overflowed
   D. the water level will have dropped
   E. the water level will have remained constant

38. A sextant is an instrument used to determine by a single   38. ___
observation the
   A. direction of true north
   B. elevation of a given place
   C. exact time at a given place
   D. latitude of a given place
   E. longitude of a given place

39. A 5-pound pail containing 25 pounds of water stands on a   39. ___
platform scale. A 4-pound piece of cork with a specific
gravity of 0.25 is floated on the water. Weights are then
placed on the piece of cork until it floats flush with the
surface of the water. The platform scale now reads
   A. 30 lb.   B. 34 lb.   C. 37 lb.   D. 46 lb.   E. 50 lb.

40. The north pole of a magnet attracted one end of a freely   40. ___
swinging bar of metal marked *A*. This shows that the bar is
   A. made of a magnetic material
   B. made of iron
   C. made of iron with a south pole at *A*
   D. magnetized with a north pole at *A*
   E. unmagnetized

41. The corn plant produces its pollen and ovules   41. ___
   A. at the same node
   B. in different rows
   C. on different plants
   D. on different flowering structures
   E. on the same flowering structure

42. Which one of the following prehistoric men appeared the   42. ___
LATEST chronologically?
   A. Cro-Magnon   B. Java C. Neanderthal D. Peking E. Piltdown

43. Tissues are to cells as organs are to   43. ___
   A. blood   B. human beings   C. organisms   D. tissues
   E. vessels

44. The number of people who die each year from cancer is in- 44. ___
   creasing because
   A. communicable diseases are better controlled and more
      people live longer
   B. it is a communicable disease
   C. it is an inherited disease
   D. malignant tumors are more prevalent than benign or
      harmless tumors
   E. medical science knows less about the disease than
      about any other disease

45. At noon on shipboard, a chronometer reads 10:00 p.m.,   45. ___
   Greenwich time. The longitude of the ship is
   A. 10° east   B. 150° east   C. 10° west   D. 100° west
   E. 150° west

46. In the East, hailstorms are MOST likely to occur in   46. ___
   A. fall   B. late winter   C. midwinter   D. summer
   E. very early spring

47. An unused electric refrigerator was placed in a room   47. ___
   which was surrounded with a perfect heat insulator. The
   refrigerator was put into opeation by connecting it to an
   external electrical circuit and at the same time its door
   was left open. During the first hour the temperature of
   the room would
   A. fall continuously
   B. fall somewhat and remain at this temperature
   C. fall somewhat and then return to its original tempera-
      ture
   D. remain constant
   E. rise

48. The *Rh* factor is of importance in the study of   48. ___
   A. fingerprinting   B. the acidity of a solution
   C. the blood   D. the determination of sex
   E. the resistance to infection

49. Which one of the following is the GREATEST advantage of 49. ___
   growing up in a large family?
   A. Each member may be able to borrow articles from other
      members.
   B. Each member may be easily provided with recreation with-
      in his family circle.
   C. Each member may be required to give and receive financial
      support.
   D. Each member may have a chance to make adjustments to him-
      self and to other people early in life.
   E. Each member may have fewer responsibilities.

38

50. Small arteries branch to form a network of capillaries.   50. ___
    In turn, the capillaries unite to form
       A. alveoles   B. arteries   C. auricles   D. veins
       E. ventricles

KEY (CORRECT ANSWERS)

1.	D	11.	D	21.	E	31.	D	41.	D
2.	D	12.	E	22.	D	32.	C	42.	A
3.	B	13.	C	23.	B	33.	C	43.	D
4.	A	14.	D	24.	D	34.	D	44.	A
5.	E	15.	A	25.	B	35.	D	45.	E
6.	B	16.	A	26.	E	36.	C	46.	D
7.	E	17.	D	27.	B	37.	E	47.	E
8.	C	18.	B	28.	E	38.	D	48.	C
9.	B	19.	C	29.	B	39.	D	49.	D
10.	C	20.	A	30.	C	40.	A	50.	D

ANSWER SHEET

TEST NO. _____ PART _____ TITLE OF POSITION _____
                                                                    (AS GIVEN IN EXAMINATION ANNOUNCEMENT - INCLUDE OPTION, IF ANY)

PLACE OF EXAMINATION _____ DATE_____
                           (CITY OR TOWN)   (STATE)

RATING

USE THE SPECIAL PENCIL.   MAKE GLOSSY BLACK MARKS.

Make only ONE mark for each answer.   Additional and stray marks may be counted as mistakes.   In making corrections, erase errors COMPLETELY.

EXAMINATION SECTION

DIRECTIONS: Each question or incomplete statement is followed by
several suggested answers or completions. Select the
one that BEST answers the question or completes the
statement. *PRINT THE LETTER OF THE CORRECT ANSWER IN
THE SPACE AT THE RIGHT.*

1. Rain is MOST directly associated with which one of the   1.____
    following cloud types?
        A. Cirrus   B. Cumulus   C. Stratus   D. Nimbus

2. Two samples of air MUST have the same dew point if they   2.____
    have the same
        A. relative humidity   B. absolute humidity
        C. lapse rate   D. capacity

3. In the continental United States of America, wind pressure   3.____
    systems USUALLY move
        A. westward and more rapidly in winter than in summer
        B. eastward and more rapidly in winter than in summer
        C. eastward at the same number of miles per day in
           winter as in summer
        D. northeast at 400 miles per day

4. Winds in low pressure systems in continental United States   4.____
    of America blow in which one of the following directions?
        A. Clockwise and outward
        B. Counterclockwise toward the center
        C. Counterclockwise and outward
        D. Clockwise and toward the center

5. Assuming proper temperatures, which one of the following   5.____
    crops grows BEST in clay soil?
        A. Wheat   B. Peanuts   C. Tobacco   D. Cotton

6. The name given to a violent circular windstorm of small   6.____
    area is which one of the following?
        A. Chinook   B. Tornado   C. Cyclone   D. Anticyclone

7. Which one of the following expressions includes the   7.____
    three others?
        A. Monsoons   B. Southeast trades
        C. Terrestrial winds   D. Prevailing northwesterlies

8. Highest tides occur soon after the time of which one of   8.____
    the following?
        A. New moon   B. First quarter moon
        C. Last quarter moon   D. None of the above

9. If the tide is lowest at 3 P.M., it will be HIGHEST   9.____
    thereafter at approximately
        A. 3 A.M.   B. 6 P.M.   C. 9 P.M.   D. 12 P.M.

10. The GREATEST ocean depths are found in the _____ Ocean.   10.
    A. Atlantic   B. Pacific   C. Indian   D. Antarctic

11. Which one of the following elements is commercially   11.
    extracted in large quantity from ocean water?
    A. Radium   B. Gold   C. Magnesium   D. Zinc

12. Large-scale ocean currents are caused by   12.
    A. erosion   B. winds
    C. boat traffic   D. tidal waves

13. Coney Island is an example of which one of the following? 13.
    A(n)
    A. barrier beach   B. atoll
    C. levee   D. spit

14. The leeward side of mountains on an island is   14.
    A. windy   B. dry   C. moist   D. cold

15. The actual mass of water vapor per cubic foot of air is   15.
    called
    A. relative humidity   B. absolute humidity
    C. dew point   D. water equivalent

16. Relative humidity is measured by which one of the follow- 16.
    ing?
    A. An anemometer
    B. Dew point apparatus
    C. Wet and dry bulb thermometer
    D. Maximum and minimum thermometer

17. At 68°F, the relative humidity BEST for human comfort is 17.
    about
    A. 20%   B. 35%   C. 50%   D. 80%

18. The horse latitudes are CORRECTLY defined as   18.
    A. regions of abundant rainfall
    B. belts of high pressure between the trade wind belts
       and the westerlies
    C. belts of light winds, calms, and high temperature at
       the equator
    D. wind belts between the westerlies and polar easterlies

19. The irregular line on the map in the doldrum belt passing 19.
    through places with the HIGHEST temperatures is called
    A. an isotherm   B. the heat equator
    C. a temperature gradient   D. an insolation line

20. Of the following, the type of cloud associated with very 20.
    high altitude is
    A. altostratus   B. cirrus
    C. altocumulus   D. cumulonimbus

21. Up to an elevation of 3 to 4 miles at the poles and 10 to   21.___
    11 miles at the equator, the lapse rate indicates that
    the temperature of stationary air
        A. *decreases* at the average rate of 3½ degrees Fahrenheit
           for each 1000 ft. elevation
        B. *decreases* 3 degrees Fahrenheit for each 100 feet of
           elevation
        C. *decreases* 10 degrees Fahrenheit for each 1000 feet
           of elevation
        D. *increases* uniformly 3½ degrees Fahrenheit for each
           1000 feet of elevation

22. Generally speaking, MOST of the world's volcanoes   22.___
        A. lie in belts which are almost identical with the two
           great earthquake belts
        B. are roughly at right angles to the earthquake belts
        C. are in the equatorial regions
        D. form no particular geographic pattern

23. The point in the bedrock at which an earthquake seems to   23.___
    center is known as its
        A. anticline B. epicenter C. focus   D. fault

24. Of the following groups, the one which contains only   24.___
    metamorphic rocks is
        A. basalt, diorite, dolomite, shale
        B. conglomerate, granite, serpentine, marble
        C. diabase, schist, obsidian, serpentine
        D. quartzite, gneiss, slate, marble

25. Diastrophism refers to which one of the following?   25.___
    The
        A. rising and sinking of the earth's surface
        B. formation of geysers
        C. erosion caused by wind
        D. movement of clouds

26. The fraction of the solid part of the earth that lies   26.___
    beneath water and ice is
        A. 1/3   B. ½   C. 3/4   D. 5/6

27. The surface of the solid part of the earth consists   27.___
    essentially of huge blocks of rock which sometimes break
    away and rise or sink.
    This action is called
        A. volcanic action   B. folding
        C. faulting   D. weathering

28. Of the following groups of materials found in the earth's   28.___
    crust, the group in which the items range progressively
    from softest to hardest is
        A. talc, fluorite, quartz, diamond
        B. feldspar, gypsum, topaz, corundum
        C. gypsum, quartz, apatite, diamond
        D. calcite, quartz, diamond, corundum

29. Which one of the following groups contains the four MOST abundant elements in the earth's crust?
    A. Oxygen, nitrogen, hydrogen, iron
    B. Nitrogen, iron, sodium, oxygen
    C. Potassium, silicon, aluminum, iron
    D. Oxygen, silicon, aluminum, iron

30. All but one of the following statements about artesian wells are true.
    The EXCEPTION is:
    A. Artesian well water is usually much colder than ordinary well water.
    B. The water in artesian wells is drawn from aquifers below an impervious layer.
    C. Artesian well water is usually harder than ordinary well water.
    D. The source of the water supply in an artesian well may be hundreds of miles from the well.

31. When oil spouts from a well as a gusher, it USUALLY does so because
    A. of the pressure of water beneath the oil or of gas above the oil
    B. air is pumped into the well
    C. of the release of great heat
    D. of the tremendous pressure of subsurface rock layers on the oil

32. The new volcano which was formed in Mexico in 1943 is named
    A. Popocatepetl   B. Mauna Loa
    C. Paricutin   D. Krakatoa

33. A narrow v-shaped valley is considered by geologists to be
    A. young   B. old
    C. mature   D. between mature and old

34. As compared with a valley made by a stream, a glacial valley is
    A. rounded and smooth   B. irregular and rough
    C. irregular and smooth D. rounded and rough

35. The branch of geology dealing with the origin of land forms is called
    A. geomorphology   B. geopolitics
    C. geomology   D. geotology

36. The farthest south in what is now the continental United States of America that the last glacier reached was
    A. Maine   B. New York   C. Kentucky   D. Alabama

37. Of the following mountain ranges, the one estimated to be the YOUNGEST is the
    A. Alps   B. Rockies
    C. Adirondacks   D. Himalayas

5

38. About 100,000,000 years ago, North America   38.___
   A. had approximately the same form as today except that
      a land bridge connected Alaska and Siberia
   B. was connected by land to Asia, South America, and
      Europe
   C. was divided into two parts by a great inland sea
   D. was connected by a land bridge to Africa

39. Of the following epochs, the one which is NOT associated   39.___
    with the Mesozoic Era is the
   A. Cretaceous   B. Jurassic
   C. Triassic   D. Permian

40. The Moh Scale measures the   40.___
   A. acidity of the soil
   B. hardness of rocks
   C. bacterial content of the soil
   D. proportion of nitrogen to potash

41. A line on a weather map indicating that warm air has been 41.___
    lifted from the earth's surface by the action of opposing
    wedges of cold air is called a(n) _____ front.
   A. cold   B. warm   C. occluded   D. stationary

42. Points of equal pressure on weather maps are connected by 42.___
    lines called
   A. isotherms B. isobars   C. isotopes   D. millibars

43. When contour lines on a topographical map are wide apart, 43.___
    it means that the area between the contour lines repre-
    sents a(n)
   A. extensive lake   B. steep rise
   C. comparatively level area D. desert

44. On a U.S. Geological Survey topographical map, the point 44.___
    at which contour lines meet represents a
   A. valley   B. hill   C. cliff   D. plain

45. The instrument among those named below which is used to 45.___
    determine latitude is the
   A. barometer   B. chronometer
   C. sextant   D. anemometer

46. The condition of *nine months of winter and three months* 46.___
    of bad weather in eastern Newfoundland is caused CHIEFLY
    by the
   A. Gulf Stream   B. Brazil Current
   C. Labrador Current   D. Sargasso Sea

47. The COMMONEST cause of hard water is the presence of 47.___
    compounds of
   A. fluorine B. calcium   C. iron   D. sulfur

48. All of the following metals are extracted from the minerals with which they are associated below EXCEPT
    A. iron from hematite
    B. uranium from pitchblende
    C. tin from sphalerite
    D. lead from galena

49. Iron pyrites, sometimes known as fool's gold, is mined CHIEFLY for use in the manufacture of
    A. costume jewelry
    B. sulfuric acid
    C. porcelain and china
    D. paint

50. Of the following acids, the one MOST often used to test for calcite is cold dilute _____ acid.
    A. hydrochloric
    B. carbonic
    C. sulfuric
    D. nitric

51. The destructive distillation of soft coal produces
    A. coal gas, bitumen, water gas, and tar
    B. ammonia, coal gas, water gas, and coke
    C. coal tar, coal gas, ammonia, and coke
    D. coal tar, coke, ammonia, and charcoal

52. If a chemist uses air displacement in a mouth-downward container for the laboratory collection of a gas, the gas is PROBABLY _____ in water and _____ than air.
    A. insoluble; heavier
    B. insoluble; lighter
    C. soluble; heavier
    D. soluble; lighter

53. To make hydrogen as a classroom demonstration, the USUAL procedure is to use hydrochloric acid and
    A. Zn
    B. Cu
    C. Hg
    D. Ag

54. The spontaneous disintegration of thorium is known as
    A. radioactivity
    B. fission
    C. fusion
    D. half-life

55. The nuclear particle with mass 1 and with unit positive charge is the
    A. meson
    B. positron
    C. alpha particle
    D. proton

56. The valence of calcium in $Ca_3(PO_4)_2$ is
    A. 1
    B. 2
    C. 5
    D. 6

57. The MOST active of the halogens is
    A. iodine
    B. fluorine
    C. chlorine
    D. bromine

58. Calcium oxide always contains 40 units by weight of calcium to 16 units by weight of oxygen. This illustrates the law of
    A. mass action
    B. multiple proportions
    C. constant composition
    D. combining proportions

59. Which one of the following is a balanced equation?   59.___

    A. $HgO \rightarrow Hg + O_2$ B. $Zn + Cl_2 \rightarrow 2ZnCl_2$

    C. $Mg + H_2SO_4 \rightarrow H_2 + MgSO_4$ D. $FeCl_3 + KOH \rightarrow Fe(OH)_3 + KCl$

60. Which one of the following is a balanced equation?   60.___

    A. $Ca(OH)_2 + Na_2CO_3 \rightarrow CaCO_3 + 2NaOH$

    B. $PbCl_2 + H_2S \rightarrow PbS + HCl$

    C. $BaCl_2 + Na_2SO_4 \rightarrow 2BaSO_4 + NaCl$

    D. $CO + Fe_2O_3 \rightarrow CO_2 + 2Fe$

61. In the reaction between $NaOH$ and H_2SO_4,   61.___
    A. the Na^+ is reduced   B. the $SO_4^=$ gains electrons
    C. the $SO_4^=$ loses electrons   D. none of the above

62. Corn oil is changed to margarine by   62.___
    A. hydrogenation   B. hydrolysis
    C. dehydration   D. hydration

63. Which one of the following compounds does NOT contain an   63.___
element common to the others?
    A. Potassium chlorate   B. Grain alcohol
    C. Hydrogen fluoride   D. Sulfurous acid

64. A noncombustible solvent for grease, the vapor of which   64.___
solvent is poisonous, is
    A. H_2O B. CCl_4 C. $NaOH$ D. C_2H_5OH

65. Which one of the following alloys contains copper?   65.___
    A. Solder   B. Sterling silver
    C. Gold amalgam   D. Stainless steel

66. A safety device in a common hydrogen generator is a   66.___
    A. pan   B. delivery tube
    C. thistle tube   D. pneumatic trough

67. Of the following scientists, the one who developed a   67.___
useful pictorial representation of the atom is
    A. Bohr   B. DeBroglie
    C. Heisenberg   D. Schrodinger

68. Which one of the following procedures is used to speed up   68.___
the reaction between iron and hydrochloric acid?
    A. Exposing the reagents to bright light
    B. Keeping the reagents cool
    C. Heating the reagents
    D. Filtering the hydrochloric acid

69. Which one of the following is an example of double replacement?

    A. $C + CO_2 \rightarrow 2CO$

    B. $KOH + HCl \rightarrow HOH + KCl$

    C. $2AgNO_3 + Cu \rightarrow Cu(NO_3)_2 + 2Ag$

    D. $SO_2 + \frac{1}{2}O_2 \rightarrow SO_3$

70. The action of aqua regia on metals converts them to
    A. nitrates   B. sulfates   C. chlorides   D. sulfides

71. When a hot saturated solution of copper sulfate cools,
    A. copper will separate
    B. nothing will happen
    C. a white solid forms
    D. blue crystals are produced

72. Given the atomic weight of aluminum as 27 and the atomic weight of chlorine as 35.5, the molecular weight of aluminum chloride is
    A. 62.5   B. 98
    C. 133.5   D. none of the above

73. The molecular weight of sucrose, $C_{12}H_{22}O_{11}$, (Atomic weights: C = 12, H = 1, O = 16), is
    A. 1   B. 45   C. 159   D. 342

74. The percent of carbon dioxide in the air is CLOSEST to which one of the following?
    A. 1%   B. .03%   C. 20%   D. 78%

75. When the molecular equation showing the reaction between Al and HCl is balanced, the coefficient before the HCl is
    A. 1 understood   B. 2
    C. 4   D. 6

76. Moore and Ross recently ascended to a height of 80,000 ft. and discovered
    A. cosmic ray bombardment from space
    B. the nature of the rings of Saturn
    C. water vapor in the atmosphere of Venus
    D. new values for the space unit, Mach

77. A reaction that goes to completion is illustrated by
    A. $KCl + I_2 \rightarrow$ B. $CuSO_4 + HCl \rightarrow$
    C. $Na_2SO_3 + H_2O \rightarrow$ D. $NaHCO_3 + H_2SO_4 \rightarrow$

78. Metallic sodium and chlorine are products of the electrolysis of which one of the following?
    A. Brine
    B. Sodium hypochlorite solution
    C. Sodium chlorate solution
    D. Molten sodium chloride

79. From 54 grams of water, one can extract how many grams of hydrogen?
    A. 1   B. 2   C. 6   D. 16   79.___

80. Which one of the following is a laboratory source of SO_2? 80.___
    A. Na_2SO_3 B. Na_2SO_4 C. Na_2S D. $NaHSO_4$

81. Which one of the following substances is used in transistors? 81.___
    A. Radium   B. Uranium   C. Germanium   D. Thorium

82. The gram molecular weight of water is 82.___
    A. 1   B. 2   C. 3   D. 18

83. Ammonia is produced by the _____ process. 83.___
    A. Solvay   B. Frasch   C. Haber   D. Flotation

84. Which one of the following substances may be used to test for proteins? 84.___
    A. $Ca(OH)_2$ B. HNO_3 C. $CuSO_4$ D. $Al(NO_3)_2$

85. The LIGHTEST of the following types of sodium particles is a(n) 85.___
    A. atom   B. molecule   C. crystal   D. ion

86. At standard pressure, 83 grams of an undissociated solute, dissolved in a 1000g. of water, elevates the boiling point 1.04°C.
    The gram-molecular weight of the solute is 86.___
    A. 41.5   B. 83   C. 86.32   D. 166

87. A science teacher wishes to demonstrate chemical change by the reaction between Fe and S, atomic weights 56 and 32, respectively.
    The weight of sulfur which should be reacted with 2 grams of iron is CLOSEST to which one of the following? 87.___
    A. 0.5   B. 1.5   C. 3   D. 4

88. Of the following raw materials, the one MOST important in the chemical industry is 88.___
    A. NaCl   B. H_2SO_4 C. $NaHCO_3$ D. Na_2CO_3

89. Water is MOST readily decomposed by which one of the following? 89.___
    A. Iron   B. Potassium   C. Magnesium   D. Calcium

90. The INCORRECT pair of items in the following couplets of compound and commercial use is 90.___
    A. $CHCl_3$ solvent   B. $COCl_2$ water purification
    C. $CaOCl_2$ bleaching   D. NaCl manufacture of HCl

91. Of the following, an example of a fully oxidized non-combustible substance is 91.___
    A. C_3H_8 B. CCl_4 C. CH_3Cl D. C_2H_5OH

92. Which one of the following is the formula for a hydro-   92.
carbon?
   A. $C_6H_{10}O_5$ B. $CHCl_3$ C. C_3H_8 D. $A_2C_2O_4$

93. The E.M.F. required to maintain an electrolysis   93.
   A. is independent of the products
   B. is the same for all ionic substances in equal con-
      centration
   C. is related to the decomposition potential
   D. depends upon the source of the E.M.F.

94. The Minuteman guided missile is different from the Atlas   94.
and the Titan that preceded it in that the Minuteman
   A. is a tactical weapon of limited range
   B. is jet powered
   C. requires high altitude launching
   D. is powered by solid fuel

95. If a gram-molecular volume of an unknown gas weighs 320   95.
grams, its relative molecular weight is
   A. 10   B. 20   C. 160   D. 320

96. When a splint which has been burning in a bottle of air   96.
goes out, the residue gas contains
   A. no oxygen   B. only carbon dioxide
   C. some oxygen   D. only nitrogen

97. In the United States, a research program recently   97.
developed extremely lightweight thermoelectric generators
using
   A. boiling heavy water reactors
   B. principles of steam regeneration
   C. thermocouples
   D. high energy linear accelerators

98. The reaction between nitrogen and hydrogen is promoted by   98.
the addition of pressure to the system.
This is BEST explained by _____ Law.
   A. LeChatelier's   B. Dumas'
   C. Dalton's   D. Charles'

99. In the Laue method of determination of crystal structure,   99.
the crystal is bombarded with
   A. neutrons   B. protons
   C. x-rays   D. alpha particles

100. The percentage composition of an oxide of iron is   100.
approximately 72.4 for iron and 27.6 for oxygen.
Given atomic weights Fe = 56 and O = 16, the formula
for the compound is
   A. FeO   B. Fe_2O_3 C. Fe_3O_4 D. $Fe_2O_3 \cdot Fe_3O_4$

101. Differentiation in structure to adapt to special function   101.___
     is illustrated by
     A. jaw and teeth of sharks
     B. beaks of birds
     C. tooth structure of mammals
     D. all of the above

102. Which one of the following terms includes all the others?   102.___
     A. Organ   B. Organism   C. Cell   D. Tissue

103. The cell membrane is permeable to all of the following   103.___
     EXCEPT
     A. sugar   B. starch   C. oxygen   D. salt

104. Sugar solution is distributed in a plant through which   104.___
     one of the following?
     A. Bast fibers   B. Xylem
     C. Sieve tubes   D. Wood ducts

105. Which one of the following processes stores energy?   105.___
     A. Assimilation   B. Respiration
     C. Metabolism   D. Photosynthesis

106. Which of the following is a factor CHIEFLY responsible   106.___
     for the rise of sap in trees during the summer?
     A. Root pressure   B. Transpiration
     C. Adhesion   D. Diffusion

107. Leguminous plants, such as vetch, are planted MAINLY to   107.___
     achieve which one of the following?
     A. Bind the soil   B. Conserve soil water
     C. Add soil nitrates   D. Prevent soil erosion

108. The gametophyte generation is the dominant one in MOST   108.___
     A. bryophytes   B. ferns
     C. grasses   D. flowering plants

109. The mapping of chromosomes has been made possible LARGELY   109.___
     through careful study of
     A. Mendel's Laws
     B. crossover percentage between linked genes
     C. ploidy
     D. mutation

110. The crucial point in animal mitosis is the division of the 110.___
     A. cell into two parts
     B. chromosomes so that each daughter cell receives a
        full set of chromosomes
     C. cytoplasm so that each daughter cell receives an
        equal amount
     D. centriole into two equal parts

111. In the development of the animal embryo, the sequence is   111.___
     fertilization,
     A. cleavage, blastula, invagination, gastrula
     B. blastula; cleavage, gastrule, invagination

C. gastrula, cleavage, invagination, blastula
D. cleavage, invagination, blastula, gastrula

112. Chordate embryos, in their development, follow a regular   112.
pattern in which distinctions among
    A. classes appear first
    B. orders appear first
    C. species appear first
    D. different chordates are not discernible

113. Among the following, the structure LEAST closely related   113.
to the others is
    A. flipper of porpoise   B. fin of shark
    C. wing of bird   D. wing of bat

114. Joshua Lederburg received a Nobel Prize for his work in   114.
    A. bacterial genetics   B. virus transmutation
    C. origin of virus   D. bacteriophage

115. The MOST important function accomplished by meiosis is   115.
the
    A. formation of a variety of haploid gametes
    B. splitting of chromosomes into two equal parts
    C. formation of polar bodies
    D. formation of identical gametes

116. An omnivorous food habit would MOST likely be associated   116
with which one of the following?
    A. Relatively unspecialized tooth structure
    B. Well-developed incisors
    C. Well-developed canines
    D. Well-developed molars

117. The energy yield of food is measured by   117
    A. a thermometer   B. a thermocouple
    C. calorimeter   D. B.T.U.'s

118. The PRINCIPAL nutrient constituent of the human body, by   118
weight, is
    A. minerals   B. fat   C. protein   D. water

119. The ULTIMATE source of food in the sea is   119
    A. plankton   B. shell fish
    C. marine worms   D. small teleosts

120. Which one of the following is NOT a protein?   120
    A. Gluten   B. Hemoglobin
    C. Chlorophyll   D. Glycogen

121. Food is moved through the alimentary canal CHIEFLY by   121
    A. muscular spasms   B. peristalsis
    C. sphincter muscles   D. voluntary muscles

122. Which one of the following is NOT a product of digestion?   122
    A. Glycogen   B. Fatty acids
    C. Amino acids   D. Glucose

123. All of the following enzymes help to digest carbohydrates 123.____
EXCEPT
    A. amylase   B. lipase   C. maltase   D. ptyalin

124. Basal metabolism is   124.____
    A. metabolic rate for minimal activity
    B. average metabolic rate
    C. metabolic rate for normal activity
    D. metabolic rate of a newborn infant

125. Each of the following is at least in part an endocrine 125.____
gland EXCEPT the
    A. pancreas   B. ovary   C. pituitary   D. liver

126. Each of the following is necessary for normal blood 126.____
function EXCEPT
    A. alpha-naphtha quinone   B. alphatocopherol
    C. folic acid   D. vitamin B_{12}

127. Red corpuscles are formed in   127.____
    A. bone marrow   B. lymph node
    C. liver   D. blood

128. Lacteals are   128.____
    A. milk glands   B. lymph capillaries
    C. lymph glands   D. blood capillaries

129. Blood does NOT distribute oxygen in which one of the 129.____
following?
    A. Frog   B. Grasshopper
    C. Whale   D. Starfish

130. The MOST effective of the following methods of increasing 130.____
the respiratory rate is to _____ in the inspired air.
    A. *increase* the amount of oxygen
    B. *decrease* the amount of oxygen
    C. *increase* the amount of carbon dioxide
    D. *decrease* the amount of carbon dioxide

131. Membranous walls, rich blood supply, and large surface 131.____
area are characteristic of the
    A. kidney   B. lung
    C. small intestine   D. all of the above

132. Of the following statements about the process known as 132.____
photosynthesis, the one which is INCORRECT is:
    A. Nitrogen is a by-product of the process.
    B. Chlorophyll and sunlight are necessary for it to take
       place.
    C. It takes place most rapidly in temperatures from
       80-90°F..
    D. A carbohydrate is the end result of the process.

133. The COMMONEST type of non-nucleated cell in the human body is the _____ cell. 133.
    A. red blood   B. white blood
    C. epithelial   D. nerve

134. The energy for muscular contraction results from the breakdown of 134
    A. ATP   B. ACTH   C. DNA   D. PAS

135. In animals, the problem of providing a fluid medium in which the sperm may reach the egg is solved by 135
    A. liberating both eggs and sperm in water with subsequent external fertilization and development
    B. liberating sperm in water with subsequent external fertilization and development
    C. liberating sperm directly into the body of the female with subsequent internal fertilization and development
    D. all of the above

136. The act of restoring a lost part by growing a new one is called 136
    A. asexual reproduction   B. regeneration
    C. growth   D. parthenogenesis

137. In the binomial system of nomenclature, each living thing is named by 137
    A. class and species   B. class and order
    C. order and family   D. genus and species

138. Chordates are characterized by 138
    A. notochord and dorsal hollow nerve cord
    B. notochord and ventral nerve cord
    C. bilateral symmetry and four-chambered heart
    D. bilateral symmetry and three-chambered heart

139. The classic experiment on spontaneous generation was performed by 139
    A. Aristotle B. Hooke   C. Brown   D. Redi

140. *Study nature, not books* was the advice of 140
    A. Linnaeus   B. Darwin
    C. Agassiz   D. Leeuwenhoek

141. Which one of the following items includes the others? 141
    A. Visual purple   B. Rods and cones
    C. Fovea   D. Retina

142. Functional damage to the brain may be studied by the use of which one of the following? 142
    A. X-rays   B. Electrocardiograph
    C. Electroencephalograph   D. Radioisotopes

143. Which one of the following organs is NOT concerned with the elimination of metabolic waste from the human body?
    A. Lungs   B. Kidneys   C. Skin   D. Spleen

143.____

144. Which one of the following is used as a test for acid ions?
    A. Eosine   B. Brom thymol blue
    C. Indophenol   D. Hyposulphite of soda

144.____

145. Penicillin was discovered by
    A. Florey   B. Ehrlich   C. Fleming   D. Waksman

145.____

146. Which one of the following animals is used in making Salk vaccine?
    A. Chick embryos   B. Rabbits
    C. Monkeys   D. Horses

146.____

147. It is generally believed that a sore throat which has been diagnosed as diphtheria should be immediately treated with
    A. toxoid   B. toxin-antitoxin
    C. streptomycin   D. antitoxin

147.____

148. Which one of the following is the MOST important recent development in the war on polio?
    A. Large scale testing of an orally administered vaccine containing live polio virus
    B. Large scale testing of an orally administered vaccine containing dead polio virus
    C. Injection of a vaccine containing live polio virus
    D. Injection of a vaccine containing dead polio virus

148.____

149. An important indicator of the degree of cumulative action of radioactive fall-out is the measurement of the amount of
    A. iodine 131 in thyroid tissue
    B. strontium 90 in bone tissue
    C. carbon 14 in epithelial tissue
    D. phosphorus 30 in tooth enamel

149.____

150. Which one of the following has been saved from extinction by conservation measures?
    A. Passenger pigeon   B. Egret
    C. Heath hen   D. Labrador duck

150.____

151. Pressure in a gas is explained by which one of the following?
    A. The kinetic theory of gases
    B. The Brownian movement
    C. Mariotte's contribution to Boyle's Law
    D. Charles' Law

151.____

152. What horizontal force is required to pull a 10 lb. loaded   152.
wooden box on a level glass plate when the coefficient of
sliding friction between glass and wood is 0.15?
_____ lb.(s).
A. 1.5   B. 6.67   C. 9.85   D. 15

153. The absolute unit of force required to accelerate one   153.
pound of mass at the rate of one foot per second is the
A. dyne   B. momentum   C. poundal   D. slug

154. The E.M.F. generated in a conductor when it is moved   154.
across magnetic lines of force depends upon
A. strength of the field   B. length of the conductor
C. speed of the conductor   D. all of the above

155. A ten pound ball is swung around on the end of a 5 ft.   155.
nylon cord.
If the velocity of the ball is 20 feet per second, what
is the centrifugal force in pounds?
_____ lb(s).
A. 1   B. 1.32   C. 25   D. 200

156. The period of a pendulum is independent of which one of   156.
the following?
A. Length of the pendulum
B. Arc through which the pendulum swings
C. Acceleration due to gravity
D. Material and mass of the pendulum

157. Where MUST the object be placed in front of a spherical   157.
concave mirror in order that the image be magnified?
A. At the principal focus
B. Beyond the center of curvature
C. At the center of curvature
D. Between the principal focus and the mirror

158. Spherical aberration in a camera lens can be reduced to   158.
a MINIMUM by using a
A. color filter   B. Polaroid filter
C. small diaphragm opening   D. large diaphragm opening

159. Chromatic aberration is USUALLY corrected by   159.
A. a double concave lens
B. a Polaroid lens
C. a color filter
D. cementing a converging lens into a compound lens

160. Astigmatism may be corrected by a _____ lens.   160.
A. bifocal   B. spherical
C. cylindrical   D. compound

161. The primary colors of light are   161.
A. red, blue, and green
B. magenta, blue-green, and yellow
C. red, blue, and yellow
D. red, orange, yellow, green, blue, and violet

162. When white light is passed through a prism, the color of light that is bent the MOST is 162.____
    A. red   B. yellow   C. green   D. violet

163. Two colors of light which together produce white light are called 163.____
    A. primary light colors   B. complementary colors
    C. additives   D. neutrals

164. The spectrum of the sun is BEST called a _____ spectrum. 164.____
    A. continuous   B. bright line
    C. absorption   D. Frauhofer

165. When white light is passed through a prism, the lights of different colors are separated because of 165.____
    A. interference   B. scattering
    C. dispersion   D. polarization

166. The quantum theory of light was proposed by 166.____
    A. Einstein   B. Newton   C. Planck   D. Huyghens

167. In an A.C. series circuit, the resistance is 40 ohms, inductive reactance is 50 ohms, the capacitative reactance is 20 ohms. 167.____
What is the TOTAL impedance?
    _____ ohms.
    A. 50   B. 70   C. 75   D. 110

168. Three resistances of 20, 30, and 60 ohms are connected in parallel to a 120 volt source. 168.____
The TOTAL resistance of the group is _____ ohms.
    A. 10   B. 110   C. 36.7   D. 40

169. The voltage across a lamp is 10 volts. The current is 2 amperes. 169.____
What is the resistance in ohms?
    _____ ohms.
    A. 0.2   B. 2.5   C. 5   D. 20

170. The maximum voltage in an A.C. circuit is 140 volts. The effective voltage is CLOSEST to which one of the following? 170.____
    _____ volts.
    A. 70   B. 98.98   C. 93.33   D. 110

171. Of the following statements, the one that is NOT true is that, in general, 171.____
    A. dense gases are better transmitters of sound waves than rare gases
    B. liquids are better transmitters of sound waves than solids
    C. liquids are better transmitters of sound waves than gases
    D. solids are better transmitters of sound waves than gases

172. Of the following statements, the one which is TRUE is: 172.
     Sound
     A. is the result of electrons passing through a magnetic
        field
     B. is the result of atomic vibrations within the molecule
     C. results when a string is vibrated in a vacuum
     D. results from a series of forward and backward move-
        ments of molecules of air

173. Which one of the following statements is TRUE?   173.
     The _____ loudspeaker.
     A. tweeter is a high frequency
     B. woofer is a treble
     C. tweeter is a bass
     D. woofer is a high frequency

174. The ratio between the friction experienced by an airplane   174.
     moving at 600 miles per hour and that experienced by an
     airplane moving 300 miles per hour, other things being
     equal, is
     A. 1:1   B. 2:1   C. 3:1   D. 4:1

175. In long distance transmission of electrical power, the   175
     line losses are reduced by
     A. high amperage and low voltage
     B. low amperage and high voltage
     C. high towers
     D. high amperage and high voltage

176. Television broadcasting uses   176
     A. ultra high frequency waves, a channel width of 6
        megacycles, and transmits an audio, video, and
        synchronizing signal
     B. high frequency waves, a channel width of 4.5 mega-
        cycles and two transmitters
     C. radio waves, a channel width of 6 megacycles and AM
        and FM signal transmission
     D. ultra high frequency waves, a channel width of 4.5
        megacycles, and transmits an audio and video signal

177. In a television receiver, the kinescope is ESSENTIALLY   177
     a(n)
     A. cathode ray oscilloscope   B. image orthicon
     C. iconoscope   D. photo cathode

178. The color TV system adopted by the Federal Communications   178
     Commission operates with
     A. 525 line interlaced scanning and picture frequency
        of 30 cycles per second
     B. 262½ line scanning and picture frequency of 60 cycles
        per second
     C. 525 line scanning and picture frequency of 60 cycles
        per second
     D. 265½ line scanning and picture frequency of 30 cycles
        per second

179. The operation of rocket engines is possible because of   179.____
     the law of
     A. conservation of energy   B. conservation of momentum
     C. gravity   D. Corolis force

180. The *escape velocity* for the earth is CLOSEST to which one 180.____
     of the following?
     A. Seven miles a minute   B. 5,000 miles per hour
     C. 25,000 miles per hour   D. 186,000 miles per hour

181. Isotopes are elements of   181.____
     A. same atomic number but different atomic weights
     B. same atomic weight but different atomic number
     C. same number of planetary electrons and the same
        atomic weight
     D. different number of planetary electrons and different
        numbers of neutrons in their nuclei

182. Radioactive elements, such as radium and uranium, are   182.____
     spontaneously disintegrating and emitting particles
     including
     A. helium nuclei, electrons, and x-rays
     B. helium ions, neutrons, and deuterons
     C. helium nuclei, electrons, and positrons
     D. electrons, x-rays, and photons

183. The amount of energy lost per mass unit particle when   183.____
     the protons and neutrons are packed together in the
     nucleus of an atom is called
     A. nuclear energy   B. the packing factor
     C. the energy level   D. thermonuclear energy

184. When a liquid expands as it freezes, the solid formed   184.____
     will, if kept in the original liquid at the freezing
     temperature,
     A. float   B. melt   C. dissolve   D. sink

185. The electrical unit which equals 6.25×10^{18} electrons   185.____
     is called the
     A. ampere   B. volt   C. coulomb   D. farad

186. The torque exerted on a bar magnet of pole strength m   186.____
     and length l, placed perpendicularly to a magnetic field
     of intensity H, is

     A. $\dfrac{Hm}{l^2}$ B. Hml   C. $\dfrac{H + m}{l^2}$ D. $\dfrac{\sqrt{H^2+m^2}}{l^2}$

187. Of the following, the BEST approximation for the angle   187.____
     of magnetic declination in New York City is
     A. 12°W   B. 12°E   C. 75°W   D. 43°N

188. An induced current in a coil has such a direction that it produces a magnetic field which opposes the motion of the magnetic field by which the current is produced.
This is known as
   A. Lenz's Law
   B. Oersted's Discovery
   C. Faraday's Law
   D. D'Arsonval's Principle

188.

189. The compound microscope was invented by
   A. Van Leeuwenhoek
   B. Huyghens
   C. Newton
   D. Galileo

189.

190. The density of water is
   A. maximum at 4°C
   B. maximum at 0°C
   C. maximum at -4°C
   D. independent of the temperature

190.

191. The fuel mixture is ALWAYS ignited by the heat of compression in the _____ engine.
   A. two-stroke gasoline
   B. multiple cylindered gasoline
   C. diesel
   D. gas turbine

191.

192. The operating frequency of a broadcasting station whose assigned wavelength is 250 meters is
   A. 12,000 cycles
   B. 1200 kilocycles
   C. 12,000,000 cycles
   D. 12 megacycles

192.

193. The BEST radiator of heat is a _____ surface.
   A. rough, black
   B. smooth, black
   C. rough, silvered
   D. smooth, silvered

193.

194. In a deep lake, the water at the bottom of the lake rarely falls below what Centigrade temperature?
   A. 0   B. 4   C. 32   D. 100

194

195. The temperature of water boiling in a pressure cooker in New York City is MOST likely to be closest to
   A. 100°C   B. 98.6°C   C. 80°C   D. 110°C

195

196. The specific heat of iron is 0.11.
The number of calories required to raise the temperature of 10 grams of iron from 20°C to 30°C is
   A. 10
   B. 11
   C. 110
   D. none of the above

196

197. Of the following, the metals which make an alloy used for very strong permanent magnets is
   A. iron, nickel, and sulfur
   B. tempered steel and silicon
   C. carefully purified iron and molybdenum
   D. cobalt, aluminum, and nickel

197

198. On a map of terrestrial magnetism, the line joining all points where a compass needle points true north is called the   198.____
    A. aclinic   B. isoclinic   C. isogonic   D. agonic

199. If both ends of a piece of steel strongly repel the south pole of a compass, we may conclude that   199.____
    A. the steel bar is not a magnet
    B. each of the two ends is a south pole
    C. the steel bar is paramagnetic
    D. the phenomenon is caused by magnetic induction

200. If a magnetic pole of 10 emu is repelled with a force of 8 dynes by a second magnetic pole 5 cm. away, the strength of the second magnetic pole is ____ emu.   200.____
    A. 20   B. 30   C. 40   D. 190

KEY (CORRECT ANSWERS)

1.	D	41.	C	81.	C	121.	B	161.	A
2.	B	42.	B	82.	D	122.	A	162.	D
3.	B	43.	C	83.	C	123.	B	163.	B
4.	B	44.	C	84.	B	124.	A	164.	C
5.	D	45.	C	85.	D	125.	D	165.	C
6.	B	46.	C	86.	A	126.	B	166.	C
7.	C	47.	B	87.	B	127.	A	167.	A
8.	A	48.	C	88.	A	128.	B	168.	A
9.	C	49.	B	89.	B	129.	B	169.	C
10.	B	50.	A	90.	B	130.	C	170.	B
11.	C	51.	C	91.	B	131.	D	171.	B
12.	B	52.	D	92.	C	132.	A	172.	D
13.	A	53.	A	93.	C	133.	A	173.	A
14.	B	54.	A	94.	D	134.	A	174.	D
15.	B	55.	D	95.	D	135.	D	175.	B
16.	C	56.	B	96.	C	136.	B	176.	A
17.	C	57.	B	97.	C	137.	D	177.	A
18.	B	58.	C	98.	A	138.	A	178.	A
19.	B	59.	C	99.	C	139.	D	179.	B
20.	B	60.	A	100.	C	140.	C	180.	C
21.	A	61.	D	101.	D	141.	D	181.	A
22.	A	62.	A	102.	B	142.	C	182.	A
23.	C	63.	C	103.	B	143.	D	183.	B
24.	D	64.	B	104.	C	144.	B	184.	A
25.	A	65.	B	105.	D	145.	C	185.	C
26.	C	66.	C	106.	B	146.	C	186.	B
27.	C	67.	A	107.	C	147.	D	187.	A
28.	A	68.	C	108.	A	148.	A	188.	A
29.	D	69.	B	109.	B	149.	B	189.	D
30.	A	70.	C	110.	B	150.	B	190.	A
31.	A	71.	D	111.	A	151.	A	191.	C
32.	C	72.	C	112.	A	152.	A	192.	B
33.	A	73.	D	113.	B	153.	C	193.	A
34.	A	74.	B	114.	A	154.	D	194.	B
35.	A	75.	D	115.	D	155.	C	195.	D
36.	C	76.	C	116.	A	156.	D	196.	B
37.	B	77.	D	117.	C	157.	D	197.	D
38.	C	78.	D	118.	D	158.	C	198.	D
39.	D	79.	C	119.	A	159.	D	199.	B
40.	B	80.	A	120.	D	160.	C	200.	A

EXAMINATION SECTION

DIRECTIONS: Each question or incomplete statement is followed by
several suggested answers or completions. Select the
one that BEST answers the question or completes the
statement. *PRINT THE LETTER OF THE CORRECT ANSWER IN
THE SPACE AT THE RIGHT.*

1. Respiration in plants occurs   1.___
   A. only on cloudy days   B. only in the night
   C. only in the daytime   D. all the time

2. The complex chemical ATP is necessary to produce   2.___
   A. fats   B. sugars
   C. proteins   D. amino acids

3. A medicine obtained from the bark of the cinchona tree is   3.___
   A. atabrine   B. pentaquine
   C. chloroquine   D. quinine

4. A radioactive element used to study photosynthesis in   4.___
   green plants is
   A. I^{131} B. C^{14} C. N^{16} D. U^{233}

5. The selectivity of a cell depends upon the   5.___
   A. cell membrane   B. nucleus
   C. cytoplasm   D. mitochondria

6. The zoologist who helped formulate the cell theory was   6.___
   A. Schleiden B. Hooke   C. Purkinje   D. Schwann

7. The brown spots on the back of fern fronds produce   7.___
   A. pollen   B. spores   C. scales   D. seeds

8. Plants without true roots, stems, or leaves are called   8.___
   A. bryophytes   B. spermatophytes
   C. thallophytes   D. pteridophytes

9. Of the following, the CLOSEST biological relative of the   9.___
   whale is the
   A. shark   B. toad   C. crocodile   D. horse

10. The process LEAST likely to result in vitamin loss is   10.___
    A. bleaching celery   B. refining flour
    C. quick freezing fruits   D. peeling vegetables

11. A trait determined by two identical alleles is said to be 11.___
    A. homologous   B. analogous
    C. heterozygous   D. homozygous

12. The nutrient that produces the LARGEST number of calories 12.___
    per gram of weight is
    A. protein   B. starch   C. carbohydrate D. fat

13. A method used to condition the soil by spreading straw, manure, or peat moss over it is
A. fallowing B. terracing C. leaching D. mulching

13.___

14. The plant that acts as an alternate host for the wheat rust is
A. gooseberry
B. white pine
C. red cedar
D. barberry

14.___

15. In the process of respiration in a plant,
A. potential energy is stored
B. chlorophyll is necessary
C. stored food is utilized
D. protein is synthesized

15.___

16. The insect that feeds on the cottony cushion scale is the
A. Ladybird bettle
B. Boll weevil
C. Tachina fly
D. Hessian fly

16.___

17. Food made in the leaves moves to all parts of a green plant through the
A. stomates B. phloem C. pith D. xylem

17.___

18. Deamination of proteins occurs MAINLY in the
A. small intestine
B. liver
C. spleen
D. pancreas

18.___

19. The chemical that plays a part in the passage of nerve impulses across the space between two connecting neurons is
A. auxin
B. colchicine
C. reserpine
D. acetylcholine

19.___

20. The gathering of white blood cells around bacteria is an example of
A. thigmotropism
B. chemotropism
C. geotropism
D. hydrotropism

20.___

21. The Islets of Langerhans are located in the
A. testis B. pancreas C. pituitary D. thyroid

21.___

22. The adrenal cortex is stimulated to secrete cortisone by
A. ATP B. ACTH C. 2, 4-D D. PAS

22.___

23. Liquid wastes are carried from the kidneys to the urinary bladder by the
A. ureters
B. urethras
C. oviducts
D. Fallopian tubes

23.___

24. The part of the brain that controls the breathing rate is the
A. medulla
B. cerebrum
C. cerebellum
D. hypothalamus

24.___

3

25. The chemicals that cause clumping of the erythrocytes in
    the blood are
    A. platelets   B. red corpuscles
    C. white corpuscles   D. plasma

26. An organism with an *open circuit* system of circulation is
    the
    A. frog   B. earthworm   C. crayfish   D. fish

27. The heart chamber that pumps blood to the aorta is the
    A. right auricle   B. right ventricle
    C. left auricle   D. left ventricle

28. The substances that are absorbed into the lacteals of the
    villi are
    A. amino acids   B. vitamins
    C. simple sugars   D. fatty acids

29. A chemical that has been used with great success in the
    treatment of tuberculosis is
    A. isoniazid   B. chloromycetin
    C. sulfanilamide   D. radioactive phosphorus

30. Ringworm disease is caused by a
    A. lichen   B. roundworm
    C. segmented worm   D. fungus

31. The organism that causes typhus fever is a(n)
    A. fungus   B. Rickettsia C. bacterium D. virus

32. Emotional behavior is controlled in the
    A. hypothalamus   B. cerebrum
    C. cerebellum   D. medulla

33. In a given sample of blood, clumping occurred with both
    A serum and B serum.
    The blood type was
    A. A   B. B   C. O   D. AB

34. Of the following vitamins, the one that does NOT aid in
    cellular oxidation is
    A. thiamin   B. niacin
    C. ascorbic acid   D. riboflavin

35. The cyton of a motor neuron is found in the
    A. posterior root ganglion
    B. anterior root ganglion
    C. gray matter of the spinal cord
    D. white matter of the spinal cord

36. An instrument that records the electrical impulses
    developed in the brain is the
    A. kymograph   B. electrocardiograph
    C. polygraph   D. electroencephalograph

3

37. The relationship between clover plants and nitrogen-fixing bacteria is a form of
    A. parasitism   B. saprophytism
    C. commensalism   D. symbiosis

38. The number of pairs of cranial nerves in man is
    A. 12   B. 31   C. 48   D. 206

39. Water pollination occurs in the
    A. water lily   B. corn
    C. spruce   D. duckweed

40. A vegetative structure that consists of an underground stem surrounded by storage leaves is a
    A. slip   B. rhizome   C. bulb   D. tuber

41. If a planarium is cut in half, each part will grow eventually into a complete organism.
    This process of forming a new organism is called
    A. conjugation   B. parthenogenesis
    C. meiosis   D. regeneration

42. Passive immunity GENERALLY lasts a
    A. few weeks   B. few months
    C. few years   D. lifetime

43. Septic tanks are used in waste disposal to
    A. break down solid wastes   B. dilute sewage
    C. aerate sewage   D. filter sewage

44. The development of the polio vaccine was made possible, in part, by the discovery that the polio viruses could be cultured in test tubes on one of the following organs of Old World monkeys:
    A. Liver   B. Thyroid gland
    C. Kidney   D. Lung

45. The scientist who discovered streptomycin was
    A. Enders   B. Fleming   C. Florey   D. Waksman

46. A sex-linked disease in man is
    A. leukemia   B. anemia
    C. hemophilia   D. erythroblastosis fetalis

47. Destruction of the red blood cells of a developing embryo may occur when the embryo is Rh _____ and the mother is Rh _____.
    A. positive; positive   B. positive; negative
    C. negative; negative   D. negative; positive

48. The scientist who FIRST used the word mutation to describe changes that he found in the evening primrose plant was
    A. Morgan   B. Muller   C. DeVries   D. Mendel

49. The study of the functioning of living organisms is called   49.____
    A. anatomy   B. pathology   C. ecology   D. physiology

50. The fact that a white guinea pig resulted from a cross   50.____
    between two hybrid black guinea pigs illustrates the law
    of
    A. segregation   B. dominance
    C. linkage   D. independent assortment

51. When a blue Andalusian rooster is crossed with a blue   51.____
    Andalusian hen, the phenotypic ratio expected among the
    offspring will be
    A. 100% blue
    B. 50% black and 50% white
    C. 75% black and 25% white
    D. 25% white, 25% black, 50% blue

52. A vitamin that contains cobalt as part of its chemical   52.____
    structure is vitamin
    A. A   B. B_2 C. B_{12} D. C

53. The two-layered cup stage that forms during cleavage is   53.____
    called the
    A. morula   B. gastrula   C. blastula   D. mesoderm

54. The one term that includes all the others is   54.____
    A. equational division   B. gamete
    C. maturation   D. reduction division

55. Organizers are chemicals that influence   55.____
    A. differentiation   B. mitosis
    C. fertilization   D. maturation

56. The developing embryo of a mammal is protected by a   56.____
    liquid-filled sac called the
    A. placenta   B. amnion   C. uterus   D. allantois

57. The seedless orange is propagated by   57.____
    A. self-pollination   B. cross-pollination
    C. hybridization   D. grafting

58. One similarity between reflexes and habits is that they   58.____
    are BOTH
    A. inborn acts   B. autonomic acts
    C. learned acts   D. automatic

59. The MOST ancient of the following prehistoric men is   59.____
    A. Heidelberg   B. Neanderthal
    C. Pithecantropus   D. Cro-Magnon

60. The theory of *Use and Disuse* was developed by   60.____
    A. Weismann   B. Darwin   C. Wallace   D. Lamarck

61. The micturating membrane in man is an example of a(n)   61.
    A. mutation   B. vestigial structure
    C. malformation   D. embryonic structure

62. The LATEST of the geological eras is called the   62.
    A. cenozoic   B. paleozoic
    C. proterozoic   D. mesozoic

63. Liquids are transported through stems and roots by the   63.
    A. epidermis   B. cortex
    C. vascular bundles   D. pith

64. An animal that is PROBABLY a link between the fish and   64.
    amphibia is the
    A. archeopteryx   B. coelacanth
    C. trilobite   D. lamprey

65. The hormone that stimulates the change of glycogen to   65.
    glucose in the liver is
    A. insulin   B. progestin   C. cortin   D. adrenin

66. The haploid chromosome number in the fruit fly, Drosophila, 66.
    is
    A. 4   B. 8   C. 24   D. 48

67. The plant in which seed dispersal by animals occurs is the 67.
    A. cherry   B. coconut
    C. witch hazel   D. milkweed

68. Blood tissue differentiates from the primary germ layer   68.
    known as the
    A. endoderm   B. endosperm   C. mesoderm   D. ectoderm

69. Of the following types of tissue, the one which is NOT   69.
    classified as connective tissue is
    A. blood   B. bone   C. cartilage   D. tendon

70. A chrysalis is a   70.
    A. pupa case   B. nymph   C. larva   D. cocoon

71. The one term that includes all the others is ____ plant.   71.
    A. herbaceous   B. flowering
    C. spermatophyte   D. annual

72. Nitrogen from the air is made available to plants by   72.
    A. decay   B. fixation
    C. denitrification   D. nitrate bacteria

73. The series of muscular waves of contraction in the   73.
    alimentary canal is called
    A. pylorus   B. peristalsis
    C. symbiosis   D. parthenogenesis

74. The corals belong to the phylum
    A. Mollusca   B. Porifera
    C. Arthropoda   D. Coelenterata
     74.____

75. Three of the following substances are narcotics.
    The one that is NOT is
    A. chlorpromazine   B. nicotine
    C. morphine   D. cocaine
     75.____

76. Hydrogen sulfide is USUALLY prepared in the laboratory
    by the action of
    A. hydrogen on hot sulfur
    B. hydrochloric acid on ferrous sulfide
    C. acid on sulfite
    D. sulfuric acid on copper
     76.____

77. An unknown gas dissolves readily in water. The water
    solution turns red litmus blue. The gas reacts with
    hydrogen chloride gas, forming white fumes.
    The unknown gas is PROBABLY
    A. nitric oxide   B. ammonia
    C. sulfur dioxide   D. hydrogen sulfide
     77.____

78. Of the following, the one whose water solution will be
    basic in reaction is 0.1 molar
    A. HCl   B. $NaC_2H_3O_2$ C. NaCl   D. $HC_2H_3O_2$
     78.____

79. An apple green flame test indicates the presence of
    A. chromium   B. sodium   C. strontium   D. barium
     79.____

80. In the balanced chemical equation for the reaction
    between copper and dilute nitric acid, the coefficient
    before the nitric acid is
    A. 1   B. 3   C. 4   D. 8
     80.____

81. The molecular weight of sodium hydroxide is 40.
    To prepare 100 cc. of a 0.1 N solution would require a
    weight of sodium hydroxide, in grams, of
    A. 0.4   B. 2   C. 4   D. 400
     81.____

82. Concentrated solutions of potassium hydroxide should be
    stored in bottles with stoppers made of
    A. glass   B. rubber   C. cork   D. aluminum
     82.____

83. White phosphorus should be stored under
    A. carbon disulfide   B. carbon tetrachloride
    C. oil   D. water
     83.____

84. It is dangerous to add concentrated sulfuric acid to
    A. calcium sulfate   B. sodium bisulfate
    C. potassium permanganate   D. clay
     84.____

85. You should instruct students to carry concentrated
    sulfuric acid
    A. very carefully   B. in a covered metal can
    C. under no circumstances   D. in a cart
     85.____

86. The formula for chloroform is   86.
    A. CH_2Cl_2 B. $CHCl_3$ C. CH_3Cl D. $C_2H_4Cl_2$

87. *Wood* alcohol is the common name for   87.
    A. ethyl alcohol   B. propyl alcohol
    C. glycerol   D. methyl alcohol

88. The FIRST thing to do if concentrated acid comes into   88.
contact with the skin is to
    A. wash with ammonia
    B. call a doctor
    C. pour sodium hydroxide over it
    D. wash with cold water for a long time

89. Hydrofluoric acid is GENERALLY stored in   89.
    A. polyethylene bottles   B. glass bottles
    C. copper jars   D. platinum bottles

90. A liter is APPROXIMATELY equivalent to a(n)   90.
    A. quart   B. pint   C. gallon   D. gill

91. The FIRST scientist to effect a nuclear reaction was   91.
    A. Rutherford   B. J.J. Thomson
    C. Chadwick   D. Fermi

92. The chemical behavior of the atom is LARGELY determined   92.
by the
    A. atomic weight
    B. number of neutrons
    C. kind of charge in the nucleus
    D. electrons

93. Radioactive substances   93.
    A. easily lose their orbital electrons
    B. have unstable nuclei
    C. gain electrons easily
    D. lack mesons

94. In the reaction $_7N^{15} + _1H^2 \rightarrow X + _1H^1$, X is   94.

    A. $_9F^{17}$ B. $_8O^{15}$ C. $_6C^{14}$ D. $_7N^{16}$

95. In the reaction $C + O_2 \rightarrow CO_2$, the weight of CO_2, in grams,   95.
produced by burning 100 grams of carbon with 100 grams of
oxygen is about (At. Wgts.: C = 12, O = 16)
    A. 100   B. 137   C. 150   D. 200

96. When sodium combines with chlorine, the sodium is   96.
    A. oxidized and the chlorine is reduced
    B. reduced and the chlorine is oxidized
    C. oxidized and the chlorine remains unchanged
    D. unchanged while the chlorine is oxidized

97. An electric spark is passed through a mixture containing 3.2 grams of oxygen gas and 0.6 grams of hydrogen gas. After the explosion and subsequent cooling to room temperature, there are in the container
    A. 3.2 grams of water and 0.6 grams of hydrogen
    B. 3.6 grams of water and 0.2 grams of hydrogen
    C. 3.8 grams of water and 0 grams of hydrogen
    D. 0.9 grams of water and 2.9 grams of oxygen

97.____

98. The columns of the modern periodic table contain elements which resemble each other in
    A. the number of neutrons B. valence
    C. density D. appearance

98.____

99. Carbon forms a large number of compounds because
    A. of the ability of carbon atoms to form covalent linkages with each other
    B. of its small ionic radius
    C. it forms triple bonds
    D. it is very active

99.____

100. The SIMPLEST way to recover silver from a solution of one of its compounds is to
    A. distill the solution B. use the thermit process
    C. add powdered zinc D. decompose the solution

100.____

101. In a chemical reaction, the valence of the element arsenic was changed from +5 to 0. All of the following statements are true EXCEPT the one stating that arsenic
    A. oxidized something else B. was reduced
    C. gained electrons D. lost protons

101.____

102. The neutralization of a base by an acid ALWAYS produces
    A. soluble products B. water
    C. gas D. sodium chloride

102.____

103. The pH of an acid solution could be
    A. 5 B. 7 C. 9 D. 13

103.____

104. The CORRECT formula of the hydronium ion is
    A. OH^- B. H_3O^+ C. H_4O^+ D. H^+

104.____

105. When $CaCO_3$ reacts with CHl, the products are
    A. CaO, H_2O and CO_2 B. $CaCl_2$, H_2O and CO_2
    C. $CaOCl$, H_2O and CO_2 D. $CaCl_2$, Cl_2, CO_2 and H_2O

105.____

106. A solution of a non-volatile solute in water
    A. boils at 100°C
    B. freezes below 0°C
    C. has a higher vapor pressure than water at the same temperature
    D. always has a volume equal to the combined volumes of solute and solvent

106.____

107. An unknown gas has a density of 1.5 grams per liter under   107.___
     standard conditions.
     Its molecular weight is about
       A. 33.6   B. 22.4   C. 11.2   D. 67.2

108. Of the following sequences, the one that CORRECTLY   108.___
     represents the non-metals in the order of their increasing
     activity as non-metals is
       A. F, Cl, Br, I   B. F, I, Cl, Br
       C. I, Cl, Br, F   D. I, Br, Cl, F

109. Carbon will NOT reduce the oxide of   109.___
       A. sodium   B. iron   C. zinc   D. copper

110. The valence of the metal in the compound $Ca_3(PO_4)_2$ is   110.___
     plus
       A. 1   B. 2   C. 3   D. 6

111. Covalent bonds are MOST commonly found in   111.___
       A. salts   B. bases
       C. inorganic solids   D. organic compounds

112. Al_2O_3 and CBr_4 are the correct formulae of the oxide of   112.___
     aluminum and the bromide of carbon.
     The formula of the compound aluminum carbide is
       A. AlC   B. Al_4C_3 C. Al_3C_4 D. Al_4C_2

113. A chalk and salt mixture could be separated into its   113.___
     components by
       A. subliming the salt out of the mixture
       B. adding water and distilling
       C. adding water, boiling, and filtering
       D. adding water, boiling, and cooling

114. The electrolysis of brine is used commercially to produce   114.___
     all of the following substances EXCEPT
       A. sodium hydroxide   B. hydrogen
       C. chlorine   D. sodium chloride

115. In the Hall process, cryolite is used as a   115.___
       A. source of aluminum   B. solvent
       C. source of fluorine   D. solute

116. All of the following are present in pig iron as   116.___
     impurities EXCEPT
       A. silicon   B. phosphorus   C. molybdenum D. sulfur

117. The compound MOST generally found in petroleum is   117.___
       A. $CHCl_3$ B. C_8H_{18} C. CH_5N D. $C_7H_{15}OH$

118. When a non-metallic oxide such as N_2O_5 is dissolved in   118.___
     water,
       A. the solution is acidic
       B. the solution is basic
       C. the solution may be either acidic or basic
       D. no chemical change occurs

11

119. In developing a photographic plate,
    A. sodium thiosulfate is used as a reducing agent
    B. it is left in the developer until all of the silver bromide has been developed
    C. no visible change takes place
    D. the exposed plate is reduced most rapidly where most light has been absorbed
     119.____

120. The plastic lucite is a polymer of
    A. methyl methacrylate   B. styrene
    C. butadiene   D. acrylonitrile
     120.____

121. MOST animal fats are classed as
    A. alcohols B. esters C. aldehydes D. acids
     121.____

122. Hydrogen should be prepared in the classroom by combining
    A. sodium and hydrochloric acid
    B. zinc and sulfuric acid
    C. potassium chlorate and hydrochloric acid
    D. iron oxide and steam
     122.____

123. The formula for baking soda is
    A. Na_2CO_3 B. NaOH C. $NaHCO_3$ D. Na_2SO_4
     123.____

124. The chemist GENERALLY credited with discovering deuterium is
    A. Hall   B. Urey
    C. Fermi   D. Oppenheimer
     124.____

125. Thermit mixture is composed of
    A. magnesium and iron oxide
    B. iron and aluminum oxide
    C. aluminum and iron oxide
    D. magnesium and barium peroxide
     125.____

126. The statement, *It is easier to raise a load with pulleys,* means that for the given load, there is a reduction in the required
    A. force B. work C. distance D. power
     126.____

127. If, when three forces are applied to a body, the body is at rest, the resultant of these forces is
    A. the weight of the object
    B. more than the largest force
    C. zero
    D. the equilibrant of the object
     127.____

128. Reducing friction has no effect on the
    A. actual mechanical advantage
    B. efficiency
    C. ideal mechanical advantage
    D. work input
     128.____

129. Machines can multiply   129.
    A. work   B. energy   C. force   D. efficiency

130. Weights of 3 lb. and 7 lb. hang from a bar which is   130.
    supported by a spring scale.
    Neglecting the weight of the bar, the weight, in pounds,
    registered by the scale is
    A. 2.5   B. 4   C. 10   D. 21

131. A body starts from rest and falls freely for four seconds. 131.
    The distance, in feet, the body will fall (neglecting air
    resistance) is
    A. 64   B. 96   C. 256   D. 512

132. The width of the film, in inches, used in a 35 mm camera 132.
    is
    A. 1   B. 1.4   C. 2.5   D. 3.5

133. The pressure cooker cooks food more rapidly because the   133.
    A. water boils more rapidly
    B. water boils at a higher temperature
    C. less water is used
    D. pressure is reduced below normal

134. Any two objects of equal weight are necessarily at the   134.
    same temperature if
    A. they contain equal amounts of heat
    B. they lose heat at equal rates
    C. neither loses heat to the other when they are in
       contact
    D. their molecules have equal average speeds

135. Heat may be measured by   135.
    A. temperature change in a known quantity of water
    B. the expansion of mercury
    C. the bending of a bimetallic strip
    D. the expansion of hydrogen

136. The quantity of heat, in calories, required to change   136.
    10 grams of ice at 0°C to water at 20°C is
    A. 100   B. 200   C. 1000   D. 5600

137. To double the pressure in a fixed volume of a gas at 0°C, 137.
    its temperature, in °C, must be raised to
    A. 100   B. 273   C. 373   D. 546

138. An object is placed 8 inches from a convex lens of 4 inch 138.
    focal length.
    The image formed will be
    A. larger than the object
    B. smaller than the object
    C. the same size as the object
    D. virtual

139. When light strikes the prisms in binoculars, it will be   139.____
    A. reflected   B. refracted
    C. dispersed   D. absorbed

140. Evidence that light is a transverse wave phenomenon is   140.____
obtained from
    A. beats   B. polarization
    C. photoelectric effect   D. interference

141. The failure of a lens to focus, at a point, light of   141.____
different colors is called
    A. interference   B. spherical aberration
    C. polarization   D. chromatic aberration

142. Two sounds of the same wavelength MUST have the same   142.____
    A. amplitude   B. frequency   C. intensity   D. quality

143. The human ear cannot distinguish tones that differ in   143.____
    A. phase   B. quality   C. intensity   D. pitch

144. Of the following, the one that is at MAXIMUM when   144.____
resonance occurs in an electrical circuit is
    A. impedance   B. resistance   C. reactance   D. current

145. Electromagnetic waves radiated into space are called   145.____
_____ waves.
    A. rectified   B. carrier
    C. stationary   D. polarized

146. A TV broadcasting station transmits the picture (video   146.____
signal) by means of _____ modulation of _____ frequency
waves.
    A. frequency; high   B. amplitude; high
    C. frequency; low   D. amplitude; low

147. The emission of electrons from certain metals when they   147.____
are exposed to light is known as the _____ effect.
    A. thermionic   B. Edison
    C. photoelectric   D. thermoelectric

148. The process of varying the amplitude of a carrier wave   148.____
is called
    A. modulation   B. regeneration
    C. oscillation   D. rectification

149. A transformer may be used to increase   149.____
    A. energy   B. power   C. voltage   D. wattage

150. An induction coil   150.____
    A. produces a large current
    B. changes AC to DC
    C. produces a high voltage
    D. steps down high voltages

151. The part NOT found in an AC generator is a(n)   151.
    A. field magnet   B. armature
    C. brush(es)   D. commutator

152. To protect a delicate watch from a magnetic field, its   152.
    case should be made of
    A. cobalt   B. aluminum
    C. soft iron   D. steel

153. The electrical device MOST similar to a galvanometer in   153.
    operation is the
    A. bell   B. electromagnet
    C. motor   D. fuse

154. A hand generator is easier to turn when the external   154.
    circuit is open.
    This is BEST explained by a principle stated by
    A. Oersted   B. Ampere   C. Ohm   D. Lenz

155. *60 cycle* current refers to   155.
    A. wavelength   B. amplitude
    C. frequency   D. velocity

156. One end of a metal rod is brought near the north pole of 156.
    a magnet, and it is noted that they attract.
    This indicates that the metal rod is
    A. a permanent magnet   B. not a magnet
    C. a magnetic substance   D. made of iron

157. One coulomb per second defines one   157.
    A. volt   B. watt   C. ampere   D. ohm

158. Electricity is stored in a   158.
    A. dry cell   B. condenser
    C. storage battery   D. generator

159. Increasing the distance between the plates of a charged   159.
    capacitor
    A. *increases* the potential difference
    B. *decreases* the potential difference
    C. *decreases* the amount of charge
    D. *increases* the amount of charge

160. A radioactive emission not bent by a magnetic field is   160.
    a(n)
    A. proton   B. gamma ray
    C. beta particle   D. alpha particle

161. $_4Be^9$ means that the number of protons in a beryllium 161.
    nucleus is
    A. 4   B. 5   C. 9   D. 13

162. *Isotopes* is the name given to elements that have
    A. the same atomic number but different atomic mass
    B. the same atomic mass but different atomic number
    C. the same atomic mass and the same atomic number but different chemical properties
    D. similar chemical properties although they differ in both atomic mass and atomic number
       162._____

163. Ionization is the basis for the
    A. Geiger counter and scintillation counter
    B. Geiger counter and cloud chamber
    C. cloud chamber and scintillation counter
    D. Geiger counter, cloud chamber, and scintillation counter
       163._____

164. Atomic mass is determined by
    A. protons   B. neutrons
    C. protons plus neutrons   D. protons minus neutrons
       164._____

165. The mass of a nucleus, as compared with the sum of the masses of the particles which compose it, is
    A. slightly greater   B. much greater
    C. equal   D. slightly less
       165._____

166. To an observer on Earth, the BRIGHTEST planet is
    A. Jupiter   B. Saturn   C. Mars   D. Venus
       166._____

167. The Russian Lunik revolves around the
    A. sun outside the earth's orbit
    B. sun inside the earth's orbit
    C. moon
    D. earth
       167._____

168. The Northern Cross lies in the constellation
    A. Cygnus   B. Bootes   C. Lyra   D. Pegasus
       168._____

169. A galaxy visible to the unaided eye lies in the constellation
    A. Andromeda   B. Ursa Minor
    C. Auriga   D. Canis Major
       169._____

170. A rock composed of angular fragments cemented together into a coherent mass is a
    A. breccia   B. tufa   C. conglomerate   D. dacite
       170._____

171. In Moh's scale of mineral hardness, quartz is number
    A. 5   B. 6   C. 7   D. 8
       171._____

172. A rock which shows foliated structure is
    A. marble   B. serpentine   C. schist   D. quartzite
       172._____

173. A river is classified as mature when it includes a
    A. chain of lakes in its course
    B. gorge
    C. series of meanders
    D. series of rapids
       173._____

174. On a Mercator projection, a straight line joining New   174.
     York City and Liverpool
     A. has constant direction
     B. has constant scale
     C. is the arc of a great circle
     D. has a larger scale near Liverpool than near New York

175. An esker is a   175.
     A. winding, roughly stratified glacial ridge
     B. linear, unstratified glacial ridge
     C. roughly circular glacial mound
     D. series of glacial elevations and depressions

176. An example of an active volcano of the *quiet* type is   176.
     A. Krakatoa   B. Mauna Loa
     C. Mt. Lassen   D. Mt. Vesuvius

177. Stone Mt., Georgia is classified as a   177.
     A. butte   B. mesa
     C. monadnock   D. volcanic neck

178. The velocity of escape of a projectile from the Earth,   178.
     in number of miles per hour, is about
     A. 7,000   B. 18,000   C. 25,000   D. 35,000

179. An outstanding example of a glacial trough is the   179.
     A. Grand Canyon of the Colorado
     B. Yellowstone Canyon in Yellowstone National Park
     C. Yosemite Valley in Yosemite National Park
     D. Zion Canyon in Zion National Park

180. The Keewatin Glacier of the Pleistocene ice age was   180.
     centered in
     A. north central Canada   B. Labrador
     C. Alaska   D. Greenland

181. Lost rivers or underground streams are MOST likely to   181.
     occur in regions whose bedrock is
     A. limestone   B. slate
     C. granite   D. conglomerate

182. The Royal Gorge of the Arkansas River represents a river 182.
     valley which is
     A. young   B. mature   C. old   D. subdued

183. Sink holes are the result of the work of   183.
     A. earthquakes   B. underground water
     C. streams   D. glaciers

184. The mineral which is LEAST susceptible to chemical   184.
     weathering is
     A. feldspar   B. hornblends
     C. augite   D. quartz

185. Of the following, the mountains of GREATEST geologic age are the
    A. Appalachians   B. Rockies
    C. Sierra Nevadas   D. Cascades

185.____

186. Laccoliths are found in
    A. domed mountains   B. block mountains
    C. folded mountains   D. volcanoes

186.____

187. The normal percentage of dissolved mineral matter in sea water (by weight) is APPROXIMATELY
    A. 1.5   B. 2.5   C. 3.5   D. 4.5

187.____

188. A shoreline formed as a result of submergence is a _____ shoreline.
    A. coastal plain   B. delta
    C. fiord   D. volcano

188.____

189. Spring tides occur at
    A. full moon *only*
    B. new moon *only*
    C. both full and new moon
    D. first and last quarter phases

189.____

190. An annular eclipse of the sun takes place at the phase of the moon called
    A. new moon   B. new gibbous
    C. new crescent   D. full moon

190.____

191. When it is noon, Eastern Standard Time, in New York City, the standard time at the 120°W meridian is
    A. 9 A.M.   B. 10 A.M.   C. 2 P.M.   D. 3 P.M.

191.____

192. On June 21, in New York City, the sun
    A. rises in the northeast
    B. sets in the southwest
    C. reaches the zenith at local noon
    D. is north of the zenith at local noon

192.____

193. The Palisades of New Jersey originated as an igneous intrusion during the period known as
    A. Eocene   B. Cretaceous
    C. Permian   D. Triassic

193.____

194. A region whose warmest monthly temperature average is 80°F, while its coldest monthly temperature average is 77°F, MUST have a climate typified as
    A. marine west coast   B. Mediterranean
    C. tropical desert   D. tropical rainforest

194.____

195. A necessary condition for the formation of sleet is a
    A. cold front   B. strong pressure gradient
    C. steep lapse rate   D. temperature inversion

195.____

18

196. The dry adiabetic lapse rate per 1000 feet is   196.
     A. 2.5°F   B. 3.5°F   C. 4.5°F   D. 5.5°F

197. The prevailing wind at 40°S latitude is   197.
     A. northwesterly   B. northeasterly
     C. southwesterly   D. southeasterly

198. The European equivalent of the American chinook wind is   198.
     known as the
     A. bora   B. buran   C. foehn   D. mistral

199. Cumulonimbus clouds are MOST likely to occur in connec-   199.
     tion with a(n) _____ air mass.
     A. mTk   B. mTw   C. cPk   D. cPw

200. At perigee, our moon's distance, expressed in miles,   200.
     from the earth is about
     A. 205,000   B. 220,000   C. 235,000   D. 245,000

19

KEY (CORRECT ANSWERS)

1. D	41. D	81. A	121. B	161. A
2. B	42. A	82. B	122. B	162. A
3. D	43. A	83. D	123. C	163. B
4. B	44. C	84. C	124. B	164. C
5. A	45. D	85. C	125. C	165. D
6. D	46. C	86. B	126. A	166. D
7. B	47. B	87. D	127. C	167. A
8. C	48. C	88. D	128. C	168. A
9. D	49. D	89. A	129. C	169. A
10. C	50. A	90. A	130. C	170. A
11. D	51. D	91. A	131. C	171. C
12. D	52. C	92. D	132. B	172. C
13. D	53. B	93. B	133. B	173. D
14. D	54. C	94. D	134. C	174. A
15. C	55. A	95. B	135. A	175. A
16. A	56. B	96. A	136. C	176. B
17. B	57. D	97. B	137. B	177. C
18. B	58. D	98. B	138. C	178. C
19. D	59. C	99. A	139. A	179. C
20. B	60. D	100. C	140. B	180. A
21. B	61. B	101. D	141. D	181. A
22. B	62. A	102. B	142. B	182. A
23. A	63. C	103. A	143. A	183. B
24. A	64. B	104. B	144. C	184. D
25. D	65. D	105. B	145. B	185. A
26. C	66. A	106. B	146. B	186. A
27. D	67. A	107. A	147. C	187. C
28. D	68. C	108. D	148. A	188. C
29. A	69. A	109. A	149. C	189. C
30. D	70. A	110. B	150. C	190. A
31. B	71. C	111. D	151. D	191. A
32. A	72. B	112. B	152. C	192. A
33. D	73. B	113. C	153. C	193. D
34. C	74. D	114. D	154. D	194. D
35. C	75. A	115. B	155. C	195. D
36. D	76. B	116. C	156. C	196. D
37. D	77. B	117. B	157. C	197. A
38. A	78. B	118. A	158. B	198. C
39. D	79. D	119. D	159. A	199. A
40. C	80. D	120. A	160. B	200. B

19

EXAMINATION SECTION
TEST 1

DIRECTIONS: Each question or incomplete statement is followed by several suggested answers or completions. Select the one that BEST answers the question or completes the statement. *PRINT THE LETTER OF THE CORRECT ANSWER IN THE SPACE AT THE RIGHT.*

Questions 1-3.

DIRECTIONS: Answer Questions 1 to 3 based on the following situation.

You are a school counselor in an academic and commercial high school. A senior boy by the name of Peter informs you that for years he has wished to prepare for the practice of medicine. His parents urged him to make this choice when an uncle, who was a doctor, promised to pay part of his college expenses, provided he enrolled in the medical course.

You have listened with interest to Peter's problem as he related it. You have talked to all of his teachers, studied his school records, checked his grades, and given him a battery of tests. All of his grades were below average. Tests revealed that he had slightly less than an average mental ability. Personality and adjustment tests revealed nothing wrong EXCEPT a slight tendency to be dissatisfied with his family relationship. His clerical aptitude test score was low. Three mechanical aptitude tests, however, revealed high promise. Further questioning revealed that for years Peter had tinkered in his own shop with tools.

It appears that unwise family pressures had caused Peter to choose a life work beyond his ability to achieve.

1. Your FIRST step in handling this problem should be to   1.____
   A. tell the parents that they must agree to a search for another life goal
   B. inform the boy's parents that their son does not have the ability to succeed in a profession
   C. confer with the boy's parents and get them to have the boy keep trying to gain entrance to a medical school
   D. see the boy's parents and suggest that they forget about his choice of a vocation for the present

2. You later arranged a meeting with Peter and during your   2.____
   interview with him, he stated that he wanted to learn
   more about various types of work before he chose.
   Under these conditions, you should
   A. advise him to take a variety of subjects as tryouts so that he will be able to make a wiser choice
   B. suggest that he learn something about the requirements of other jobs

      C. take him to the library and show him books to read
         on various types of work and try to given him insight
         into his abilities and interests
      D. tell him you feel that he is old enough to decide now

3. After thinking about it, Peter finally decided to prepare   3._
   for work as a garage mechanic.
   You should then
      A. advise him to change to a trade school and take auto
         mechanics or machine shop and do that kind of work
         during the summer
      B. advise him to drop chemistry and biology but not
         give up completely the idea of becoming a doctor
      C. advise him to remain in school and take several
         more science subjects
      D. try to interest him in getting a job in a garage
         and attending night school

4. You are a judge in a juvenile court in a large city. A   4._
   young girl fifteen years of age is brought before you.
   She is charged with the theft of a dress, perfume, and
   handbag from a large department store. The total value
   of the articles is $437. This is the first time the girl
   has been caught. She is from a middle class family. Her
   mother works in a factory in the daytime, and her father
   is employed in a local bank as an assistant cashier.
   Their combined income is about $40,000 a year. She is an
   only child. Her school record is good, and one test showed
   that she had better than average mental ability.
   After having had a talk with the girl, it is your duty to
   make a decision. You FIRST would
      A. give her a severe scolding and release her, but make
         her pay the bill
      B. counsel with the girl and her parents and then give
         her another chance
      C. talk with the mother to find out whether the girl
         had ever been neglected
      D. inform the girl that you are thinking of sending her
         to a girls' training school

5. Wally is a bright five-year-old boy in a kindergarten   5._
   group. Every day he wastes the time of the group by being
   slow in putting away materials at the end of the activity
   period. You, his teacher, know that at home his toys are
   picked up and put away by his mother or father when he
   tires of them. He is an only child.
   You should
      A. tell his parents to force him to pick up things at
         home so that he will put away his materials when he
         is at school
      B. tell him to hurry because the group is waiting for him
      C. help him to put away his materials so the group will
         not be forced to wait
      D. send the group to the gymnasium to play a game which
         Wally likes, and have Wally lose out on the fun while
         he puts away his materials

6.   Jimmy, a first-grade pupil, is active on the playground.   6.___
      In the schoolroom, however, he refuses to take part and
      frequently cries when told to do so.
      In trying to remedy this situation, you, as his teacher,
      should
          A. advise him to take part at once because you think
             that he is afraid
          B. ask his parents to keep him at home for a year in
             the belief that he is not yet mature enough to
             begin school
          C. keep harmony in the class by permitting him to take
             part when he chooses to do so
          D. encourage him to take part gradually

7.   Ralph, who is in the sixth grade, likes to make things   7.___
      with tools and seems to enjoy helping you keep the library
      books in order and the room decorated nicely. He finds
      arithmetic very difficult and often avoids it. He plays
      truant quite often.
      In handling this truancy problem, you should
          A. discuss why his offense is serious and try to get
             him to see the error of his ways
          B. attempt to discover the causes of his difficulty
             and tell him you will excuse him from arithmetic if
             he does not skip school
          C. compliment him on his mechanical ability and at the
             proper time assign him mechanical work in which
             arithmetic would be useful
          D. tell him that staying out of school is an offense
             not to be tolerated

8.   Harry sprinkled a foul-smelling drug around the classroom. 8.___
      The odor was so bad that it made some of the pupils ill
      and thus almost broke up school for the day. When the
      teacher discovered who did it, she forced Harry to apologize
      to the school and to stand before the class each morning
      for a week taking a smell of the drug from a vial which
      she kept in her possession.
      In your judgment, this form of punishment
          A. will cure him
          B. is not quite severe enough for the offense
          C. was carried on too long even though it produced the
             desired results
          D. is apt to fail

9.   For more than a month, various articles had been disappear- 9.___
      ing from the lockers in the school hallway. Finally, the
      instructor caught Jerry going through the coats in the
      lockers. He admitted the thefts. The instructor knew that
      Jerry's parents were very poor. He had no spending money,
      and his meals did not meet his needs.
      His instructor should
          A. give him a weekly amount which he can pay back sometime
             and also give him an apple, a sandwich, or candy when
             possible
          B. help him find work so that he can take care of his own
             needs

    C. show him that a thief always gets caught and then promise him a still worse penalty if he does it again

    D. make an example of him by telling the students that he stole the articles

10. Jack, in the eighth grade, is always doing something to attract the attention of his classmates. He makes *bright* remarks during class, insists on talking more than his share of the time, acts up as he walks around the room to obtain a laugh, and even dresses, walks, and combs his hair in an unusual manner to attract attention. His teachers think that

    A. he should be separated from the group or otherwise punished until he learns not to disturb

    B. the best way to handle him is to join with his classmates in smiling at his remarks and tricks because this cannot do a great deal of harm

    C. the teacher should give him the attention he desires whenever he earns it by doing something worthwhile

    D. the teacher should refuse to notice his behavior so it will return to normal again

10._

11. The teacher has noticed lately that Mildred, age eight, answers out of turn, speaks when others are speaking, and wants to be the center of attention in every activity. She pouts or cries if another child is selected to do something for the teacher which she wishes to do. She has no sister but has a new baby brother. The MOST probable explanation of her behavior is that

    A. her behavior changed because she now has new duties at home

    B. she is no longer the center of attention at home and is seeking more attention at school

    C. she is being disobedient because she has been spoiled from babyhood

    D. Mildred is probably suffering from some illness

11._

12. You are an employment officer. It is your duty to talk with and refer individuals who are trying to secure work. There have been many inquiries regarding a particularly fine automotive mechanic's job in a well-known shop in the city. It offers a good chance to anyone who obtains it. It is up to you to fill this opening from a large group of men applying for this work. You should select the man who

    A. showed that he knew his trade and showed you the best set of written references and recommendations from his former employers

    B. appeared to be most highly recommended by such previous employers as you were able to contact and answered the trade questions most satisfactorily

    C. told you he had the best training and had the longest experience in the automotive field

    D. appeared the most intelligent and answered the oral trade questions correctly

12._

13. As head nurse in a leading hospital, you are faced with   13.___
a serious problem. Two of your very efficient nurses
are unable to cooperate and to avoid trouble. You have
attempted to improve the situation by talking to both of
them but their attitudes and relations have not improved.
It would be BEST to
   A. dismiss the less efficient nurse and secure a more
      satisfactory employee to take her position
   B. overlook their attitude toward each other as much
      as possible
   C. assign each to unpleasant duties and thereby attempt
      to teach both that they should try to cooperate
      better with each other
   D. place them on duty in different wards of the hospital
      so that they will not need to work together

14. You are a nurse in a city hospital assigned to a patient   14.___
who demands too much of your time, thus causing you to
neglect other duties.
The situation would BEST be handled agreeably by
   A. referring her case to the hospital authorities
   B. doing things requested by her to avoid offending her
   C. explaining pleasantly but firmly why you are unable
      to grant all of her requests
   D. paying no attention to her occasionally so she will
      not ask so often

15. You are a social case worker from a public welfare agency.   15.___
You are charged with advising and assisting poor families
which supposedly are in need of financial or medical aid.
You are asked to investigate a family of six small children
whose father is a ne'er-do-well and who is in a drunken
condition most of the time. The mother has been frail
and sickly for years.
Under these conditions, you should
   A. give them a monthly allowance despite the father's
      drinking
   B. refuse them all help so that the father might feel
      forced to work
   C. take the children from the family and advise the
      mother to secure a divorce
   D. give them a monthly allowance and have the father sent
      to a sanitarium or other institution for medical help

16. Virginia is an attractive girl in the ninth grade with   16.___
ability somewhat above the average. She is nervous and
worries a great deal about her schoolwork and about life
in general. Her mother is very anxious for her to excel
in school. She criticizes Virginia if her marks are not
high and urges her to work harder.
If you were Virginia's teacher, the method you would use
in helping Virginia is to
   A. show the other pupils what fine work Virginia is
      doing, using her case as a model to inspire the others
   B. talk to the mother, explaining that it may be
      dangerous to urge Virginia to earn high marks

C. encourage Virginia and her mother to continue as
    at present since it is likely to lead to high
    scholarship
D. tell Virginia that she should not study hard

17. The attitudes of three teachers in discussing the   17.__
     behavior of their pupils is shown in the four paragraphs
     that follow.
     Which do you regard as BEST from the standpoint of
     development of the child?
        A. When a child does what is wrong, he should be with-
            drawn from the group so that he may think over his
            poor behavior.
        B. Teachers should watch children, stopping them promptly
            the instant they get into mischief. Privileges should
            be temporarily withdrawn because of offenses.
        C. When a child misbehaves, he should be punished.
        D. When a child misbehaves, the adult should explain
            what the right mode of behavior is and why it is right.

18. Teacher X will never admit that she is wrong. Every   18.__
     question in the classroom is taken as a challenge to her
     authority. Every comment on her work is regarded as unfair
     criticism. She makes sarcastic comments to her fellow
     workers but never apologizes. She can usually prove to
     her own satisfaction that she is right. She interrupts
     friends or students so often that no one is able to finish
     a discussion in her presence.
     If you were the principal, you would
        A. put up with the behavior since in a few more years
            she will be obliged to retire
        B. tell her that she may lose her position if she does
            not change
        C. have a serious talk with her and force her to see her
            behavior is educationally unsound
        D. arrange for a psychiatrist to help her to understand
            her behavior and alter it

19. Dale shows shyness on the playground. He seems afraid to   19.__
     enter into the games and is so awkward when he plays that
     the boys do not like to choose him on their side. You
     are the director.
     How can you assist him in overcoming this fear? You should
        A. give him some easy task connected with the games, such
            as keeping score
        B. allow him to watch or to do something with another
            pupil
        C. advise him to learn to play
        D. insist that he get into the games and play

20.   A ten-year-old boy in the fourth grade suddenly begins   20.____
      to stutter. He is ashamed, and the children in his class
      are amused.
      The teacher should
        A. advise the parents to keep him out of school for a
            while because of his nervousness
        B. compel him to recite in front of the class so that
            he will cure his stuttering
        C. tell him he can stop if he wants to and then attempt
            to overlook the condition if it occurs again
        D. refer him to a clinic for help

KEY (CORRECT ANSWERS)

1. D		11. B	
2. C		12. B	
3. A		13. D	
4. B		14. C	
5. D		15. D	
6. D		16. B	
7. C		17. D	
8. D		18. D	
9. B		19. A	
10. C		20. D	

TEST 2

DIRECTIONS: Each question or incomplete statement is followed by several suggested answers or completions. Select the one that BEST answers the question or completes the statement. *PRINT THE LETTER OF THE CORRECT ANSWER IN THE SPACE AT THE RIGHT*.

Questions 1-8.

DIRECTIONS: If you were judging social workers, which of the following personality traits would you consider the MOST important for a successful person in this type of work? Select ONE in each group, and mark its letter in the space at the right.

1. A. Aggressive and persuasive
    B. Determined and hard working
    C. Prudent and careful
    D. Helpful and kindly   1.___

2. A. Ambitious and spirited
    B. Tactful and diplomatic
    C. Persuasive and overbearing
    D. Cautious and prudent   2.___

3. A. *Slippery* and critical
    B. Pleasant appearing and apologetic
    C. Selfish and self-reliant
    D. Well-balanced and interested in people   3.___

4. A. Persevering and determined
    B. Considerate and understanding
    C. Outstanding and superior
    D. Friendly and spirited   4.___

5. A. Sympathetic and condescending
    B. Determined and superior
    C. Practical and experienced
    D. Self-confident and changeable   5.___

6. A. Sociable and sincere
    B. Self-reliant and theoretical
    C. Overbearing and forward
    D. Agreeable and congenial   6.___

7. A. Self-confident and assured
    B. Energetic and tactless
    C. Intelligent and ambitious
    D. Industrious and tolerant   7.___

8. A. Enthusiastic and eager
    B. Cheerful and apologetic
    C. Cordial and tolerant
    D. Analytical and intelligent   8.___

9. Geraldine, a junior in high school, is boasting constantly 9.___
    about something that she has done, or about the members of
    her family. Her companions think that she is conceited.
    A close study of her case shows the following possibilities.
    The MOST likely cause of her boastful conduct is that
       A. her father is a prominent man in town, highly respected
          by his fellow citizens
       B. she has ability above the average and generally earns
          good marks
       C. she lacks self-confidence and occasionally hints to
          her teacher that she is not quite as capable as her
          classmates
       D. she has been spoiled by having had too much attention

10. Skippy, a high school senior, is a poor athlete. No matter 10.___
    how hard he tries, he seems unable to do well in sports.
    This worries him. He has expressed the opinion that he
    does not amount to much. He has had a physical examination
    and his poor athletic ability is not due to physical causes.
    Skippy can *probably* be helped if
       A. his teachers urge him to put forth every effort to
          become good in athletics
       B. teachers let him alone to fight the battle that
          everyone must fight sooner or later when he learns
          that someone else is better than he
       C. his teachers study his case and help him to discover
          other things that he can do well
       D. the coach places him in a special class known as the
          awkward squad and teaches him to improve his athletic
          ability

11. In order to help a child to avoid developing the feeling 11.___
    that others are ALWAYS better than he is, you should
       A. assist him in becoming as successful as possible in
          the things he attempts
       B. try to get him to see that he is as competent as
          anyone else
       C. tell him never to admit that he is beaten
       D. help him to be as successful as possible in the things
          he attempts and help him to do some one thing
          especially well

12. With pupils of extremely low mental ability, it is MOST 12.___
    justifiable to
       A. give them the same work as the others get but realize
          that it will take them longer to do it
       B. give them the same type of work as the others get
          but less of it
       C. assign more extra curricular work and less from the
          regular curriculum; for example, use more handwork
       D. place all of them in manual arts courses

13. You are a personnel manager in a large industrial plant   13._
    engaged in the manufacture of vital instruments. It is
    your job to maintain good employee-employer relationships,
    increase the amount of work done, and keep the men happy
    and satisfied in their work. In other words, you are
    active in keeping up high standards of work by keeping
    everyone happy.
    One of your experienced employees, Mr. Ryan, is engaged
    in the final inspection of shuttle o-rings. He apparently
    has fallen down in his work rating without any known
    reason. He holds an important job and must maintain a
    high degree of skill. The plant physician, after a
    thorough physical examination, says there is nothing wrong
    with him physically.
    Under these conditions, you should
       A. suggest that he might lose his job if he does not
          increase the quality and amount of work he does
       B. talk with him and attempt to determine what is
          causing his trouble or what is worrying him
       C. drop a word of praise occasionally so he might be
          helped to do better
       D. suggest that it might help if he changed to a
          different type of work

14. Suppose that you found that Mr. Ryan was upset at work   14._
    because of difficulties with his wife and his envy of a
    man who was promoted over him.
    You should
       A. try to explain to him why this man was promoted over
          him
       B. to satisfy him, tell him that your plant promotes
          those first who were employed first, and casually
          suggest that his wife drop in to see you
       C. give him some marital advice and suggest that he may
          be better off if he separated from his wife for a
          while
       D. tell him you are interested only in his output and
          that he will have to work out his personal affairs
          by himself

15. You are a Red Cross director with an army unit in the   15._
    field. A soldier, Jones, approaches you and tells you
    there is serious illness in his family, and he would like
    to go home. You agree, but upon looking into the matter
    the next day, you find that no one is actually sick in
    the soldier's family.
    Under these conditions, you should
       A. take no further action at present but later get the
          man a furlough because you can see that he is under
          serious strain and may become very ill
       B. treat it as a humorous incident but be on the lookout
          so that it does not occur again
       C. notify the commanding officer and get his opinion
       D. deny the request and try to find out the real cause
          for the man's behavior

16. If Jones then saw you again, you should   16.____
    A. tell him to pour out his troubles to you
    B. scold him for his actions and explain the seriousness
       of such dishonesty
    C. explain that taking vacations whenever he feels like
       it is impossible; offer assistance and try to find
       something to interest him
    D. explain to him in a nice manner that you have
       shortened his furlough a few days

17. Jones then told you that he was sick and tired of the   17.____
    army and wanted to get away from it for a while.
    You should
    A. warn him of what would happen if he deserted and
       obtain a furlough for him
    B. notify his commanding officer that the man should
       be watched
    C. suggest an appointment be made for him with the
       psychiatrist
    D. refuse to interest yourself in his problem because
       it is not your concern

18. If Jones also told you that his first sergeant was   18.____
    picking on him, you should
    A. look into the matter to determine the truth by
       talking to a few people who know him
    B. call the soldier's commanding officer and tell
       him about the situation
    C. tell him to forget the incident since it really
       was not very serious
    D. try to arrange to get the soldier transferred to
       another company

19. You are a dean in a secondary school. An intelligent   19.____
    child, Bob, sixteen years of age who is about to fail,
    has been referred to you. Prior to this time, the boy
    has been a good student and a very likable boy. Suddenly,
    he began to neglect his work.
    Under these conditions, you should
    A. go to the principal and suggest that the boy be
       deprived of a few privileges around school until
       his behavior improves
    B. have a casual talk with the boy
    C. learn about the boy's home life and outside activities
    D. have a talk with the boy and tell him he must apply
       himself

20. If you should have a talk with Bob, your FIRST step will   20.____
    be to try to
    A. make him feel that by improving his behavior it will
       please you
    B. gain his confidence so he will feel free to tell his
       problem
    C. impress him with the importance of your position
    D. show him that he is developing some bad habits

21. You discover that one reason for Bob's poor attitude is the fact that he feels he is being left out of things. Knowing this, you should
    A. ask his friends to aid him in his studies
    B. force him to engage in sports
    C. tell him not to worry as things are bound to turn out all right
    D. seek the help of his friends

21.__

22. If, in two months, you heard nothing more concerning Bob, you should
    A. have one of his teachers send him to you
    B. look into his current activities and then drop in and talk to him about how well he is progressing in his classes and social relations
    C. inquire about him and then drop in casually and observe him
    D. look at his school record to determine whether he had improved

22.__

23. Near the close of the school year, you notice a great improvement in Bob's behavior, and his grades have improved.
    You then should
    A. call the boy in and tell him you were disappointed in the amount of improvement shown because you knew he could do better
    B. say nothing to him but inform his parents that he has improved
    C. go to him and comment on his splendid improvement
    D. give him a two-day holiday as a reward for the splendid improvement shown

23.__

24. Which of these teacher's opinions is CORRECT?
    A. Mr. W. -"*I think some children are naturally quite mischievous and must be dealt with sternly.*"
    B. Mr. X. -"*I have a pupil who causes a great deal of trouble. After I scold him, he quiets down and behaves himself.*"
    C. Mr. Y. -"*Since every bit of misconduct has a cause, we should not be angry with a child who misbehaves any more than we should get angry at one who is ill.*"
    D. Mr. Z. -"*Most misconduct can be traced right back to the home. It is the parents' fault.*"

24.__

25. You are a social case worker from a public welfare agency. One of your cases is Mr. Backus, an aged man whose failing health makes nursing care necessary. Mr. Backus is dependent upon relief. An agency reports that he suffers from *senility and paralysis*. His only son is confined in the Veterans Hospital. There are no other relatives. Mr. Backus is receiving $320 per month, but he feels he should be receiving at least $600 per month on which to live since the high cost of living makes it very hard to get along on less. He has no savings. His landlady says that she does not wish to have him remain there because she cannot care for an invalid.

25.__

After a complete investigation of this case, you then should
  A. arrange to increase Mr. Backus' pension to $600 a month and then try to get the landlady to keep him
  B. place him in a home for old people at public expense
  C. increase his pension to $600 a month and make arrangements with the owner of a nursing home to care for Mr. Backus
  D. try to have the son support him

———

KEY (CORRECT ANSWERS)

1. D			11. D
2. B			12. C
3. D			13. B
4. B			14. A
5. C			15. D
6. A			16. C
7. D			17. C
8. C			18. A
9. C			19. C
10. C			20. B

21. D
22. B
23. C
24. C
25. C

———

ANSWER SHEET

ST NO. _____ PART _____ TITLE OF POSITION _____

(AS GIVEN IN EXAMINATION ANNOUNCEMENT - INCLUDE OPTION, IF ANY)

ACE OF EXAMINATION _____ DATE _____

(CITY OR TOWN)   (STATE)

RATING

USE THE SPECIAL PENCIL.   MAKE GLOSSY BLACK MARKS.

	A B C D E		A B C D E		A B C D E		A B C D E		A B C D E
1	⋮⋮⋮⋮⋮	26	⋮⋮⋮⋮⋮	51	⋮⋮⋮⋮⋮	76	⋮⋮⋮⋮⋮	101	⋮⋮⋮⋮⋮
2	⋮⋮⋮⋮⋮	27	⋮⋮⋮⋮⋮	52	⋮⋮⋮⋮⋮	77	⋮⋮⋮⋮⋮	102	⋮⋮⋮⋮⋮
3	⋮⋮⋮⋮⋮	28	⋮⋮⋮⋮⋮	53	⋮⋮⋮⋮⋮	78	⋮⋮⋮⋮⋮	103	⋮⋮⋮⋮⋮
4	⋮⋮⋮⋮⋮	29	⋮⋮⋮⋮⋮	54	⋮⋮⋮⋮⋮	79	⋮⋮⋮⋮⋮	104	⋮⋮⋮⋮⋮
5	⋮⋮⋮⋮⋮	30	⋮⋮⋮⋮⋮	55	⋮⋮⋮⋮⋮	80	⋮⋮⋮⋮⋮	105	⋮⋮⋮⋮⋮
6	⋮⋮⋮⋮⋮	31	⋮⋮⋮⋮⋮	56	⋮⋮⋮⋮⋮	81	⋮⋮⋮⋮⋮	106	⋮⋮⋮⋮⋮
7	⋮⋮⋮⋮⋮	32	⋮⋮⋮⋮⋮	57	⋮⋮⋮⋮⋮	82	⋮⋮⋮⋮⋮	107	⋮⋮⋮⋮⋮
8	⋮⋮⋮⋮⋮	33	⋮⋮⋮⋮⋮	58	⋮⋮⋮⋮⋮	83	⋮⋮⋮⋮⋮	108	⋮⋮⋮⋮⋮
9	⋮⋮⋮⋮⋮	34	⋮⋮⋮⋮⋮	59	⋮⋮⋮⋮⋮	84	⋮⋮⋮⋮⋮	109	⋮⋮⋮⋮⋮
10	⋮⋮⋮⋮⋮	35	⋮⋮⋮⋮⋮	60	⋮⋮⋮⋮⋮	85	⋮⋮⋮⋮⋮	110	⋮⋮⋮⋮⋮

Make only ONE mark for each answer.   Additional and stray marks may be
counted as mistakes.   In making corrections, erase errors COMPLETELY.

	A B C D E		A B C D E		A B C D E		A B C D E		A B C D E
11	⋮⋮⋮⋮⋮	36	⋮⋮⋮⋮⋮	61	⋮⋮⋮⋮⋮	86	⋮⋮⋮⋮⋮	111	⋮⋮⋮⋮⋮
12	⋮⋮⋮⋮⋮	37	⋮⋮⋮⋮⋮	62	⋮⋮⋮⋮⋮	87	⋮⋮⋮⋮⋮	112	⋮⋮⋮⋮⋮
13	⋮⋮⋮⋮⋮	38	⋮⋮⋮⋮⋮	63	⋮⋮⋮⋮⋮	88	⋮⋮⋮⋮⋮	113	⋮⋮⋮⋮⋮
14	⋮⋮⋮⋮⋮	39	⋮⋮⋮⋮⋮	64	⋮⋮⋮⋮⋮	89	⋮⋮⋮⋮⋮	114	⋮⋮⋮⋮⋮
15	⋮⋮⋮⋮⋮	40	⋮⋮⋮⋮⋮	65	⋮⋮⋮⋮⋮	90	⋮⋮⋮⋮⋮	115	⋮⋮⋮⋮⋮
16	⋮⋮⋮⋮⋮	41	⋮⋮⋮⋮⋮	66	⋮⋮⋮⋮⋮	91	⋮⋮⋮⋮⋮	116	⋮⋮⋮⋮⋮
17	⋮⋮⋮⋮⋮	42	⋮⋮⋮⋮⋮	67	⋮⋮⋮⋮⋮	92	⋮⋮⋮⋮⋮	117	⋮⋮⋮⋮⋮
18	⋮⋮⋮⋮⋮	43	⋮⋮⋮⋮⋮	68	⋮⋮⋮⋮⋮	93	⋮⋮⋮⋮⋮	118	⋮⋮⋮⋮⋮
19	⋮⋮⋮⋮⋮	44	⋮⋮⋮⋮⋮	69	⋮⋮⋮⋮⋮	94	⋮⋮⋮⋮⋮	119	⋮⋮⋮⋮⋮
20	⋮⋮⋮⋮⋮	45	⋮⋮⋮⋮⋮	70	⋮⋮⋮⋮⋮	95	⋮⋮⋮⋮⋮	120	⋮⋮⋮⋮⋮
21	⋮⋮⋮⋮⋮	46	⋮⋮⋮⋮⋮	71	⋮⋮⋮⋮⋮	96	⋮⋮⋮⋮⋮	121	⋮⋮⋮⋮⋮
22	⋮⋮⋮⋮⋮	47	⋮⋮⋮⋮⋮	72	⋮⋮⋮⋮⋮	97	⋮⋮⋮⋮⋮	122	⋮⋮⋮⋮⋮
23	⋮⋮⋮⋮⋮	48	⋮⋮⋮⋮⋮	73	⋮⋮⋮⋮⋮	98	⋮⋮⋮⋮⋮	123	⋮⋮⋮⋮⋮
24	⋮⋮⋮⋮⋮	49	⋮⋮⋮⋮⋮	74	⋮⋮⋮⋮⋮	99	⋮⋮⋮⋮⋮	124	⋮⋮⋮⋮⋮
25	⋮⋮⋮⋮⋮	50	⋮⋮⋮⋮⋮	75	⋮⋮⋮⋮⋮	100	⋮⋮⋮⋮⋮	125	⋮⋮⋮⋮⋮

ANSWER SHEET

TEST NO. _____ PART _____ TITLE OF POSITION _____

PLACE OF EXAMINATION _____ DATE _____
(CITY OR TOWN)   (STATE)

RATING

USE THE SPECIAL PENCIL. MAKE GLOSSY BLACK MARKS.

	A B C D E		A B C D E		A B C D E		A B C D E		A B C D E
1	:: :: :: :: ::	26	:: :: :: :: ::	51	:: :: :: :: ::	76	:: :: :: :: ::	101	:: :: :: :: ::
2	:: :: :: :: ::	27	:: :: :: :: ::	52	:: :: :: :: ::	77	:: :: :: :: ::	102	:: :: :: :: ::
3	:: :: :: :: ::	28	:: :: :: :: ::	53	:: :: :: :: ::	78	:: :: :: :: ::	103	:: :: :: :: ::
4	:: :: :: :: ::	29	:: :: :: :: ::	54	:: :: :: :: ::	79	:: :: :: :: ::	104	:: :: :: :: ::
5	:: :: :: :: ::	30	:: :: :: :: ::	55	:: :: :: :: ::	80	:: :: :: :: ::	105	:: :: :: :: ::
6	:: :: :: :: ::	31	:: :: :: :: ::	56	:: :: :: :: ::	81	:: :: :: :: ::	106	:: :: :: :: ::
7	:: :: :: :: ::	32	:: :: :: :: ::	57	:: :: :: :: ::	82	:: :: :: :: ::	107	:: :: :: :: ::
8	:: :: :: :: ::	33	:: :: :: :: ::	58	:: :: :: :: ::	83	:: :: :: :: ::	108	:: :: :: :: ::
9	:: :: :: :: ::	34	:: :: :: :: ::	59	:: :: :: :: ::	84	:: :: :: :: ::	109	:: :: :: :: ::
10	:: :: :: :: ::	35	:: :: :: :: ::	60	:: :: :: :: ::	85	:: :: :: :: ::	110	:: :: :: :: ::

Make only ONE mark for each answer.   Additional and stray marks may be
counted as mistakes.   In making corrections, erase errors COMPLETELY.

	A B C D E		A B C D E		A B C D E		A B C D E		A B C D E
11	:: :: :: :: ::	36	:: :: :: :: ::	61	:: :: :: :: ::	86	:: :: :: :: ::	111	:: :: :: :: ::
12	:: :: :: :: ::	37	:: :: :: :: ::	62	:: :: :: :: ::	87	:: :: :: :: ::	112	:: :: :: :: ::
13	:: :: :: :: ::	38	:: :: :: :: ::	63	:: :: :: :: ::	88	:: :: :: :: ::	113	:: :: :: :: ::
14	:: :: :: :: ::	39	:: :: :: :: ::	64	:: :: :: :: ::	89	:: :: :: :: ::	114	:: :: :: :: ::
15	:: :: :: :: ::	40	:: :: :: :: ::	65	:: :: :: :: ::	90	:: :: :: :: ::	115	:: :: :: :: ::
16	:: :: :: :: ::	41	:: :: :: :: ::	66	:: :: :: :: ::	91	:: :: :: :: ::	116	:: :: :: :: ::
17	:: :: :: :: ::	42	:: :: :: :: ::	67	:: :: :: :: ::	92	:: :: :: :: ::	117	:: :: :: :: ::
18	:: :: :: :: ::	43	:: :: :: :: ::	68	:: :: :: :: ::	93	:: :: :: :: ::	118	:: :: :: :: ::
19	:: :: :: :: ::	44	:: :: :: :: ::	69	:: :: :: :: ::	94	:: :: :: :: ::	119	:: :: :: :: ::
20	:: :: :: :: ::	45	:: :: :: :: ::	70	:: :: :: :: ::	95	:: :: :: :: ::	120	:: :: :: :: ::
21	:: :: :: :: ::	46	:: :: :: :: ::	71	:: :: :: :: ::	96	:: :: :: :: ::	121	:: :: :: :: ::
22	:: :: :: :: ::	47	:: :: :: :: ::	72	:: :: :: :: ::	97	:: :: :: :: ::	122	:: :: :: :: ::
23	:: :: :: :: ::	48	:: :: :: :: ::	73	:: :: :: :: ::	98	:: :: :: :: ::	123	:: :: :: :: ::
24	:: :: :: :: ::	49	:: :: :: :: ::	74	:: :: :: :: ::	99	:: :: :: :: ::	124	:: :: :: :: ::
25	:: :: :: :: ::	50	:: :: :: :: ::	75	:: :: :: :: ::	100	:: :: :: :: ::	125	:: :: :: :: ::

ANSWER SHEET

EST NO. _____ PART _____ TITLE OF POSITION _____

(AS GIVEN IN EXAMINATION ANNOUNCEMENT - INCLUDE OPTION, IF ANY)

PLACE OF EXAMINATION _____ DATE____ _____

(CITY OR TOWN)   (STATE)

RATING

USE THE SPECIAL PENCIL.   MAKE GLOSSY BLACK MARKS.

Make only ONE mark for each answer.   Additional and stray marks may be counted as mistakes.   In making corrections, erase errors COMPLETELY.

ANSWER SHEET

TEST NO. _____ PART _____ TITLE OF POSITION _____
                                                    (AS GIVEN IN EXAMINATION ANNOUNCEMENT - INCLUDE OPTION, IF ANY)

PLACE OF EXAMINATION _____ DATE____ _____
                        (CITY OR TOWN)   (STATE)

RATING

USE THE SPECIAL PENCIL. MAKE GLOSSY BLACK MARKS.

	A B C D E		A B C D E		A B C D E		A B C D E		A B C D E
1		26		51		76		101	
2		27		52		77		102	
3		28		53		78		103	
4		29		54		79		104	
5		30		55		80		105	
6		31		56		81		106	
7		32		57		82		107	
8		33		58		83		108	
9		34		59		84		109	
10		35		60		85		110	

Make only ONE mark for each answer.   Additional and stray marks may be
counted as mistakes.   In making corrections, erase errors COMPLETELY.

	A B C D E		A B C D E		A B C D E		A B C D E		A B C D E
11		36		61		86		111	
12		37		62		87		112	
13		38		63		88		113	
14		39		64		89		114	
15		40		65		90		115	
16		41		66		91		116	
17		42		67		92		117	
18		43		68		93		118	
19		44		69		94		119	
20		45		70		95		120	
21		46		71		96		121	
22		47		72		97		122	
23		48		73		98		123	
24		49		74		99		124	
25		50		75		100		125	